Getting Russia Wrong

Getting Russia Wrong

The End of Kremlinology

PATRICK COCKBURN

VERSO

London · New York

First published by Verso 1989
© Patrick Cockburn 1989
All rights reserved

Verso
UK: 6 Meard Street, London W1V 3HR
USA: 29 West 35th Street, New York, NY 10001-2291

Verso is the imprint of New Left Books

British Library Cataloguing in Publication Data
Cockburn, Patrick: the end of Kremlinology.
    Getting Russia wrong
    1. Soviet Union. History
    I. Title
    947

ISBN 0-86091-264-7
ISBN 0-86091-977-3 pbk

US Library of Congress Cataloging-in-Publication Data
Cockburn, Patrick.
    Getting Russia wrong : the end of Kremlinology / Patrick Cockburn.
        p.   cm.
    ISBN 0-86091-264-7 : $40.00. — ISBN 0-86091-977-3 (pbk.) : $13.95
    1. Soviet Union—Politics and government—1985-   2. Glasnost.
3. Soviet Union—Economic conditions—1976-   4. Cockburn, Patrick—
Journeys—Soviet Union.   5. Soviet Union—Description and travel—1970-
6. Foreign correspondents—Great Britain—Biography.
I. Title.
DK288.C63 1989
947.085′4—dc20

Typeset in Times by Leaper & Gard Ltd
Printed in Finland by Werner Söderström Oy

Contents

Acknowledgements   vii

PART I: The Rules of the Game   **1**

A Siege within a Siege: Foreigners in Moscow   3

PART II: The End of Kremlinology: The Politics of the Gorbachev Era   **23**

Mikhail Gorbachev and the End of Kremlinology   25

     The Death of Chernenko; Gorbachev as Leader; The Switch from Economic to Political Reform; The Fall of Yeltsin

PART III: Ethnic Politics   **63**

Gorbachev and the Soviet Nationalities   65

     The Last Wilderness; An End to the Cavalry Charge; Siberian Tigers; Kazakhstan: The Virgin Lands; Alma-Ata Before the Riots; On the Iranian Border; Corruption in Georgia; Backlash as the Barons Fall; Digging up Rashidov; Furs and Films in Leningrad; Stalingrad Revisited; The Army's Role in Armenia

PART IV: Glasnost, Corruption and Chernobyl   **103**

Glasnost   105

     Soviet Censorship: The Beginnings of Glasnost; Gorbachev, the Press and Glasnost; The *Admiral Nakhimov* Sinks; The Release of Sakharov; Second Chance for Soviet Media; *Life and Fate*; Vital Statistics Revealed; Political and Social Clubs; Soviet Intelligentsia and Glasnost

Corruption   125

     The Clampdown on Alcohol; Penalising the Black Economy; Gastronom Number One; Siberian Gravediggers; Fall in the Death Rate; Mr and Mrs Shushkov Go to Jail

Chernobyl   137

    The Kremlin Reacts to Chernobyl; May Day Dances; Boris
    Shcherbina; Useless Secrecy; Moscow Admits Chernobyl
    Underestimated; Chernobyl Disaster Leaves Three Vital
    Questions Unanswered; The Results of Chernobyl; The Site
    of the Disaster

PART V: The Economy and the Impulse for Reform   **151**

    Radical Objectives; Oil and Energy: The Exhaustion of
    Brezhnev's Economic Policy; Agriculture: The Ball and Chain;
    The Prices Test; Opening to Moonlighters; Why Soviets Buy
    Cars; At Togliatti Car Plant; Wages and Prices; Economic
    Change Promises Quick Improvement to Soviet Lifestyle;
    Dawn of the Enterprise Culture; Joint Ventures with Western
    Companies; The Shift to Radical Economic Reform; Soviet
    Economic Motor Changes up a Gear

PART VI: Foreign Policy and the Military   **191**

    Memories of War; Before the Geneva Summit; After the
    Geneva Summit; Reykjavik Summit; Stability between the
    Superpowers; Military Influence on the Wane in the Kremlin;
    Air Defence Flaws; A Tactical Retreat; Moscow and the
    Burden of the Arms Race

PART VII: Afterword   **211**

    Unusual Flowers   213

Index   221

Acknowledgements

I would like to thank the Carnegie Endowment for International Peace in Washington, DC, for providing the friendly home where much of this work was written.

A version of "A Siege within a Siege" has appeared in *Granta* in spring 1989; "Mikhail Gorbachev and the End of Kremlinology" in *World Policy Journal*, spring 1989; and "Gorbachev and the Soviet Nationalities" in *Foreign Policy*, March 1989. Most of the narrative pieces appeared in the *Financial Times* between 1985 and 1988.

PART I

The Rules of the Game

A Siege within a Siege: Foreigners in Moscow

I left Lebanon for the Soviet Union in 1984. In January the army had mutinied and the government lost control of Beirut, its defeat complete and unmistakable. The President held only his palace, in which he was occasionally shelled by artillery in the surrounding hills. In Moscow, by contrast, the political battle for the succession to Leonid Brezhnev, who died in 1982 after eighteen years in power, was eerily invisible. In Lebanon journalists and diplomats watched the battles in the hills above Beirut to find winners and losers. In Moscow the equivalent staging posts in the leadership crisis were state funerals when the coffin of the latest Politburo member to die was carried through Red Square. Surviving members of the leadership watched the funeral from on top of Lenin's red granite tomb while journalists and diplomats, standing in reserved areas just below, stared up in an effort to diagnose the progress of their various ailments.

There were four important deaths. Leonid Brezhnev and his successor Yuri Andropov died in the two years before I arrived, and in the next six months they were followed by Marshal Dmitri Ustinov, the Defence Minister, and Konstantin Chernenko, President and General Secretary of the Communist Party. Soviet officials, like hospital spokesmen, issued optimistic bulletins up to the moment when television and radio switched to solemn music. The death of Ustinov was first publicly revealed when two American journalists went to a hall close to the Kremlin where the world chess championship was taking place. They found the door to the hall closed and a short note pinned to it cancelling the day's game. Curious to know why, they knocked on the door until it was opened by a cleaning woman holding a mop; she said she was doing the floor to prepare for the lying-in-state of the marshal, who had died the previous night. Pleased with the scoop, the two journalists went back to their office but, worried by the lowly status of their source, decided— since, like everybody else in the Soviet Union, she was ultimately employed by the state—to attribute their information to "a Soviet official".

3

The cleaning woman's promotion to more respectable rank in the interests of credibility indicated the edginess of journalists deprived of the normal professional rituals of interview, briefing and press conference. In fact their worries were exaggerated. Despite all the secrecy, the main features of what was happening in the Soviet Union were obvious enough: the old order, the wartime generation, was dying. Difficult though it was to believe, peering up at the elderly men standing on Lenin's tomb, Soviet conservatives, the leaders who wanted to do things the way Brezhnev had done them, were weak. They needed a younger and healthier candidate as an alternative to Mikhail Gorbachev, and did not have one. The best they could do after the death of Yuri Andropov early in 1984 was to appoint Brezhnev's old aide Konstantin Chernenko to succeed him.

Chernenko, white-haired and gasping for breath because of his emphysema, looked like a malevolent caricature of the old leadership, and by the end of the year he had disappeared from public view. We asked the official spokesman where he was, but were told that he was resting in his dacha on the outskirts of Moscow. He made only one macabre appearance in what looked like a bungled attempt by Soviet television to prove that he was still animate. It showed him standing upright to receive a delegation, but obviously supporting himself with an effort by gripping the back of a chair with both hands. When the leader of the delegation tried to give Chernenko a bunch of red flowers, he was too weak to take them. Twice he raised his right hand a few inches off the chair, but the effort was overwhelming and the hand fell back.

A few weeks later I went to Chernenko's funeral, which was interrupted by a surprisingly touching incident. Everybody, from the Politburo to the crowds outside the GUM department store on the other side of Red Square, was in a good mood. The leadership crisis was finally over. Behind me in a walkway below the level of the square special KGB troops, in their dress uniform of gold braid and Persian lamb fur hats, were laughing and smoking cigarettes. Then, as I was about to go home, Mrs Chernenko, who looked like any elderly peasant woman in a Moscow market, threw herself on the coffin before they could take it away. For a few minutes, the funeral came to a halt while she lay there sobbing.

In Beirut the last president to die was Bashir Gemayel, blown up by a bomb in a suitcase as he addressed a party meeting in 1982. As I watched large yellow bulldozers clear away the rubble, the sense of life exterminated seemed to mark a definable frontier between old and new. In Moscow the process of change was less dramatic. Three presidents died in three years, but they were old men and their deaths did not have the same impact. As a result much of the next three years was spent arguing about the significance of what had happened. Intellectuals in the capital at first said they expected "Brezhnevism without Brezhnev". Visiting pundits wrote carefully hedged articles about "continuity and change in the Soviet Union", never committing themselves to how much they expected of either. And a few years later, as change became visible, Soviets I knew always asked me: "Could it be reversed?" Minute incidents were nervously examined for evidence of a return to Brezhnevism.

It was a good moment, as Lord Northcliffe had advised journalists, not to lose one's sense of the superficial. The generation of leaders shaped in the thirties and forties by Stalin and the War had finally died. Gorbachev was a child during the last war. The six months when the Germans held the village in the southern steppes where he lived had not marked him. Moreover, the men in the Kremlin might be moribund, but the way people lived in the Soviet Union had been transformed since the death of Stalin. Gorbachev was the product as well as the promoter of change. Surprisingly, journalists and diplomats who had spent the past three years in a prolonged deathwatch were often reluctant to accept that something significant and irreversible had occurred. The foreigners with the best track record over the next four years were those who believed that the state funerals in Red Square marked a change as explosive and irreversible as the death of Gemayel. There might be a more authoritarian alternative to Gorbachev, but not a return to Brezhnev.

Foreign journalists in Moscow lived in peculiar conditions. The government could never make up its mind whether it regarded them as spies, whose efforts to obtain information should be thwarted at every turn, or people whom it needed to cultivate and influence. Torn between these two approaches, it tried both at once. The Foreign Ministry organised trips for journalists who, on their return to Moscow, read articles in the press in which the author said that correspondent X, so far from showing gratitude for Soviet hospitality, had behaved in a manner difficult to distinguish from straight espionage. The pieces, too evidently based on KGB reports, were written in the pained tone of the trusting friend whose confidence had been betrayed. The message was that while foreign correspondents might be admitted to the Soviet Union, they were subject to a sort of quarantine. Ordinary Soviet citizens should approach with care.

Living conditions mirrored the same schizophrenia. There were some three hundred full-time journalists in Moscow in 1984, living in twenty foreigner-only apartment blocks in different parts of Moscow. The entrance of each was guarded twenty-four hours a day by grey-coated police who recorded the name of anybody entering or leaving the building. Foreigners with passports were allowed in, but ordinary Soviets were stopped unless accompanied by a resident. Inside their apartments foreigners assumed that any word they said could be monitored by the KGB through bugs in the walls.

I lived in a nine-storey brown building, built by German prisoners of war in the late 1940s, opposite the Puppet Theatre on the ring road which encircles central Moscow. Conditions were not uncomfortable. My predecessor as *Financial Times* correspondent was expelled a year before I arrived, but before this happened he had expanded the small *Financial Times* apartment by taking over the Argentine Trade Office next door. When I moved in the only signs of previous Argentine occupation were large box-like air conditioners inserted in three of the windows. Given Moscow's five-month-long winters and summers of intermittent warmth, the air conditioners seemed a touching piece of optimism on the part of the departed Argentine diplomat. They never worked but removing them was complicated, so I stuffed the vents with brown paper and left them in place for the next three years.

The rest of the building was divided between journalists and diplomats. The next-door apartment was occupied by Colonel Miroslav Popovic, the Yugoslav military attaché, whom I often met in the evening as he left in full dress uniform to attend some military function. Three floors above me lived Antero Pietela, the *Baltimore Sun* correspondent, while the ground floor was rented by the *New York Times*. The mixture of journalists and diplomats was also reflected in the cars in the court-yard. The two could easily be distinguished because the authorities, in order to make foreigners highly visible, gave each profession a different-coloured number plate: red for diplomats and yellow for correspond-ents. Diplomatic plates began with a D, correspondents with a K and businessmen with an M, the first three digits after the letter indicating the nationality of the owner, Britain being 001 and Zimbabwe 115.

In the courtyards of most foreigner-only buildings in Moscow it was diplomatic plates which predominated. In the expatriate community as a whole diplomats outnumbered journalists by ten to one and this gave to day-to-day life a formal, hierarchical flavour. The hierarchy stretched from ambassadors of the major powers such as the United States, Britain and West Germany at the top, down to nannies at the bottom. The latter occupied a peculiar position. Foreign ministries across the world, fearing that the sexual seduction of the single diplomat would be rapidly followed by political betrayal, liked their embassy staff to be married and there were therefore numerous children in need of tending. This was not difficult to arrange. One of the few ways a girl, just graduated in Russian from university, could get a visa to live in Moscow was to work as a nanny. Unfortunately, many of the girls, more interested in Tolstoy and Turgenev than in the care of diplomatic offspring, discovered on

arrival that they had to work long hours for little pay. Social discontent
mounted and, in a development which would not have surprised Marx,
fuelled a movement of religious revivalism. The nanny of one journalist
took to leaving notes around his apartment on which were written
slogans of a religious character. One day he told me that on getting out
of bed that morning he had found a note in one of his slippers which
read simply: "Guard me, Lord Jesus. Satan is in this house."

Nannies were not alone in responding to the social claustrophobia
which flowed from the enforced intimacy of members of the expatriate
community. I escaped once a day by taking long walks through central
Moscow which, apart from the six-lane highways built by Stalin, had
changed little since 1917. Immediately beside the buildings where I lived
was Trubnaya Place, the centre of Moscow's thieves' district before the
Revolution but now dominated by the Central Market, a series of large
dilapidated halls where peasants from outside Moscow came to sell fruit,
meat, honey, butter, flowers and vegetables. Prices were high. A kilo of
meat which cost 2 roubles* in the state meat shop sold here for 8
roubles. Uzbeks and Kazakhs from Central Asia and Armenians and
Georgians from the Caucasus could charge enough for a suitcase full of
flowers and fruit from their private plots to fly to Moscow and back and
still make a profit. I asked what had happened to the old red-light
district. Some Soviet friends who lived nearby said that thieves had
responded to the Revolution by moving the centre of their activities a
mile north of Trubnaya to an area close to the Riga railway station,
where men just out of prison could easily rent a room, and they had
established a sort of headquarters in a rundown restaurant.

Visitors to Moscow often claimed that it was grey and lifeless. I did
not understand why they chose grey, since in summer the city was
coloured a light mud brown, while in winter it was white. I much
preferred it to Leningrad, where the baroque city was scraped, cleaned
and restored. In Moscow Stalin widened Gorki Street and built highways
to the suburbs, but most of the city was untouched. Churches and
monasteries turned into offices and apartments in 1917 retained their
primary Russian colours: pale pink, pale green, dark red and cream. In
1984 restorers were only beginning to change this. I used to walk around
the remains of the fourteenth-century fortified Convent of the Nativity
of the Virgin, close to my house, where the inhabitants looked at me
with suspicion. I thought this was because my clothes marked me as a
foreigner, but a man coming out of an apartment in a modern block of
flats in the convent grounds told me that people living there were
worried that the convent might be turned into a historic monument and

---

*For the purposes of this book, 1 rouble = £1.10. (100 kopecks = 1 rouble.)

its present inhabitants removed. They had suspected I was an official somehow involved in their eviction.

Travelling out of Moscow itself was more complicated. All foreigners had to give two working days' notice in writing or by telex to the Foreign Ministry if they planned to go beyond the outer ring road. It was then up to the Foreign Ministry to object. If you heard nothing, you could go and, in fact, the closed areas, visits to which were never permitted, were well known. They included most border areas, the Urals, where much of the defence industry was located, the rocket testing ranges in Kazakhstan and large portions of the Far East. Greatest difficulty occurred when travelling close to Moscow because it was permitted to use some of the roads radiating from the capital, but not others. Some roads were peculiarly confusing because part of the way they were legal and then, for no very obvious reason, became illegal. I was frequently stopped on the road to Istra, a fortified monastery thirty miles west of Moscow built by an exiled patriarch of the Russian Orthodox Church in the seventeenth century, apparently because it was close to an artillery testing range.

Individually none of these restrictions was very onerous for foreigners in Moscow, but taken together they exerted enough pressure to provoke self-isolation, the classic symptom of siege mentality. To neutralise the threat, a besieged community begins to caricature the besiegers as malevolent but contemptible, demonic but with feet of clay. "What is the Soviet Union? Upper Volta with rockets!" said a journalist to me during my first days in Moscow. At dinner a week later a diplomat repeated the remark. Over the next three years I heard the same nervous joke, a mixture of derision and defiance, a dozen times. It reminded me of Christians in Beirut and Protestants in Belfast, whose conversation was filled with the same sort of reassuring but misleading humour. A simplified and unchanging image of the enemy provided the glue which held their communities together. Any criticism of this picture was a sign of disloyalty, but the price of cohesion was ignorance. Lebanese Christians and Ulster Protestants were extraordinarily ill-informed, sometimes fatally so, about the aims and resources of the other side.

I tried to remember that the worst that could happen to me was probably expulsion. After all, I was in Moscow only because my predecessor as *Financial Times* correspondent had been expelled in retaliation for Soviet journalists, accused of espionage, being thrown out of London. There was obviously going to be another round of expulsions, but I thought I was probably safe because the *FT* had suffered last time. Finally, in September 1985, the dozen or so resident British correspondents were summoned to the British Embassy, housed in some splendour across the Moskva River from the Kremlin, and told that half of us were being expelled. I drove away from the Embassy with Robin Gedye, the newly arrived *Daily Telegraph* correspondent, who complained sadly: "After three weeks in Moscow entirely devoted to putting together the Habitat furniture, laying linoleum in the kitchen and trying to exterminate the cockroaches, I find myself suddenly expelled for impermissible activities."

If the Kremlin's aim was to keep diplomats and foreign journalists ignorant of what was happening in the Soviet Union, then the Cold War in miniature it waged against them was psychologically quite effective. A Western military attaché told me that he and three other officers had been specially trained for four years to maximise their effectiveness in Moscow. On their arrival in the Soviet capital, however, two of the officers were so jinxed by the number of potential pitfalls about which they had been forewarned that they refused to leave the safety of their embassy. Assuming that the Kremlin saw foreigners in Moscow as a security problem, here was a Soviet success. But they also paid a price for the quarantine system because diplomats and journalists posted to Moscow became rabidly anti-Soviet. In the interests of secrecy the Soviets created an information vacuum. They could not complain too much if it was filled by the hostile views of dissidents and Western diplomats. I pointed this out to a young Soviet diplomat. He said: "Don't forget we are just as paranoid as you."

Almost every famous Russian born in the nineteenth century, from Tchaikovsky to Gogol, had spent part of his life on the long boulevard which ran a few hundred yards behind where I lived. Statues, small museums and frequent plaques recorded their presence. After 1917 the houses of aristocrats and the prosperous middle class, which lined the boulevard, were mostly converted to offices and the presence of prominent Soviets who had worked there was also recorded. Walking along Strastnoy Boulevard close to Pushkin Square at the end of 1984, I noticed a square bronze plaque showing an eager bespectacled face. Underneath was a short message which said that it was in this building that Mikhail Koltsov had edited the magazine *Ogonyok* (Little Light) in the 1930s. His name was familiar. My father, then a correspondent for the *Daily Worker*, knew him well during the Spanish Civil War, where Koltsov was both a correspondent for *Pravda* and an emissary of Stalin. Many of the Russians who had fought or advised in Spain died in the purges, and Koltsov may have singled himself out by denouncing informers in a series of articles in *Pravda* in early 1938. When he returned from Spain for the last time in December, he was arrested and shot.

Back in the apartment I looked up Koltsov's name in my father's autobiography. He described Koltsov—and the bronze plaque gave the same impression—as having "one of the most expressive faces of any

man I ever met. What his face principally expressed was a kind of enthusiastically gleeful amusement—and a lively hope that you and everyone
else would, however depressing the circumstances, do your best to make
things more amusing still." Later, as the Spanish Civil War ground
towards its gruesome conclusion and supporters of the Republic

> became truly cynical, despairing, without faith or enthusiasm for anything, I
> found myself looking forward more and more eagerly to conversations with
> Koltsov, journeys in his company, estimates from him of the course of affairs.
> He was a man who could see the defeat for what it really was, could assume
> that half the big slogans were empty, and a lot of the big heroes stuffed, or
> charlatans, and yet not let that bother him at all, or sap his energy and enthu-
> siasm.

In the final days of Chernenko, all this seemed pertinent. Russians with
faith, energy or enthusiasm were hard to find. I felt the need, like my
father fifty years before, to talk to somebody who had not escaped into a
protective envelope of cynicism and passivity. This was difficult. I used
to have dinner with a friend called Sergei in the Aragvi, a Georgian
restaurant just off Gorki Street, where we would have careful conversations about the future of the Soviet Union. Shying away from direct
criticism of affairs in the Kremlin, he invented a satirical game in which
we took turns to suggest institutes designed to remedy Soviet failings
(Brezhnev usually responded to problems by setting up an institute to
cope with them). I remember we drew up plans for an institute devoted
to spreading humility through the Soviet Union. Beneath the enormous
frescoes of Tblisi and the Georgian mountains which covered the
Aragvi's walls, we discussed the relative humbleness of different Soviet
leaders and which of them had sufficiently furthered the cause of humility to deserve an award from our institute.
  Conversations with Soviets of any official standing were allusive and
often irritating because they were full of little nods and winks suggesting
that if only the person you were talking to was free to speak his mind, he
could reveal where the body was buried. Dissidents and refuseniks (Jews
denied exit visas) were more forthright, but embittered and unreliable
on anything other than personal experience. They often echoed information they had heard on foreign radio stations. Soon after I arrived I had
dinner with a family of refuseniks who had, at great expense, acquired a
joint of lamb. The father made some point of interest about what was
happening in the Kremlin. I asked him how he knew and he said: "I read
it in the *International Herald Tribune.*" The problem was that by the
mid 1980s there was no longer a "dissident movement" in the sense of
people who held small meetings, issued publications and had some form
of common programme. Rather, there was a group of individuals who

shared a common, and usually unpleasant, fate. The dissident movement which had existed ten years before had been crushed by exile, prison and the renewal of the Cold War. Individuals such as Roy Medvedev, living in a neat little apartment like a ship's cabin in north Moscow, still produced an alternative interpretation of current political events, but it was almost entirely for Western consumption.

At times it was difficult not to admire the thoroughness with which the authorities tried to isolate embassies and newspaper offices. A British diplomat told me how, in the early 1980s, the British ambassador, believing that the Embassy should have more contact with Soviet intellectuals, had invited 150 of them to the Queen's birthday party, the main diplomatic festivity of the year, on the Embassy lawn. When the day of the party came, just three of the intellectuals turned up. Even by Soviet standards this was on the low side, so the Embassy drivers, all Soviets, were asked if they had, in fact, delivered the invitations. They admitted that, noticing that many of the artists and painters lived in distant outskirts of Moscow, they had wanted to avoid the long drive to deliver each invitation individually. Instead, they had handed them over to the Soviet Ministry of Culture to pass them on to the appropriate intellectuals, with whom the Ministry was presumably in contact.

Enraged that the idleness of drivers had sabotaged his plans—for he assumed that the only Ministry of Culture response would have been to burn the invitations after putting a black mark against the names of those invited—the ambassador said that if this happened again he would fire them all. Under threat of the sack the following year the Embassy drivers diligently drove to distant suburbs of Moscow and walked up long flights of stairs to deliver an invitation personally into the hands of each novelist, painter or poet. But the Ministry had a longer reach than the Embassy imagined. Come the Queen's birthday the ambassador impatiently awaited their arrival but, looking around the Embassy lawn an hour after the party started, he was disappointed to note that only three intellectuals had turned up—and those were exactly the same three who had turned up the year before.

Anecdotes like this were at first dampening to the spirits, but in a few months I realised that attempts to isolate a few thousand foreigners in Moscow, a city of nine million, were absurd. It might have been possible under Stalin, but by the 1980s the memory of the terror had faded. In 1986 the Georgian director Tenghiz Abuladze was finally allowed to show his symbolic film *Repentance*, about Stalin and the purges. It was the first fully and openly anti-Stalinist film for years, and for the Moscow intelligentsia a landmark in the Gorbachev thaw. Its popular impact was less clear. Walking out of a cinema in Moscow, Mikhail Gefter, a historian of Stalinism, heard two Muscovite women discussing

the film. As he passed, he heard one woman say to the other in a
shocked voice: "Who would have believed that sort of thing goes on in
Georgia?" There was nervousness about associating with foreigners, but
no real fear. A friend said to me: "When you enter a room with thirty
Russians in it, fifteen of them will rush away from you, because they
think that associating with a foreigner might lose them their job. But
fifteen of them will rush towards you because they are curious to meet a
foreigner, would like to practise their English or think they can persuade
you to buy them a video in the West." He was a little optimistic about
the number of Soviets attracted rather than repelled by the idea of meeting a foreign correspondent, but overall his picture of their response
turned out to be correct.

None of the fifteen was likely to know anything about what was
happening in the Kremlin, but this did not matter. There was obviously a
lot more to what made the Soviet Union tick than some mechanism
located in the Politburo. Incidents like the non-attendance of Soviet
intellectuals at the Queen's birthday party were misleading, chiefly
because the lengths to which the Ministry of Culture had gone to
prevent them attending suggested that they might have passed on some
vital piece of information, which could have provided the key to understanding the Soviet Union. It strengthened the belief, a notorious occu-
pational disease of journalism, that greater access in the shape of
interviews and briefings from those in authority leads to greater understanding of what is happening. In Moscow the delusion was even
stronger than elsewhere because it was supported by the academic traditions of Sovietology which saw the Kremlin as a sort of spaceship hovering over Soviet society and exerting total control over the population. If
this was true, then the obvious—indeed, the only—course for a journalist
wishing to know what was happening was to locate and talk to somebody on board, if not in charge, of the spaceship.

There was some truth in this, but after a few months in Moscow it was
obvious that the spaceship crew, so far from being in total command,
were trying with some desperation to respond to developments which
they did not control. The way people lived had changed in mundane but
important ways. Lenin and Stalin had ruled a country of villages. Under
Khrushchev and Brezhnev, even as the men at the top became moribund, people shifted into the cities, went to university and watched television. Only by keeping both eyes very firmly fixed on the Kremlin was
it possible to avoid seeing that the daily life of an ordinary Russian had
changed more since the death of Stalin in 1953 than the life of the
average American or Italian over the same period. Willingness and
ability to use coercion had also ebbed, and Moscow was full of interesting loopholes in the authority of the state. For instance, just outside the

Foreign Ministry, a skyscraper on the Garden ring built by Stalin in the early fifties, was a small triangular park. You did not have to look at it for very long to see that it was largely inhabited by prostitutes and black-marketeers, curiously indiscreet in their pursuit of the hard currency of tourists staying in the nearby Beograd Hotel. There was, it emerged, a reason for this. By coincidence the park lay exactly on the boundary line dividing two Moscow police districts, and each had said that the other should be responsible for policing it. For years the girls and black-marketeers could ply their profitable trades while the jurisdictional dispute was unresolved.

To some of the expatriates in Moscow these changes were superficial, masking, designedly or not, the unchanging face of the Soviet state. There was also an understandable desire on the part of some experts whose lives had been devoted to trying to predict Soviet actions by examining past precedents not to admit easily to the idea of fundamental change which must deflate the value of their own accumulated know-ledge. Experts on any country instinctively—and usually rightly—deride the idea that anything new has happened, but Russia has some special attraction to people who believe that Gorbachev is only a recycled Khrushchev and Stalin a replay of Peter the Great or Ivan the Terrible. It is politically and intellectually comforting, since it requires no extra thought, to believe that we are simply seeing old patterns repeated. All problems should respond to traditional remedies.

A diplomat told me of an early adherent of this approach who had advised the British Foreign Office in 1917, just after the Bolsheviks had seized power. The Western Allies were worried that the revolutionaries would sign a separate peace with Germany. Experts on Russian affairs were consulted on how to influence the new leadership. Few had anything useful to suggest until one elderly official put forward a novel plan. He said that during his many years of dealing with Russians he had noticed their fondness for decorations. He therefore proposed that Britain award Lenin a knighthood and Trotsky some lesser but still worthwhile honour to encourage them to break off talks with Germany.

Glasnost 1986

On New Year's Eve 1985 Nick Daniloff—then *US News and World Report* correspondent in Moscow—and I went to interview the first deputy editor of *Ekonomicheskaya Gazeta*, the main economic news-paper, to ask him about prospects for economic reform. As we sipped tea and ate biscuits, invariably offered when interviewing Soviet officials, he beamed at us but denied that anything out of the ordinary was happening. "We have discussions, yes, but we also had discussions about the economy in the 1920s, 1930s, 1940s, 1950s, 1960s and 1970s," he said. "Maybe not in the 1940s," said another member of the paper's staff sitting beside him. Walking out of the office after two hours listening to him deny anything was happening, we noticed a workman in the corridor removing a name plate from the door. We asked him why and he said the chief editor of the paper had just been replaced.

The first deputy editor, on Soviet newspapers often the man in charge of the day-to-day running of the publication, was clearly trying to respond to two contradictory pressures. Even after Gorbachev had been in power for two years and Moscow was awash with glasnost, provincial officials balanced nervously between total openness and complete secrecy. Some found it difficult to get into the spirit of the new party line favouring diversity of opinion. Early in 1987 I flew with a small party of journalists from Moscow to Khabarovsk, a city on the Amur River bordering China, run for years by an elderly member of the Central Committee called Cherny. The Foreign Ministry guides took us to a building overlooking the Amur, where we were led into a room containing some forty specialists on the region. The first question asked was on relations with China and was answered by a grey-haired professor in the front row. A second was put about the economic effects of permafrost in the region, and the same man answered it. The professor spoke and the specialists sat in silence behind him for forty-five minutes before the meeting ended.

By then, total secrecy was out of fashion. The turning point was the nuclear disaster at Chernobyl in April 1986. It, more than anything else, proved to the Kremlin the impossibility of confining greater openness to peripheral issues and trying to keep catastrophes secret. The Politburo's first reaction to the news of the nuclear experiment which had gone wrong at its nuclear power plant in the Northern Ukraine was to cover it up. Only when radioactive clouds were detected over Sweden and Finland did it admit that anything had happened. The emphasis was on reassurance. Soviet television showed Ukrainian folk dancers whirling about in Kiev as evidence that foreign reports of the accident were exaggerated. Ten days later the Ukrainian Health Minister appeared on television in Kiev to warn people to stay inside and to wash their hair at least once a day. By then you could go down to Kievski station, close to my office, and watch the arrival of trains from Kiev packed with children sent by their parents to Moscow for safety.

Gorbachev faced a political disaster. A central aim of his foreign policy was to reduce demonisation of the Soviet Union in the West. He had declared a unilateral ban on nuclear tests to raise the credibility of the Soviet commitment to arms control. Now, as a result of Chernobyl, people from Finland to North Wales were being advised to avoid going outside in the rain. Worse, the Kremlin, by creating an information vacuum about the prospects of Russians and the rest of Europe getting radiation sickness, made itself vulnerable to any rumour. Chernobyl caught fire just after midnight on 26 April. By the following Tuesday the pressure for news was enormous. It seemed to me, listening to the BBC World Service and reading the Reuters wire, that doctors in homes for the mentally disturbed across Europe were assuring patients that if they drank their hot chocolate and passed a quiet night, they too would be allowed to give press and radio interviews about what exactly was happening at the core of the reactor.

Late that afternoon I saw that *United Press International* was running a story which quoted sources in Kiev as saying that 2,100 people had died, far in excess of the number admitted by the Soviets. This seemed to me very unlikely. I knew and distrusted the author of the piece. Russian rumours, like Chekhov short stories, tend to be filled with convincing bits of supporting detail which I did not think he would be able to resist. At about 10.30 in the evening, the last moment you could correct a front-page first-edition story in the *Financial Times*, I rang up the office in London and asked them not to run the story, or at least to print it in a manner that showed we did not believe it. This they did, but for the Soviet Foreign Ministry the *UPI* story was a godsend. Every time, over the next few months, they were accused of suppressing or distorting information about Chernobyl, the Foreign Ministry spokesman recalled that the Western press had said that 2,000 people had died. By then also they were in a stronger position to make denials. Ten days after Chernobyl the Soviet press started to report what had happened. The foreign press section of the Foreign Ministry, by Park Kulturi Metro station, gave press conferences and briefings.

Chernobyl marked the real beginning of glasnost on major events for the foreign press in Moscow. The Foreign Ministry learned quickly how to deal with the media. A year later I went on one of a series of press trips to Chernobyl intended to reassure Soviets and foreigners that everything was under control. It was expertly organised. In Chernobyl itself, a typical Ukrainian wooden village twelve miles from the plant, bushes and fruit trees were beginning to grow in through the windows of the abandoned houses. The only people in the village streets were soldiers dressed in military fatigues, their faces covered by white surgeons' masks. Closer to the plant the soldiers were cutting down a pine forest withered by the radiation. In Pripyat, a town of 50,000 where the workers from the plant had once lived, its gardens now stripped of topsoil which had been buried in pits, the television crews rushed to film a clothesline on which were still hanging an abandoned shirt and underpants, bleached by a year of sun and rain. "The wind blew them down but I had them replaced," said the Ukrainian in charge of the party. The press department was beginning to understand visual cliché.

The months after Chernobyl coincided with the dismantling of most of the censorship system. Gorbachev had started making critical speeches from the moment he was elected and had made Alexander Yakovlev head of the Central Committee's Propaganda Department the previous August. This was important, because it gave him influence over the appointment of editors. From early 1986 new, radical editors started to be appointed: Ivan Frolov at the party's monthly theoretical magazine *Kommunist*, Vitali Korotich at Koltsov's old magazine *Ogonyok*, now in colour but moribund, and Yegor Yakovlev at *Moscow News*, a propaganda weekly for foreign consumption published in half a dozen languages and unreadable in all of them. Georgy Markov, head of the Writers' Union for fifteen years, the man held responsible by many Moscow intellectuals for giving Brezhnev a literary award for his war memoirs, was kicked upstairs. In December Andrei Sakharov returned to Moscow after six years' exile in Gorki.

At first, Moscow intellectuals were dubious that these changes meant very much. In 1985 they had believed that Gorbachev meant only Brezhnevism without Brezhnev. Even after the release of Sakharov they remained prone to believe that some reactionary article in an obscure magazine meant that liberal reform was about to go into reverse. Their mood zigzagged between euphoria and despair. Twice, when Gorbachev went on holiday in the summers of 1986 and 1987, every journalist in Moscow heard detailed stories that he had been wounded by an assassin. On the first occasion *Pravda* tried to disprove this by publishing a picture of Gorbachev standing alone and unharmed. Rumour-spreaders then countered by saying that the absence of Raisa indicated that the assassin had missed Gorbachev and hit her. Everybody was jumpy, but glasnost created euphoria among intellectuals, journalists and Foreign Ministry officials with whom expatriates normally had to deal.

I went to see Korotich at *Ogonyok*, whose offices were now close to *Pravda*. He said: "If we fail to rebuild now we'll lose everything. We must destroy all these stone and concrete people, and do something more human, more democratic. That is the only way to live in the modern world." Given the contrast between Korotich and the type of official with whom I had previously dealt, the corniness of some of this did not grate. One day I drove to the offices of *Kommunist*, housed in a large eighteenth-century mansion behind the Pushkin Museum. Ivan Frolov, the editor, was surprised to see me. He said that his secretary had got the time of the interview wrong, but since I had come, he would talk to me for fifteen minutes. In fact he spoke for two hours. I remembered that in *Under Western Eyes*, Joseph Conrad spoke of "the Russians' love of words. They gather them up; they cherish them, but they don't hoard them in their breasts; on the contrary they are always ready to pour them out by the hour or by the night." Maybe the torrent of words was simply the result of ending half a century of self-censorship. I learned to be careful about the traditional warm-up question at the start of an interview because it might elicit a forty-minute response.

In Gorbachev's first two years, it was a comparatively small group of intellectuals and publicists, mostly from within the party, who made the running. They were progressives like Georgi Arbatov, director of the USA and Canada Institute, and Yevgeny Primyakov, head of the World Economy Institute, commentators such as Fyodor Burlatsky and Alexander Bovin, and poets like Yevtushenko and Voznesensky, who had survived and sometimes flourished under Brezhnev without loss of all critical faculties. Others who had been shunted out of the political mainstream during the 1970s began to return; the most important was Alexander Yakovlev, appointed head of the Propaganda Department of the Central Committee after ten years as ambassador to Canada. Here was an important difference between the thaws under Gorbachev in the 1980s and Khrushchev in the 1950s. Progressive members of the party who began to be promoted to influential jobs in 1985 would not have survived under Stalin. Repression under Brezhnev was more benign. A popular saying summed up the fate of senior officials who had lost their jobs under past leaders: "Stalin shot them, Khrushchev sacked them and Brezhnev made them ambassadors."

For correspondents in Moscow this group of officials and journalists began to replace dissidents and diplomats as a source of information. Many of them had learned their political skills as professional survivors during the Brezhnev era, which often made them tricky to deal with. The first time I met Korotich he took me into his office in *Ogonyok* and then, as the interview proceeded, he began to peer around and open drawers in his desk in a mystified way. Finally he jumped to his feet, saying: "This isn't my office!" and explained that as a result of building work he had accidentally taken me into his deputy's office in mistake for his own. As we moved next door to his real office, similar in size and appearance to the one we had just left, I felt a glow of sympathy for Korotich. In most Soviet newspapers there was no question of the editor making such an error, if only because his office was twice as big as anybody else's.

In the following weeks I quoted Korotich's little error to friends as proof that here was a new and more modest breed of Soviet editor. A few months later I met a Soviet friend who had just finished acting as translator for a visiting American. He said that they had visited

Ogonyok to interview Korotich, who spoke enthusiastically of perestroika and glasnost. The visitor was impressed, but what had particularly
persuaded him of the reality of change in the Soviet Union, the translator added, was a simple but significant incident. Halfway through the
interview, Korotich had started to look around his office in surprise,
then sprung to his feet and finally, with profuse apologies for taking
them to the wrong office, led them to his own room next door.

I did not resent Korotich's manoeuvre. He was a thousand times
better than his enemies. Despite all the talk of the Moscow intelligentsia
supporting Gorbachev, the number prepared to do anything about it was
quite limited and of these he was one of the most effective. There was in
any case, in the first eighteen months of glasnost, still a freshness and a
sense of excitement in uninhibited conversation with Soviet journalists
and officials released from past constrictions. It was also inevitable that
this period would end. Interviews, however frank, netted less and less
shockingly new information the longer glasnost continued. At the end of
1987 *Ogonyok* itself published a cartoon showing a fish in a fish tank to
which a radio reporter is holding up a microphone and asking: "What
do you think about glasnost?"

By then there were more interesting questions to ask, because Gorbachev's revolution from above was beginning to get a response from
below. People began to set up political clubs and groups. It was possible
to move outside the circle of progressive members of the establishment.
Visitors compared the atmosphere in Moscow to Britain and the USA
in the 1960s. Moribund magazines, unread for years, were taken over by
radicals. I started to visit the offices of one of these, called *Twentieth
Century and Peace*, whose offices lay just off Pushkin Square at the top
of a dark, crumbling staircase smelling of urine. People were becoming
more confident and daring. In Leningrad a local radical leader, wishing
to focus public attention on a demonstration he was holding, dressed up
some of his supporters in the dark leather jackets favoured by the KGB.
During the meeting crowds watched in amazement when the KGB men
debated with him the issues of the day, making, as they did so, some
extraordinarily frank and damaging admissions about the past behaviour
of the Leningrad KGB.

I found the change in atmosphere invigorating, but by 1988 the opening up of society outside the expatriate community made the claustrophobia within less easy to bear. There were certain professional
advantages in the way the government, in 1984, had treated journalists
as spies and told them as little as possible. In obtaining information from
a government anywhere in the world, a journalist is compelled to act
either as a messenger or as a spy. In London or Washington the role of
messenger inevitably predominates because the only way the journalist

can obtain the information he needs on a regular basis is if somebody in the government voluntarily gives it to him. The revelations about Watergate, considered the apogee of successful investigative reporting, required a struggle for power within the administration waged by selective leak and information acquired through judicial proceedings against officials. A journalist can clearly be an independent and effective investigator or spy, but even here he must act also as a conduit for information, a messenger for somebody in the higher or lower reaches of government who wants to make information public.

There is nothing necessarily demeaning in the role of messenger, but it does demand a degree of intimacy with the government. In Moscow it was something of a relief to be regarded as a spy, however ineffective; or, at best, as a permanent outsider. This was a disaster only if you believed, as did some Kremlinologists, that everything which made the Soviet Union and its 285 million inhabitants tick was explained by some mechanism located in the Politburo. If this were true, then lack of access through leak or interview with the men at the top was a crippling disadvantage. But if, on the contrary, you believed that much of what these men did in the Kremlin was a response, sometimes desperate and often wrongheaded, to a changing political and social landscape outside its walls, then the absence of news conferences and briefings made no difference. In some respects it was an advantage, and I rather regretted the passing of the old system in autumn 1986.

The press section of the Foreign Ministry began to announce enough news at press conferences to make it impossible not to attend. They learned that to control the way an event is reported you must deluge the press and television with information from the very first. When, for instance, soon after Chernobyl, a Soviet grain carrier cut in half a cruise ship called the *Admiral Nakhimov* in the Black Sea, drowning 398 passengers and crew, the news was immediately announced at a late press conference. When the USA claimed that its Moscow embassy was bugged, the Soviet side instantly responded by holding an exhibition of monitoring devices removed from Soviet Embassy buildings in Washington. There was a hiccup in the new détente between foreign journalists and the Foreign Ministry when Nick Daniloff was arrested and jailed for a week at the end of 1986, but otherwise the Kremlin had evidently decided that it was in its interests to treat journalists in Moscow as messengers spreading news of Gorbachev rather than spies.

1988: Visitors

Moscow was now filled with foreign visitors who had come to check on the state of health of perestroika and glasnost. Their arrival was greeted by resident correspondents with the same enthusiasm as soldiers in the First World War greeted generals on a brief visit to the front line. Visits by American publishers and editors were particularly feared by their employees, who had to organise restaurants, hotels, interviews and receptions for them. The payoff was that the Soviet Foreign Ministry, impressed by the presence of the owners of newspapers and television stations, would grant interviews with hitherto inaccessible Politburo members. This calculation was sometimes correct, but did not necessarily benefit the local correspondent. In May 1988 Mrs Katharine Graham, owner of the *Washington Post* and *Newsweek*, came to Moscow to interview Gorbachev in the Kremlin. She took with her four senior staff members from the newspaper and the magazine, but at the last moment excluded the *Washington Post* and *Newsweek* Moscow correspondents. The *Newsweek* correspondent refused to attend Mrs Graham's party celebrating the big interview, and soon afterwards left the magazine.

From the point of view of understanding what was happening in Moscow, all these visits suffered from a common and insurmountable difficulty. Their aim was to write about how far the Soviet Union had changed and would change under Gorbachev. The problem was that few of the visitors knew what the Soviet Union had been like in 1985 and therefore could not judge the extent to which it had shifted since. As a result, most wrote pieces which said there was continuity in the midst of change, hedged a little on the balance between the two, but usually put the heaviest bet on the Soviet Union changing very little.

This may have had something to do with the hotels. After a few months watching visitors it became obvious that their optimism or pessimism about perestroika depended less on the enormous number of interviews they conducted than the state of their accommodation. Here the Hungarians handled things much better. At the same time as their economic experiment got under way in the late sixties they constructed on the Danube, in central Budapest, three or four first-class hotels where the food was good and the waiters spoke English. The aim was to earn hard currency from tourists, but the effect was to impress visiting journalists and diplomats with the success of the Hungarian economic experiment. They wrote reports suggesting that here was real change just as correspondents in Moscow, who had failed to get their breakfast, were writing about the inflexibility of the Soviet system.

In fact all the visitors tended to make the same mistake. Before I went to Moscow I had met pundits in hotel lobbies and ministerial offices in Lebanon and Northern Ireland. Visitors to both countries, after routine comments about the hopelessness of the political situations, would often brighten up and suggest escape routes from the crisis. These were usually imaginary, or at best overoptimistic, because the pundits failed to realise that the countries were too small—in the sense of being under siege by too great enemies, at home and abroad—to allow the room to manoeuvre needed for development and change. Visitors to Moscow over the last four years have made the opposite mistake. It was not that they exaggerated the difficulties facing the Soviet Union—offices filled with ossified bureaucrats and factories with obsolescent machinery—but they almost invariably underestimated the range of options open to a vast and powerful country. They could try one thing, one approach, and if that did not work, try something else. In Lebanon and Northern Ireland, everybody felt too vulnerable to take chances like that.

In one sense, reporting the Soviet Union was easy in 1984 and for the next three or four years. The journalists and diplomats who predicted events correctly were those who assumed that fundamental change was taking place and that Gorbachev was part of those changes. "The Kremlinologists should all have resigned with Gromyko," said one Western ambassador to me in 1985 after some colleague had warned him of the essential conservatism of the Soviet system. These changes had not started with Gorbachev and would not have ended even supposing Moscow rumour had for once been right and he had been assassinated in 1986 or 1987. The impulse for change was so strong that whenever it hit an obstacle it became more, not less, radical. As a result, for most of this period Gorbachev's political strength in the Politburo was greater than it looked because he was going with the tide. Examine the composition of the Politburo and Central Committee, as Kremlinologists largely advised, and he looked vulnerable; look at the overall political and social environment in which the Politburo and Central Committee operated and to which it had to respond, and it was evident that he was impossible to replace.

Gorbachev benefited by going with the tide, but by the same token he was also far less in control of it than he claimed to be. The Soviet Union might have more options than smaller and weaker countries, but was Gorbachev the man to take advantage of them? In 1985, just after he became General Secretary of the party, I thought that to British ears his rhetoric about industrial renewal and managerial revolution seemed familiar, evoking memories of Harold Wilson as Labour Prime Minister after winning the general election in 1964. There was the same glibness and tactical agility masking a policy of drift. By the time I left I had come to feel this was unfair. Gorbachev had started to dismantle the fortress into which Lenin and Stalin had turned the Soviet Union. He had done so more effectively than had seemed possible when Chernenko was buried, even if it was evident that he did not know precisely what he intended to put in its place. He was ending the long siege, and with it the Cold War in miniature, the siege within a siege, in which foreigners in Moscow had lived since the Revolution.

March 1989

PART II

The End of Kremlinology: The Politics of the Gorbachev Era

Mikhail Gorbachev and the End of Kremlinology

Historical analogies have multiplied alarmingly since Mikhail Gorbachev became General Secretary of the Soviet Communist Party in 1985. Sympathisers with Gorbachev's reforms compare him to President Roosevelt, doing for Soviet socialism in the 1980s what his predecessor did for American capitalism in the 1930s—modernising it in order to maintain it. Others, hopeful or fearful of a more total reformation and break with the past, speak of Martin Luther as the more instructive parallel, while comparison with Peter the Great remains popular among those who claim that nothing much ever changes in the Soviet Union, and then only under the iron heel of the state. Western academic specialists and Kremlinologists, on the other hand, often prefer a more recent analogy: looking at Gorbachev's career as a reformer they say they see parallels, many of them ominous, with the rise and fall of former Soviet leader Nikita Khrushchev. The implication, comforting to many in the West, is that what is happening in Moscow today is not so original as might at first sight appear and recent reforms are, in any case, continually vulnerable to conservative counterattack, perhaps culminating—like the fate of Khrushchev in 1964—in the overthrow of Gorbachev and the reversal of all the changes he has introduced.

Expert opinion on Gorbachev and the chances of successful reform has always tended towards gloomy prophecy. Since the death of Leonid Brezhnev in 1982 it has emphasised the strength of conservatives and vested interests at the top, insoluble economic problems and the inability of the system to adapt. At first expectations of many Western Sovietologists were categorically negative. In 1983 Lieutenant General William Odom, then head of the National Security Agency and a leading expert on the Soviet Union, expected "sound and fury about domestic reform accompanied by little actual change", while abroad, "we can expect threats to end détente." Over the next five years predictions by Sovietologists became more circumspect, though still flavoured by warnings of doom. After the Soviet party conference in June 1988 Peter Reddaway, Director of the Kennan Institute for Russian Studies in Washington, concluded a survey of Gorbachev's position by noting:

> Ominous issues are the current economic situation, about which delegates
> expressed considerable alarm, the intractable and mounting problem of keep-
> ing the national minorities under control, and the smouldering opposition in
> the Eastern European countries. These are the biggest threats to perestroika
> and Gorbachev. However much Gorbachev manoeuvres, any or all of them
> could play into the hands of Ligachev [Yegor Ligachev, presumed leader of
> the conservative opposition in the Politburo] and the forces he represents.

The depressed tone of this and other speculation about the Soviet Union
owes much to two important legacies of classic Kremlinology. The first
is a methodology of accumulating past precedents, almost regardless of
historical context, and using them as a guide to present events. Patterns
of political behaviour from Khrushchev's era are assumed to be a sound
precedent for behaviour under Gorbachev. Limited weight is given to
the political impact of major social changes such as urbanisation, the
spread of higher education or Gorbachev's ability to communicate
directly with the population through television in a way Khrushchev
could not. A second legacy is an exaggerated focus on the Politburo and
the top ranks of government, as if the Soviet state were an independent
entity hovering over the rest of society and unaffected by its development. Here the fact that many specialists on the Soviet Union work for
or are associated with Western governments may be of importance in
producing an assumption that initiatives must come from the top down
and any disorder or disruption of the existing system must count against
Gorbachev. At the end of 1987, for instance, Lieutenant General Odom
returned to questions of Soviet reform to ask: "Is Gorbachev bent upon
fundamental change in the system? If he is, the chances he can control it
are small, virtually nil."

It is not that Sovietology is always wrong in its description of potential or actual crises. Peter Reddaway is right in saying that the Soviet
Union faces serious problems in the troubled economy, ethnic relations
at home and the uncertainties in its relations with Eastern Europe.
Sovietologists are correct to point to division and conflict in the Politburo and Central Committee. The error comes rather in the conclusions
drawn about the political consequences of these difficulties and the
assumption that they block reform. In fact the pattern of Soviet politics
since Gorbachev became General Secretary has been quite different:
impediments to reform have increased the pace of change and shifted it
in a more radical direction. Major crises such as Chernobyl and the
prolonged war in Afghanistan have produced radical solutions rather
than reinforcing the status quo.

To illustrate this point, it is worth looking at the three problems raised by Reddaway as possibly "playing into the hands of Ligachev" and threatening reform—the economy, the nationalities question, and Eastern Europe. Of these, the potential impact of opposition in Eastern Europe has not really been tested, since the situation there has not deteriorated sufficiently to demand a response from the Soviet leadership. Domestic economic problems and nationalist unrest, on the other hand, have already presented real and pressing challenges to Gorbachev. Yet the lesson in each case is that where obstacles have been encountered in the process of reform, the Kremlin has had no choice but to seek a more rather than less radical solution.

For example, the increasingly evident failure of limited administrative reform to solve Soviet economic problems in 1985 and 1986 led to the adoption, at a plenary meeting of the Central Committee in June 1987, of a radical economic agenda that sought to change fundamentally the basis on which the economy was run. Similarly, Moscow appeared to learn a lesson from the failure of its policy towards the Armenia–Azerbaijan conflict. Instead of the party standing in the way of local demands and thus losing political influence, it has sought to become their advocate. In early 1988 Armenian demands for the return of the enclave of Nagorno–Karabakh led to demonstrations, riots, and a massacre—events the Soviet leadership failed to foresee or prevent. But Moscow's response to nationalist unrest in the Baltic republics of Estonia, Latvia and Lithuania later in the year was both more adroit and more radical, seeking to co-opt the energy of protesters demanding autonomy and channel it into support for reform—even if this meant making a fundamental change in the relations between Moscow and the non-Russian republics.

Gorbachev and his supporters are clearly conscious that they need a sense of crisis to force through change. In the economy it is they who have stressed the intractability of the problems, the seriousness of which are taken in the West as weakening the Soviet leader and possibly even driving him from office. It was Gorbachev in 1987 who first started talking of the economy being in "a pre-crisis situation". Pro-reform economists write long articles about the seriousness of the crisis in the economy which Soviet citizens face. Their alarm is heartfelt, but it also serves two vital political purposes: it mobilises public opinion behind reform, and it puts pressure on the Politburo and Central Committee to sanction fundamental change. Gorbachev has always been extremely adroit at creating a political atmosphere conducive to his aims. Before the 1987 plenum on the economy he summoned a heavily publicised meeting of experts and supporters of perestroika to describe what was wrong and what needed to be done. Again, in the days before his reshuffle of the Politburo on 30 September 1988, Soviet television gave blanket coverage of his tour of the Siberian city of Krasnoyarsk, where people vociferously complained of lack of food, housing and services. In other words it is Gorbachev, not his opponents, who has raised the political temperature by emphasising the seriousness of economic conditions.

The key to the discovery of the dynamic and general direction of Soviet politics in 1985–88 is knowing why this strategy worked. Why did the Soviet leadership consider they had little option but to opt for radical solutions? Gorbachev and his chief Politburo ally Alexander Yakovlev may be skilled at political manoeuvring, but the Central Committee, which supported fundamental economic and political change in 1987 and 1988, was largely inherited from Leonid Brezhnev. Again and again Western specialists emphasised the conservatism of the system and the strength of vested interests, yet one of the real surprises of the last four years is that active conservative opposition to reform has been so ineffectual. This made Gorbachev stronger than he looked. Where he was weak, his opponents were even weaker. They lacked an alternative leader and an alternative economic policy at a moment when even the most conservative recognised that some change was necessary. In 1964, when Brezhnev and Kosygin took over leadership in the Kremlin from Khrushchev, it was still possible for a Soviet conservative to argue that the existing system was fundamentally sound and needed only to be run more efficiently. Twenty years later this argument had little credibility, and Gorbachev himself constantly defended reform by saying that whatever the difficulties, nobody else had come up with a credible alternative.

In fact the Soviet Union had evolved enormously under Brezhnev, fundamentally altering the way Soviet politics worked. Gorbachev was a product of change as well as a catalyst for reform. Thus the cards were always stacked a little more in his favour than was evident to observers abroad, who were frequently hampered by a methodology which had an inbuilt bias towards the belief that Soviet society cannot and does not change. Analogies between Khrushchev and Gorbachev are relevant as a guide to current events only if we assume that the political situation under both men was largely the same. In other words, the methodology used to analyse the Soviet Union presupposed a static situation in which historic precedents could be expected to repeat themselves and, given this assumption, expert opinion naturally warned that changes were limited, vulnerable and reversible. Moreover, because the traditions of Sovietology indicated that the impulse for change in Moscow should be limited, it had difficulties in explaining the dynamics of reform. Why, for instance, every time reform encountered an obstacle such as continuing economic stagnation or a crisis such as Chernobyl, did it always opt for more rather than less change? Why was it that again and again conservative men in the Politburo and Central Committee, who would have preferred things to remain as they were, felt they had no practical alternative but to go along with changes aimed at transforming the way their society was run?

It was in the tradition of Western perceptions of the Soviet Union to seek and find the dynamic for reform in the Politburo and, more especially, in Gorbachev himself. It also followed from this that the pace of reform was dictated by a prolonged struggle between reformers and conservatives, led by Gorbachev and Ligachev respectively. There was much to be said for both views. In 1985 Gorbachev had launched a revolution from above, and the initiative for change had come from the Politburo and the party secretariat. This was sometimes taken to imply that perestroika had shallow roots, was somehow accidental or artificial in its origins, and therefore vulnerable to counterattack by conservative members of the Politburo. In fact the opposite conclusion should have been drawn. The very fact that the Politburo and the Central Committee, often portrayed as caricatures of an aging oligarchy, felt that change had come was a measure of the bankruptcy of the more conservative solutions they might have preferred. At the party conference in June 1988 a conservative delegate warned that the party was like a plane taking off for an unknown destination, but he was immediately attacked by another delegate of some seniority, who said that whatever lay over the horizon, it could not be as bad as the marsh in which their plane was currently stuck. By the mid 1980s, doing nothing had come to seem very risky indeed.

By the same token, the least likely outcome of the struggle for reform would be a return to Brezhnevite orthodoxy. Although from 1986 onwards specialists and non-specialists alike asked if perestroika and glasnost were reversible, there was never any real constituency at the top for a return to pre-1982 norms. Part of the confusion over the reversibility of change comes from the misuse of labels. Names like reactionary, conservative, moderniser, reformer and radical frequently described attitudes rather than factions, and these attitudes changed with the political situation. Reactionaries and conservatives in the Politburo, in the sense of those who wanted to preserve the status quo of 1964–82, lost their crucial battles in the three years between the death of Brezhnev and the election of Gorbachev. Their last success was the selection of Konstantin Chernenko to succeed Yuri Andropov as General Secretary in 1984. In the first two years of Gorbachev men like Andrei Gromyko, Foreign Minister for twenty-eight years, Yegor Ligachev and KGB chief Konstantin Chebrikov were seen as modernisers, implementing administrative reforms and getting rid of corrupt party bosses such as Viktor

Grishin in Moscow and Dinmukhamed Kunaev in Kazakhstan. In other words, the definition of a Politburo conservative changed between 1985 and 1988.

The political struggles at the top of the party between 1985 and 1988 were never a clean-cut fight between conservatives and radicals but a messy conflict between men who generally accepted that they had to make drastic changes in order to modernise. As a result the essence of the political situation was not combat between organised factions in the leadership but fluidity, shifting alliances and combinations. From mid 1987 the differences between Politburo members who might be described as radical and those who wanted more limited change did become sharper and more visible, but it is also important to appreciate the strength of the glue holding the leadership together. Being conservative on one issue did not mean being conservative on all. To give an example: in August 1988 Ligachev, often seen as the leader of the conservatives, made a speech in Gorki in which he reaffirmed his belief in class struggle as a vital constituent of world politics and Soviet foreign policy. This contradicted a speech by Eduard Shevardnadze in July in which the Foreign Minister had deprecated the class struggle as a determinant of the way the Soviet Union handled its relations with other states. Here the ideological differences between the two were clear and unambiguous. But it is important also to realise that Ligachev never came out against the withdrawal from Afghanistan, a more substantive and potentially divisive issue; nor is there any evidence that he opposed it. In other words, Ligachev was defending what he considered a fundamental part of Leninism, but not the political inheritance of Brezhnev.

Gorbachev himself caught the Soviet political mood well. Addressing a meeting of newspaper editors last September, he said the key feature of politics was that "the old and new are living side by side, comrades, side by side, and they are in conflict." And it is this conflict, a struggle which is going on at every level of society, which produces "an intricate mosaic of moods, confused thoughts, illusion, impatience, irritation". He might have added that he himself had increased perplexity in Moscow and abroad about the radicalism of changes being contemplated by his use of a quite deliberate and effective political tactic. The one factor which might have brought together the disparate but numerous party functionaries with misgivings about the direction Gorbachev was taking was Gorbachev himself. Not wanting to make conservative sentiment within the Politburo and the Central Committee gel, he was always careful never to identify conservative factions but to attack conservative attitudes. The political situation may have been naturally fluid, but Gorbachev did all he could to keep it that way. Boris Yeltsin, the populist party leader in Moscow, was very publicly dismissed by Gorbachev in October 1987 after he had openly criticised Ligachev to the Central Committee for opposing perestroika. This provoked divisions at a moment when Gorbachev did not want them and he was quick to join the attack on his former supporter, although many of the accusations levelled against Yeltsin by Moscow party officials could have been levelled equally against Gorbachev himself.

This tactic of not provoking division at the top was rooted partly in weakness—not in the sense that Gorbachev was in any danger of being overthrown, but in the difficulty of persuading the Politburo and the Central Committee that radical steps were necessary to modernise the country. Even in 1988 committed radicals in the Politburo, on whose support Gorbachev could always count, were probably limited to Eduard Shevardnadze, Alexander Yakovlev and, after the Politburo reshuffle of 30 September, Vadim Medvedev. But the tactic was also part of the much broader strategy which has flavoured Soviet politics over the last three-and-a-half years: Gorbachev and the other reformers have repeatedly said that the party is the only instrument which can carry out reform in the Soviet Union. At the same time they are clearly conscious that almost nothing needs reform as badly as the party itself. Responding to this situation, Gorbachev has tried to shake up the party without splitting it. "We are responsible for preventing the country from being split into camps, for keeping people from head-on clashes," he said just before he became President. "We know all about 'firing at headquarters' from China. And it took fifteen years to try to understand what they had done."

By "firing at headquarters" Gorbachev meant launching a drastic purge of the top party leadership, and by ruling it out—and it was doubtful in any case that such a purge was feasible without provoking a backlash—he doomed himself to a complicated process of cajoling and persuading the rest of the leadership into accepting changes about which they were apprehensive. Not that Gorbachev and the victors in the 1982–85 leadership battle had not clearly targeted some of their opponents on the Politburo such as Grishin, Kunaev and Grigorii Romanov, the former boss of Leningrad. All three were the antithesis of the rejuvenated party, purged of corruption, which Gorbachev and Ligachev both said they wanted.

But although the removal of conservative members of the Politburo and the chief organs of state went smoothly there were, from the beginning, deep misgivings in what reformers saw as the two main areas of conservative strength: the middle ranks of the party outside Moscow, in the shape of regional first secretaries, and the top ranks of the state apparatus, such as the heads of ministries and state committees in Moscow. Their conservatism was generally passive, but they were able to use their bureaucratic strength to sidetrack or dilute reform. Their inertia created extreme frustration among supporters of reform. At the party conference the actor Mikhail Ulyanov said that everybody criticised bureaucrats as the invisible agents who silently smothered change, and compared the bureaucracy to the Abominable Snowman: "There are lots of tracks everywhere; everything is trampled down, but no one has set eyes on one." His point was to emphasise the residual strength of the bureaucracy but he also, unconsciously, identified its political weakness: the very invisibility of which he complained made it difficult to challenge Gorbachev.

In any case, the silent stifling of reform by the bureaucracy, the fate of Kosygin's economic reforms in the 1960s, had become much more difficult because of two fundamental changes in the political environment. The first was glasnost, which emerged in 1986 as censorship was relaxed, Brezhnev holdovers such as the Minister of Culture and head of the Writers' Union were removed and a number of radical editors were appointed to magazines and papers such as *Kommunist*, *Ogonyok* and *Moscow News*. Glasnost, the open expression of a diversity of views, rapidly fostered the development of public opinion and limited the bureaucracy's monopoly of information, which had been a key buttress of its authority. At first, in autumn 1986, criticism was focused on important but ultimately anodyne subjects such as the erection of a hideous new war memorial in Moscow or the pollution of Lake Baikal, but by 1988 debate had shifted towards discussion of more serious topics such as Soviet foreign policy and the future of socialism. Old orthodoxies came under attack, and in an important change in the political atmosphere there was an explosion in popular expectations: economic, political and cultural. People expected more from the government, and this increased pressure on the party to implement radical change.

It was this explosion of expectations which provoked the second major change in the political environment—the rise of mass political participation. The most important feature of Soviet politics between 1982 and 1987 was the struggle of the elite to break from its old routines. This effort was in response to a series of challenges: the need to modernise the economy, compete with the West and raise the living standards of the people. But the elite was *not* responding to any threat to its position from any existing or potential political opposition. There were dissidents, but they were individuals who shared a common fate rather than members of a dissident movement. Even when public opinion began to develop as a political force in 1986–87, it did not impinge on the authority of the party. Gorbachev himself said, in speeches in Krasnodar and Khabarovsk in autumn 1986, that political reform must come at the same time as economic change, but it was over a year before his revolution from above began to elicit a mass political response. When it did so it was for a cause and in a region which caught Gorbachev by surprise: mass demonstrations by Armenians demanding the return of Nagorno-Karabakh, followed four months later by mass agitation in Estonia and the two other Baltic states.

These developments interacted with struggles in the leadership to dictate the pace and trajectory of reform, and from summer 1987 onwards, they also put increasing strain on the consensus within the Politburo. The danger from Gorbachev's point of view of the Yeltsin affair in October that year was that almost for the first time modernisers like Ligachev and Chebrikov in the Politburo were coming together with reactionaries lower down in the party apparatus to sack the Moscow party boss. Not surprisingly, Gorbachev and Yakovlev showed no hesitation in throwing Yeltsin overboard. Friction within the party was clearly increasing. In March a sort of conservative manifesto, purporting to be a letter from a Leningrad schoolteacher called Nina Andreyeva, was published in *Sovietskaya Rossiya*, a major newspaper, and in April firmly rebutted by *Pravda*.

But it was only at the party conference in June that the conflict among the leadership became really visible. Ligachev attacked Yeltsin and the radical press, reminded delegates of the party's past achievements and issued a subtle warning to Gorbachev about the role in his election as General Secretary of members of the Politburo now seen as too conservative. There was no change, as had been expected, in the membership of the Central Committee. In July Eduard Shevardnadze made a speech to his own Foreign Ministry officials strongly criticising the past conduct of Soviet foreign policy and thus, by implication, the policy of President Gromyko, Soviet Foreign Minister for the twenty-eight years up to 1985. In August Ligachev made a speech in Gorki reasserting the importance of class struggle in foreign policy, and defended the party's record.

How great a threat did this pose for Gorbachev? Did Ligachev want to replace him, and was he ever in a position to do so? A few days after the party conference ended in July Roy Medvedev, a dissident historian under Brezhnev but by 1988 a supporter of Gorbachev, summarised Ligachev's position in an interview:

On his own Ligachev represents the union of the old and the new. He is opposed to corruption, alcoholism and parasitism. However, he believes in order imposed by the party by dint of declarations and wants to keep the country under the CPSU's close control—especially the press and television, which he believes should broadcast only political programmes. It is clear that many conservatives and the entire apparatus have a natural defender in him.

This was a reasonable, if somewhat jaundiced, description of Ligachev's political position by summer 1988, but his disquiet had been slow to surface publicly. After 1985 Ligachev, although often pilloried as a reactionary by Moscow intellectuals, had played a useful political role for Gorbachev by forming a link between the old and the new and by keeping in check the fears of the party apparatus. If Ligachev had not existed, it might have been necessary to invent him. Only at the party conference in June did Ligachev begin to speak of the role played by three Politburo members—Andrei Gromyko, Mikhail Solomentsev and Viktor Chebrikov—in making Gorbachev General Secretary with, perhaps, the implication that what they could do in 1985, they could undo in 1988.

Yet in his most conservative utterances Ligachev principally criticised what he deemed the excesses of perestroika. He never really developed a credible alternative programme, and above all an alternative economic policy, and this was a critical failing because the need for economic change, admitted even by otherwise reactionary members of the Central Committee, had been the main motor for reform since the death of Brezhnev in 1982. In so far as there ever was a programme of "moderate perestroika" it had been tried in 1985–86, when Gorbachev and Ligachev had combined to fire inefficient ministers and administrators, crack down on corruption and try to run the existing system more effectively through better strategic control at the top, balanced by better managers at the bottom. Ligachev announced the near-record 1986 grain harvest as the first fruits of improved administration, but the first good news also turned out to be the last. The dividends of moderate perestroika were very limited.

If the struggle in the Politburo had been between outright conservatives and radicals, Ligachev's inability to show how he could be a more effective moderniser than Gorbachev would not have mattered. As it was, it made it far more difficult for him to compete for the leadership. This impression of weakness seems to be confirmed by the Politburo reshuffle of 30 September: Ligachev was shifted from his number two position to head agriculture, and Chebrikov lost his position as head of the KGB. Andrei Gromyko and Solomentsev, two Politburo members mentioned by Ligachev at the party conference in a context which implied that they stood with him, were retired. Gorbachev replaced Gromyko as president and Vadim Medvedev, whose speeches had always been radical, entered the Politburo.

This was not a total knockout victory for radicals over conservatives, but it did leave Gorbachev in a much stronger position. Neither the armed forces nor the KGB, possible centres of resistance to change, were now headed by a full Politburo member. In the weeks since the reshuffle Ligachev had been notably less vocal, and even in the management of agricultural policy much of the running had been made by Gorbachev and Viktor Nikonov, the Politburo member who was party secretary for agriculture. In brief, the intermittent conflict between modernisers and radicals in the Soviet leadership, which began to heat up in summer 1987, concluded with a shift in the balance of power towards the radicals or—perhaps a more accurate label—towards those leaders with fewest inhibitions about introducing radical change.

Reviewing the history of the period between 10 March 1985, when Gorbachev became General Secretary, and 30 September 1988, when he became President, what other lessons can be learned about the dynamics of change? A difficulty here is that the actions and plans of the leadership became much more visible under Gorbachev, in contrast to the obscurity of conflicts in the Kremlin between 1982 and 1985. But the decisive moments in the struggle between reformers and conservatives—conservative in the real sense of wishing to conserve the Brezhnev legacy in a way Ligachev did not—took place in this period, not later. The key victories for reform were the election of Yuri Andropov in 1982 and Mikhail Gorbachev in 1985, while the weakness of the conservatives in the leadership was evident in their inability in 1984 to produce a more credible candidate as General Secretary than Konstantin Chernenko, who was ill for most of his one year in office. Once Gorbachev was General Secretary he was extraordinarily difficult to displace because of the strength of the office and because his opponents had no alternative candidate. The party and state bureaucracy, able to use their administrative strength to dilute or block reform, could not turn tactical setbacks for Gorbachev into political defeat.

There was a further consequence, less flattering to Gorbachev, which flowed from the perception, common among foreign observers and Soviet intellectuals alike, that the dynamic and pace of reform were determined by the balance of power within the Politburo. There was some truth in this, but it also led to an exaggerated idea of the degree to which Gorbachev himself had a programme and a plan. In fact many of his difficulties flowed not from political opposition but from the intractability of the problems he faced, with no clear plan—and this was above all true of the economy—for how he should tackle them. This was masked because from 1986 Gorbachev was clear about his long-term objectives: a less authoritarian society, a modernised economy, and no inhibitions about the radicalism of the measures needed to achieve these ends. His opponents, though occasionally vocal about what they did not want, had no real alternative programme. From Gorbachev's point of view there were advantages in denying potential opposition a target, but for all the Soviet leader's confidence and vigour in pursuing reform, the lack of a clear strategy stored up difficulties for the future.

Emphasis on the strength of Gorbachev's political position does not mean that the direction he took after 1985 did not cause deep and pervasive resentment in the party apparatus, the middle- and lower-level officials whose authority was threatened. Yet there was not much they could do about it. Traditions of obedience and the fact that they were essentially administrative officials made them ineffective and inexperienced in organising political opposition. They might applaud Ligachev at the party conference, but there is no sign that this affected the outcome of conflicts at the top. The very political impotence of the Communist Party of which Gorbachev frequently complained, its inability to persuade in contrast to its ability to administer, made it difficult to organise an effective opposition. For example, the publication of the Nina Andreyeva letter in March, and the lack of any reply from pro-reform writers until April, was taken as a sign of conservative strength. Somebody had got the letter published and discussed, and prevented any response. But as a conservative counteroffensive the letter was a nostalgic and unconvincing appeal to old party nostrums. To combat Gorbachev, conservatives needed to match his populist appeal with populism of their own, and the letter showed limited capacity to do so.

Ironically, if Gorbachev's plans to detach the party from its role as economic administrator and increase its role as a political body able to convince as well as coerce come to fruition, it will be much easier—indeed, necessary—to organise factions in the future. How else, if the Soviet Union is to remain a one-party state, is it to become more democratic? Any return to real political life in the Soviet Union *must* mean that real conflicts are aired within the party and expressed in the press outside it, and the expression of differences must mean, at some stage, the formation of factions. This is not as alarming as it seems to Soviet and foreign observers. The Bolsheviks openly debated whether or not to launch the October Revolution in 1917 and opposition groups within the party were banned only in 1921. Failure to adopt any mechanism through which conflicts in the leadership could be expressed paved the way for Stalin's despotism. Gorbachev tolerates differences within the leadership (perhaps because he has no choice) but the real need is for rules of the political game, defining the consensus within which differences can be expressed. If this does not happen, "democratic centralism" will remain a contradiction in terms.

Since economic reform has been the motor for change since the death of Brezhnev, it is not surprising that Gorbachev's failure to produce economic results is often seen as undermining perestroika. Robert Gates, deputy director of the Central Intelligence Agency, voiced this belief when he declared, in October 1988: "Popular hostility is growing, as disruption and dislocation brought about by change result in economic setbacks and a worsening situation for the consumer." In fact, it is Gorbachev's supporters who have highlighted these failures, using them as a stick to attack the economic record of Brezhnev and to argue that the model of the command economy developed in the 1930s is obsolete. The pattern of the period from 1985 to 1988 was for the failure of economic reforms—though these were very limited—to raise the standard of living to strengthen Gorbachev's hand, not weaken it. But this tactic cannot be used for ever. By the end of 1988 reforming economists, worried that continuing disappointment of popular expectations might discredit perestroika, called for the Soviet Union's scarce hard currency to be spent on importing food and consumer goods.

The main economic developments under Gorbachev do not show a disastrous slide in performance but rather a continuation of the pre-Gorbachev trend of modest increases in output and no improvement in quality. In the first nine months of 1988 national income rose by a respectable 4.7 per cent over the same period in 1987 and production of meat, milk and eggs increased faster than the five-year plan decreed. Why, then, is there a general perception among Soviets that economic conditions are growing worse, not better? Two trends may have contributed to this perception. First, as the State Committee for Statistics reported in October: "Wages in many enterprises rose faster than labour productivity. The population's monetary income exceeds the goods and services available." Without price increases this means that the degree to which demand exceeds supply is expressed by ever-longer queues. Secondly, and less quantifiably, there is an increase in discontent at food and consumer goods shortages because Gorbachev's arrival in power led to an explosion of expectations in 1985–86. Domestic output has not risen fast enough to meet this demand—indeed, without price increases demand will always exceed supply—and there has been no attempt so far to emulate the Hungarians in the early 1970s when they bolstered reform by rapidly increasing imports of scarce consumer goods and foodstuffs.

The failure to produce economic results did not discredit perestroika because Gorbachev and the reformers could still blame deficiencies on Brezhnev and the command economy. The excuse was all the easier to use because no serious economic reform was introduced during Gorbachev's first three years in power. This may have been because the leadership did not realise the seriousness of the situation. Gorbachev now says: "We underestimated the whole depth and weight of the distortions and the past years' stagnation. There was a lot we simply didn't know and are seeing only now." He therefore spent his first year looking for increases in output and quality through changes in personnel, administration and investment. A new quality control organisation was established in 1987 but had to curtail its activities in the face of protests from management and workers alike.

It was only in June 1987 that the Central Committee endorsed an agenda for economic reform condemning the command economy as obsolete and establishing radically new objectives for the economy, though not stating how they were to be attained. The State Enterprise Law, giving financial independence to enterprises, was introduced at the beginning of 1988 but the central ministries and state committees (Gosplan and Gosnab, in charge of the distribution of resources) retained most of their old authority. Changes were often introduced in addition to, instead of replacing, existing methods even where they contradicted each other. How, for instance, was an enterprise to be financially independent if it did not control its own prices? The results of this approach were spelled out at the party conference by Leonid Abalkin, a leading reform economist and head of the Economics Institute. He said that in the present five-year plan (1986–90) it was necessary to go either for quality or for quantity and, true to Soviet tradition, the government had refused to give up its demand for more, rather than better, goods. Abalkin said it could not have both: "By continuing to opt for purely quantitative, volume economic growth we are unable to solve the problems of fundamentally improving output quality, retooling the national economy, and improving its efficiency, and we cannot turn the economy round towards the consumer."

Gorbachev was slow to see this. The reformers around him were astute politicians, but few had experience of macroeconomics. He never had a group of experienced Politburo members and party secretaries in charge of the economy in the same way as Shevardnadze, Gromyko, Yakovlev and Dobrynin were in charge of foreign policy. Economists like Abel Agenbegyan and Leonid Abalkin remained outside the Central Committee and it was dubious, in any case, whether they knew how to make the transition from a centrally planned and administered economy.

Not that everything which went wrong was the result of poor planning or failure to innovate. Objective factors over which nobody in the Soviet Union had any control also hit the economy. Under Brezhnev the development of the oil fields of Western Siberia had occurred just in time to take advantage of the jump in oil prices in 1973. The Soviet Union became one of the world's largest oil exporters, and by 1984 oil and gas together earned more than half its hard currency earnings. The decline in the price of oil has therefore had a very serious impact on the economy, costing the state 40 billion roubles in lost revenues between 1985 and 1988 and wiping out, from the consumer's point of view, the slender benefits of administrative change in the mid 1980s. It may also have contributed to the need—despite an early commitment by Gorbachev to do the opposite — to keep investing large sums in the energy industries.

The lesson of the last four years is that the frustration of economic reform and its failure to produce results have invariably pushed the party leadership to adopt more, not less, radical measures. There has been a general consensus at the top that they must do something about the economy, but between 1985 and 1988 no real agreement on how and when the necessary structural changes should be introduced. Given this disagreement, it was no bad thing that the state was slow to act. The whole course of Soviet economic development since 1929 has been distorted by attempts to modernise and change too fast. Effective economic change is really feasible only in the 1990s. Introduced too early, without a clear idea of how to implement a new price system, wholesale trade and domestic competition, it could damage the credibility of reform. It also needs to be accompanied by social policies such as higher pensions, job retraining and other measures which soften the impact of reform on individual workers and employees.

The danger is that continuing disappointment of heightened popular expectations of improved living standards will begin to erode political support for perestroika before it is really introduced. This support is vital because few of the reforms now being considered are politically anodyne in their impact, either on the party bureaucracy or on public opinion. For instance, it is easy enough to announce, as a general policy, that in future loss-making enterprises can go bankrupt, but what happens when the local party leadership in Georgia or Irkutsk allies itself with the appropriate ministry in Moscow to demand that an exception be made in favour of some local plant threatened with closure? It is through such exceptions that Soviet and East European economic reforms have been eroded in the past. A further test of the political strength of the government will come with the introduction of price changes, which will generally mean rises. Will strikes and demonstrations erupt? This has been the critical moment for reforms in Poland and Yugoslavia, and it will be a real measure of Gorbachev's popular support. Above all else, he needs—if he is to minimise the social and political friction inevitable in economic changes—to ensure that reform is seen as the channel through which people can escape from shortages and poor-quality goods.

Popular pressure for reform is a function of the social transformation of Soviet society since the 1920s. Economic management might have stuck essentially in the same mould it took in the 1930s, but there has always been more to what makes the Soviet Union tick than this. Over the last fifty years the growth of cities, the development of industry and the spread of education have transformed the way ordinary Soviet citizens live their lives. A central question of Soviet politics now is the degree to which these social changes have provided a new constituency for Gorbachev and reform. And if they have, will he be able to create a party that channels the energies and expresses the frustrations of a newly active public opinion?

The social differences are enormous, not just between the Soviet Union of Lenin and the Soviet Union of today, but between the times of Khrushchev and Chernenko. Stalin and the Leviathan state he built in the 1930s were rooted in the social and economic backwardness of the country. At the time of the 1917 Revolution, 70 per cent of the Russian population was illiterate. By the middle of the 1970s the majority of children could expect to be in school up to the age of seventeen or eighteen. In 1959 the majority of workers had only four years in elementary school. By 1979 the proportion of manual workers with only elementary education had fallen to 18.5 per cent. In higher education the number of students rose from 1.5 million in 1953 to over five million in 1978. There was a new generation to which Brezhnev's government had, by the 1970s, less and less to offer.

The semi-military style and organisation of Stalin's state machine was effective in the 1930s in forcing the pace of industrialisation regardless of cost, but half a century later its methods were unnecessarily primitive and counterproductive. It still had its old capacity to concentrate resources to cope with specific crises, such as President Reagan's banning the sale of US equipment to build an oil pipeline in 1981, but otherwise it perpetuated the inefficiencies which had been inevitable in the 1930s. In meeting, or even understanding, the needs of a semi-modern Soviet Union, the old system was clearly becoming obsolescent.

Social changes also transformed the political environment. Urbanisation means not only that some 180 million people now live in cities—compared to 56 million before the last war—but that 97 out of 100 families in these cities own a television set. Not that a better-educated and more sophisticated population necessarily spells the end of authoritarian government; in the Soviet Union it might not have done so if all the government had wanted was obedience. But by 1986 it was becoming clear that Gorbachev wanted and needed to win popular support for reform, and this in turn meant allowing a diversity of opinion and a freer press. The development of a well-educated society did not by itself change the political system, but the government knew that to achieve its ends, to avoid inertia, it had to be able to persuade people to act.

To appreciate the impact of higher levels of education, the introduction of television and high readership of newspapers (*Pravda* 11.5 million, *Izvestia* 7 million) on Soviet politics, compare the impact of the two intellectual "thaws": the first under Khrushchev in the late fifties and early sixties; the second under Gorbachev since 1986. The heroes of the first thaw were novelists such as Solzhenitsyn and poets like Yevtushenko. The literary magazine *Novy Mir* was the flagship of liberal reform. A quarter of a century later the pattern is different: the heroes of the Gorbachev era come from the mass media and cater to a mass audience. Film-makers like Tenghiz Abuladze and Yefim Klimov, editors like Vitaly Korotich of *Ogonyok* and Yegor Yakovlev of *Moscow News*, television programmes like "The Twelfth Floor", are the new protagonists of change. In the first thaw hundreds of thousands, perhaps millions, were affected; in the second the advocates of change reach tens, and ultimately hundreds, of millions.

But it is Gorbachev himself, and above all Gorbachev on television, who has dominated the Soviet media since 1985—another fact which makes it difficult for conservative members of the Politburo to dispose of him by a conspiracy. A surprising aspect of Western speculation about the balance of power in the Kremlin since 1985 is that specialists will consider at length the attitude towards reform of traditional state institutions such as the KGB, secretariat, Central Committee and armed forces, but neglect to consider the political impact of Gorbachev's ability to appear at will on "Vremya", the nine o'clock news, which runs on all three channels.

Yet it is through his appearances on television that Gorbachev has been best able to control the political atmosphere and affect the political agenda. Important meetings of the Central Committee are preceded by Gorbachev tours of the provinces. It was, for instance, in speeches in Khabarovsk in the Far East and Krasnodar near the Black Sea in autumn 1986 that he first announced that political change was a central component of economic reform. No other member of the Politburo has achieved this degree of public visibility—indeed, Gorbachev has been quite successful in outflanking official party and state institutions by appointing his own supporters as spokesmen who explain policy to the media. Thus the spokesman for the crucial Central Committee meeting on the economy in June 1987 was Dr Abel Agenbegyan, a Gorbachev adviser, who is not on the Central Committee.

Social change may have provided a constituency for reform, but is Soviet society conservative overall? How true is it that the average Soviet factory worker has low expectations and no desire to sacrifice low prices, minimal rent and a guaranteed job in return for a higher standard of living in the distant future? The growth of an urban and educated population may favour a less despotic government, but by the same

token society is much less malleable in the 1980s than it was in the
1930s, when 27 million people poured from the villages into the cities.
A Soviet citizen in Moscow today, living almost rent free, guaranteed a
job and very cheap transport, has a lot to lose as well as gain from radical change.

These are reasonable doubts, but a further argument is sometimes
used: that the Soviet Union is somehow instinctively conservative, suspicious of innovation, and always has been since before Peter the Great.
There is certainly some truth in this for the thirty years after the death of
Stalin in 1953, but in the half-century before Stalin died Soviet society
had changed enormously. Professor Moshe Lewin, historian of the development of Soviet society, eloquently catalogues the successive crises:

> The Russo–Japanese war, the revolution of 1905, one world war, another two
> revolutions in 1917, a shattering civil war (1918–20), which also contained
> international participation, occupations and a war with Poland, and next, after
> a short breathing space (1922–28), the collectivisation of agriculture, hectic
> industrialisation, a cascade of crises created by that collectivisation and indus-
> trialisation, bloody purges and the whole topped by another war.

The traumas which tore through Soviet society between 1904 and 1953,
and the reaction to them after the death of Stalin, explain the instinctive
conservatism of the so-called era of stagnation under Brezhnev. But it
was not a reaction shared by the postwar generation, and this was what
made the generational change in the leadership in 1984 so significant.
No doubt the traumas of the past still have an influence, but Gorbachev's general strategy has been to assume that he is dealing with a
population which welcomes experiments, originality and vigorous
pursuit of the new.

As a generalisation it is true that in 1985 the development of Soviet
society had reached a stage conducive to changes in the country's economic and political framework. But this generalisation tends to obscure
the enormous problems which resulted from the diversity of the country.
The Soviet Union has fifteen republics, and twenty-two nationalities
with more than one million members. There is a wide variation in their
level of social and economic development as well as their political traditions. Each is being affected differently—and is reacting differently to—
the impact of perestroika and glasnost. This does not mean that
relaxation of central control inevitably results in the release of centrifugal forces threatening the break-up of the Soviet Union, but it does
mean that serious reform was always going to be complicated by Soviet
ethnic politics, and there was always the risk that it would unwittingly
explode what *Pravda* called "landmines laid by the past".

The political implications of the Armenian riots and demonstrations were serious. First, they struck at a fundamental thesis of reform. Gorbachev had always defended freedom of expression by saying that what people wanted to express would not shake the political framework of the state. This was true in Moscow, but not in Yerevan. Armenia was the first occasion when Gorbachev's revolution from above had led to a mass response from below and the energies released were destructive, not creative. The loss of control had also shown that the party faced the danger that in trying to rely less on coercion and more on persuasion, it could end up having neither as an instrument of authority. Moreover, Gorbachev himself had made mistakes. As one of the first Soviet leaders without experience of the non-Russian republics and nationalities, he had failed early on to rule out boundary changes in favour of Armenia, changes which he could not realistically grant because of hostile Azerbaijani reaction and the precedent it would set for other nationalities in a similar situation.

On the positive side, Soviet security was never really in danger. Demonstrators have demanded incorporation of Nagorno–Karabakh, not self-determination for their own republic. But Gorbachev had been bidding for more than just obedience and the maintenance of law and order. Even though riots and demonstrations might pose no long-term political threat, the denial of Armenian demands led to the alienation of a whole community which Gorbachev might have expected to back him in support of reform.

In the Baltic republics Gorbachev seemed to have learned from failure in the Caucasus. From March 1988 the local parties in Estonia, Latvia and Lithuania sought to reanimate themselves politically by adopting demands for greater local control. They supported—indeed, may even have largely created—popular front organisations outside the party whose demands were not far from outright self-determination. The aim was clearly to channel local energies so they would support, not undermine, reform. Vaino Valyas, new leader of the Estonian party, warned a meeting of his Central Committee in September: "If we in the party continue to be unable to express the interests of the main political and social communities in the republic, independent movements outside the party will appear." He explained that the political changes in Moscow after 1985 had, paradoxically, damaged the popular prestige of the Estonian party because the leadership had been more interested in impressing the centre with its pioneering zeal for perestroika than in doing anything about it. Valyas said that it was only through backing autonomy and political reform—and supporting the efforts of the Popular Front—that the party could regain credibility as the political body capable of shaping the future of Estonia. This was because the people of

Estonia saw only one solution to their problems: "The autonomy of the republic and its sovereignty in solving problems pertaining to its people and its land."

Developments in Estonia and the other Baltic republics are important because they show the party fighting to regain political legitimacy. For Moscow there is a major opportunity—and there are dangers. The opportunity is to broaden the political base of the party, to channel the political energy of the demonstrators behind reform. The dangers are that the political situation will spiral out of control, the popular fronts will begin to rival the Communist Party, and the desire for autonomy will become a demand for independence. The declaration by the Estonian Supreme Soviet in November that it had a right of veto over central legislation clearly created anxiety in Moscow that instead of the party co-opting local nationalism, it might be victim of the reverse process. A further danger is that while a political experiment in Estonia, with a population of just 1.5 million (40 per cent of them Russian) is controllable, what happens there may set a precedent for the Ukraine, with 50 million people.

Yet Gorbachev has no choice but to ride the tiger of political resurgence among the Soviet nationalities. Most of the demands for local political, cultural and economic control in the Baltic fit in well with his own programmes. Furthermore, the demands are coming from the educated urban elite, product of the Soviet Union's postwar development and the very constituency on which Gorbachev wants to rely as proponents of perestroika and glasnost. It is not support he wants to alienate.

Conventional wisdom correctly held that to innovate at home, Gorbachev needed tranquillity abroad. The reasons went much deeper than a wish to transfer resources from the military to the civilian sector or inability to compete with the USA. While the Soviet leader continually spoke of the need to defuse the idea of the Soviet threat as a factor in Western politics, he also needed to deflate the concept of the Western threat in Soviet eyes. The Russian system of government, both before and after 1917, was moulded far more than that of other states by fear of external attack by superior powers, not by impulses in its own society. It was this fear which had fostered the authoritarian tradition inherited from the Tsars and perfected by Stalin. In 1931 Stalin had said: "We lag behind the advanced countries by fifty to a hundred years. We must make up this distance in ten years. Either we do this or they crush us." Fear of hostile attack, however exaggerated by paranoia and cultivated in order to contain centrifugal forces at home, was the ultimate justification for turning the Soviet Union into a fortress able to withstand open assault or slow siege. The fact that it did both with success ensured that the habits of siege mentality grew deep roots.

A shift to a more confident and relaxed attitude towards the outside world came essentially with the rise to power of the postwar generation. This brought about a transformation of Soviet attitudes. Leonid Brezhnev had made himself a marshal, awarded himself four Hero of the Soviet Union medals (the Soviet equivalent of the Medal of Honor) and promoted Malaya Zemlya, an unsuccessful battle in which he had participated in 1943, into a major turning point of the Second World War. By contrast Gorbachev never fought in the war and his instinct has been to seek security through political rather than military means. The sense of insecurity, which flavoured popular attitudes as much as Politburo policies from 1945 to 1985, began to ease.

Gorbachev's supporters were very conscious of the link between liberalisation at home and selling Soviet foreign policy abroad. Just as in the past hardliners in the Kremlin had used the foreign threat to justify authoritarian measures at home, so now party liberals and progressives used the foreign policy benefits flowing from glasnost to justify greater freedom for their own people. When Gorbachev came to power the Soviet Union had some 2,500 people in jail for political and religious offences, for which it paid an inordinate political price in terms of international discredit, far in excess of the security threat posed by the prisoners. There is no doubt that the reformers around Gorbachev did want to limit the arbitrary use of power by extending legal rights, but an important card for Soviet liberals had been the negative impact abroad of arbitrary government. The new approach was very successful. By 1987, revelling in its newfound popularity, the Kremlin had become so deeply conscious of the repercussions of its domestic politics on foreign opinion that when Boris Yeltsin was dismissed senior party officials gave more information to the foreign press than they did to their own. Unofficial political clubs in Moscow accused the authorities of practising "an information apartheid" in favour of foreigners and against their own citizens.

A further example of fresh ingredients in Soviet foreign policy and the way it interacted with domestic policy is the withdrawal from Afghanistan. The military situation, despite stepped-up US supplies to the guerrillas and the provision of Stinger anti-aircraft missiles, scarcely changed between 1985 and 1988, with no sign of an end to the stalemate. The Soviet forces were not losing ground, but so long as they could not invade Pakistan and cut guerrilla supply lines, they could not win. The real change was that Afghanistan was more of a political liability in 1986–87 than it was in 1981–85. Soviet foreign policy in 1986–87 was on the offensive, seeking to influence public opinion abroad and persuade it of the Soviet Union's peaceful, non-aggressive intentions. And it was doing so very successfully in Western Europe as well as the USA. In West Germany, for instance, between 1981 and 1988 the number of people who say they believe that the Soviet Union does threaten world peace and the USA does not dropped from 71 per cent to 11 per cent. The presence of Soviet troops in Afghanistan clearly threatened these gains in Soviet credibility and also blocked improvement in relations with China and Japan. There was also a less obvious motive for Soviet withdrawal: the influence on the Kremlin of attitudes towards the war inside the Soviet Union. The war had never been popular, but under Gorbachev this unpopularity was of much greater political importance than under Brezhnev, because now there was a government in Moscow trying to cultivate public opinion in favour of reform. Political alienation because of an unwinnable war was now a much more serious matter.

How far was the Soviet Union impelled to negotiate in order to relieve the economic burden of the arms race? From 1985 some Soviet specialists—such as Yevgeni Primyakov, head of the Institute of World Economy and International Relations—argued that a mirror-image response to increased US defence procurement had in the past heavily damaged the smaller and technically more backward Soviet economy.

Ending the arms race is vital if consumption and agriculture are to receive priority over heavy and defence industries in the allocation of resources. Up to the end of 1988 Gorbachev had not made this massive and basic shift in investment and general expenditure. Then, early in 1989, he announced that there would be a 14.2 per cent cut in the Soviet defence budget, including a 19.5 per cent fall in procurement. The timing of this announcement was probably dictated by political conditions at home and abroad and was also influenced by the fact that the lead-up to the next five-year plan in 1991 makes it important to take decisions now transferring resources from the military to the civilian sector. The size of the transfer—some 18 to 20 billion roubles—is important, since it is about the same as the *entire* yearly budget for machine-building, or half the total spent on housing annually.

Some of the reduced spending on defence is the result of Gorbachev's announcement in December 1988, at the United Nations in New York, that the Soviet Union would unilaterally cut its forces by 500,000 men and 10,000 tanks. Indeed, the cuts as ultimately spelled out are even more wide-ranging. They include 800 aircraft, an important Soviet concession given that aircraft modernisation has been a significant element in Soviet defence growth in the 1980s. Air defence within the Soviet Union, an important part of its present military establishment, is also likely to be cut back, as is the navy, and in private Soviet generals speak of unilateral cuts in naval strength in the Baltic, Black Sea and Pacific.

Other economic advantages from détente include better trade relations with the West, access to high technology, bank credits and joint ventures. Yet the benefits of these are smaller than they look. Increased borrowing was not dependent on renewed détente. In the mid 1980s it was Soviet fear of dependency on Western banks, not difficulty in obtaining credit, which limited borrowings. The Chinese experience shows that Western companies are chary of joint ventures in Communist countries. The stumbling block is that foreign companies want access to the domestic market and payment in hard currency, while the government wants access to high technology and exports to the West. And these initiatives do not get around a more basic problem: the price of the Soviet Union's oil and gas has slumped. Worse, their price is denominated in dollars, so by 1987 the Soviet Union had to sell five times as many barrels of oil to buy one West German machine tool as it had at the height of the boom in oil prices. Damage caused to the economy by the fall in the oil price so far outweighs economic benefits flowing from détente.

Overall, Gorbachev's foreign policy has been extraordinarily successful. He made improved and stable relations with the USA a priority in 1985 and by the end of 1988 had met President Reagan five times while Eduard Shevardnadze, his Foreign Minister, had met George Shultz, his US opposite number, some thirty times. In the eyes of the world he had achieved visible political parity with the USA in a way which had eluded Brezhnev. This enormously reinforced his authority and prestige at home as successive summits focused all attention on him and improved his ability to force changes on the party machine.

Not all this was Gorbachev's own doing. There were signs, even before he became General Secretary, that the second Cold War which had started in the late 1970s was on the wane. In 1984 President Chernenko offered a resumption of talks with the USA. The crisis of Soviet foreign policy at the beginning of the decade—marked by the collapse of détente in 1979–80, the invasion of Afghanistan, the rise of Solidarity in Poland, China's war with Vietnam and the election of President Reagan—had largely passed. Fears in Moscow that the first Reagan administration would be willing and able to translate its anti-Soviet attitudes into effective anti-Soviet policies had never been realised.

Opportunities in foreign policy were there, and Gorbachev was quick to seize them. Despite the anti-Communist rhetoric of President Reagan, the underlying prospects for USA–Soviet relations in 1985 were better than at any time since 1945. Most important, the two key foundations of the first period of détente agreed by Nixon and Brezhnev—Soviet parity with the USA in Intercontinental Ballistic Missiles (ICBMs) and a final settlement of European territorial boundaries such as the status of Berlin—were still in place. The two other main areas of superpower competition, the Third World and China, were no longer likely to create the sort of conflict which had destroyed détente in the 1970s. It was not that either side had become less able or willing to compete, but that there was less to compete about and there were therefore fewer points of friction. Ever since 1945 the Soviet Union and the USA had competed for power and influence in the Third World, where newly independent states were emerging from the break-up of the European empires. The collapse of the last of them, the Portuguese Empire, in 1974 had produced a final spasm of competition in Angola and Mozambique, where the USA accused the Soviet Union of exporting revolution and the Soviets responded that the USA was exporting counter-revolution.

By the 1980s, this had changed. As Alexander Bovin, senior Soviet commentator, wrote in 1988: "World revolution is not on the agenda. Therefore the thesis of the Soviet Union's support for the world revolution has become useless." Third World states struggling to break free from overt imperial control had largely achieved their aims, and the nation-states they had created were increasing in military and political strength. The intervention of the USA in Lebanon in 1982–84, the most important single attempt by Washington to change the balance of power in the Third World during the first Reagan administration, effectively ended when 258 US marines were blown up by a bomb in Beirut. Five years later, on 15 February 1989, the last Soviet troops pulled out of Afghanistan. The message of the 1980s was not that the Soviet Union had lost the Cold War but that the capacity of *both* superpowers to intervene in Third World countries was becoming limited.

The frequent analogies between Mikhail Gorbachev and past Soviet leaders, from Peter the Great to Nikita Khrushchev, do contain a clue to the dynamics of change in the Soviet Union in the 1980s, but the clue lies not in the similarities between Gorbachev and Khrushchev, but in the differences. Soviet society had developed enormously between 1964 and 1984. It was the system of government—Stalin's legacy of the state as a fortress built to manage the economy, crush domestic dissent and repel hostile attack—which failed to evolve at the same pace. The very failure to introduce reforms in the 1960s meant that by the time Gorbachev came to power the impulse for reform was far stronger than it had been twenty years before.

This does not mean that Gorbachev's triumph is inevitable. On the contrary, his ability to blame shortcomings on conservative inertia and sabotage has frequently masked his own lack of coherent policy on the economy and the nationalities. The reshuffle of the Politburo in Gorbachev's favour and his election as President strengthens his authority but also ensures that he will have to take a greater measure of responsibility for failure. A more authoritarian alternative to Gorbachev is possible, but it would have to steal a lot of his political clothes to succeed. It could not simply offer a return to the Soviet Union of Brezhnev; it would have to have broad popular appeal and offer a solution to economic problems which Gorbachev has failed to address or resolve. Here the danger point for Gorbachev may not come now but, as in China, at a point when economic reform is showing results. Less radical members of the leadership can then say that perestroika has shown it can work but should not be carried to excess. The secret of Gorbachev's success since 1985 has been that he has assumed that the impulse for change in the Soviet Union was far greater than has been believed by the rest of the party leadership or by observers abroad. "Visiting Moscow today is like visiting a hothouse where unusual flowers are growing," wrote one Western foreign editor in October 1988, "but outside the hothouse, the Russian landscape is largely unchanged, if not impervious to change." In fact, quite the reverse was true. The landscape had changed and was changing. Gorbachev needed to develop political institutions and beliefs which were the vehicle for change and able to express the frustrated political energies pent up under Brezhnev. But by the end of 1988 the near-martial law in Armenia and Azerbaijan and the continuing demonstrations in the three Baltic republics showed how difficult this was going to be.

February 1989

The Death of Chernenko

"We're hoping," said a woman buying clothes in a large department store two hundred yards from where President Konstantin Chernenko was lying in state yesterday when asked what she thought about the change in Soviet leadership. Overall, however, the President's death on Sunday did not seem to have had much impact on the shoppers. "They are all the same," said a young woman in a fur hat and winter coat. "It doesn't make any difference whether it's Brezhnev, Chernenko or Gorbachev."

A little closer to the Kremlin, outside the green and white Hall of Columns, a long queue of people was waiting to file past the bier. There was very limited security, but the police occasionally stopped the traffic in central Moscow to let past convoys of buses filled with representatives from factories and offices deputed to attend the lying-in-state.

The relaxed attitude of the police is in keeping with the low-key tone of Mikhail Gorbachev's first twenty-four hours as General Secretary of the Soviet Communist Party. Chernenko is getting the normal funeral honours, but no more. His picture, surrounded by a black border, appeared on Page 2 of *Pravda*, while the only photograph on Page 1 was of Gorbachev.

Inside the Hall of Columns — the Club of the Nobility before the Revolution, whose ballroom was first used for an official lying-in-state at the death of Lenin in 1924 — a long procession of mourners filed past the bier. To the left of this ever-moving queue an orchestra played solemn music, while to the right of the bier were rows of chairs for Chernenko's family. Anna Dmitrievna Chernenko, his widow, and his daughter were sitting in the first row of seats yesterday. The atmosphere was solemn but relaxed.

As generals and senior party officials took turns to visit the Hall, a group of French press photographers in jeans and check shirts hopped about taking photographs. Officials did not seem concerned.

Though the official obituaries are as fulsome as is to be expected, Chernenko had little opportunity to make much impact on the Soviet people. He was in office for only thirteen months, for part of which he was seriously ill and did not appear in public. Chernenko also had the disadvantage of seeming to be the physical embodiment of the old guard who rose to senior positions at the time of Khruschev's fall and have stayed there. By 1982, the year President Leonid Brezhnev died, the average age of the Soviet ministers was over sixty.

The vigorous application of the present economic experiment, the effort to reduce the power of the ministries by decentralising management at the bottom and centralising planning decisions at the top, all require substantial changes in personnel of both party and state if they are to be successful. It will also become clear over the next year how far Gorbachev can exercise his authority within the ten-man Politburo, most of whom were appointed under President Brezhnev. They include such stalwarts as Viktor Grishin, the Communist Party boss for Moscow, who has been a member since 1971, and Nikolai Tikhonov, the Prime Minister, who is seventy-nine.

In retrospect, Chernenko's thirteen months in power may seem an interregnum, but his funeral today will be impressive enough. The commission in charge of the obsequies, headed by Gorbachev, announced yesterday that at 1.40 p.m., "at the moment his body is lowered into the grave", artillery salvoes "shall be fired in Moscow" and other major cities. "At the same moment," the commission has ordered, "all the enterprises and organisations throughout the territory of the Soviet Union, with the exception of enterprises with a continuous production cycle, shall stop work for five minutes; a three-minute salute shall be sounded by hooters in factories, plants, railways and sea and river ships."

13 March 1985

Gorbachev as Leader

Since Mikhail Gorbachev became General Secretary of the Soviet Communist Party, people at home and abroad have asked if his election marks a real change in the Soviet Union. They know that the country's foreign, economic and domestic policies have been largely frozen in the same mould since 1964. Is the mould now breaking?

Gorbachev seems to have no doubt. "The ice is beginning to shift," he told a meeting in Moscow last summer, and by the end of the year the shift was evident in the top ranks of the Communist Party and state. Half of the twelve members of the ruling Politburo have been in office for only two years. The Prime Minister and the three top economic officials have been replaced in the past three months. The latest resignation is that of Viktor Grishin, head of the Moscow Communist Party.

The elevation of Andrei Gromyko to the presidency after twenty-eight years as Foreign Minister has also produced a rapid change in the way the Soviet Union deals with foreign states. Gorbachev's decision to seek a summit meeting with President Reagan in Geneva in November showed the Soviet Union to be as interested in influencing world opinion as it is in negotiating diplomatic agreements. "Changing the political atmosphere" became the new slogan in Moscow.

But the change in the leadership and the altered tone in foreign policy do not reveal the degree to which Gorbachev has the will or the capacity to change the lives of the 280 million citizens of the Soviet Union.

He was elected leader primarily as a proponent of economic reform. Within months he was calling for "a revolution" in the way the economy is managed; and the Soviet press is filled with plans for new economic initiatives. The talk of new technology, better plans and improved management are all reminiscent of the newly elected Harold Wilson in Britain in 1964, but it is still too early to know if the rhetoric of reform will wither as Gorbachev encounters political and economic obstacles. It is impossible to predict how he will cope with them because Gorbachev is a new type of Soviet leader. He and the men around him are the first of the post-1945 generation, largely unmarked by Stalin and the War, to hold supreme power in the Soviet Union.

Gorbachev was born in 1931, the son of a peasant family which farmed near Stavropol in the plains below the Caucasus mountains. At nineteen he went to study law at Moscow University, where he stayed until 1955.

As a student he joined the Communist Party, a year before Stalin died, and it was in the party that he rose rapidly when he returned to Stavropol. At thirty-nine he became the First Secretary, the senior party official, in his home area. Politically well connected and in charge of one of the richest agricultural areas of the Soviet Union, Gorbachev was well qualified to move to Moscow in 1978 as the Party Secretary in charge of agriculture.

His rise had been rapid, but he was still some way from the centre of power. There was no reason to suppose that by 1980 he would be a voting member of the Politburo or by 1983 the principal deputy of Yuri Andropov, the Soviet leader who succeeded Leonid Brezhnev. Denied the leadership when Andropov died, Gorbachev was firmly positioned as President Chernenko's heir apparent for a full year before succeeding as General Secretary in March.

Gorbachev was the chief beneficiary of the leadership crisis which had progressively paralysed the Soviet government since the mid 1970s. He benefited from being one of the few men of ability in their fifties at the top at a time when the need for leadership was all the more pressing because the last years of Brezhnev saw economic growth decline as détente collapsed. In the first administration of President Reagan, the Kremlin took the confrontational attitudes in the White House very seriously, always fearful that high US defence budgets presaged military action.

These worst fears were not realised. After 1982 there was some recovery in economic growth, the Soviet army did not invade Poland

and President Reagan showed few signs of translating ideological militancy into action on the ground. But it was the pressures from abroad, added to the economic difficulties at home, which gave a sense of urgency to the need to end the paralysis of leadership and propelled Gorbachev forward into the key position of power in the Soviet Union.

He had already shown he was an able politician. "He may have a nice smile but he has teeth of steel," Andrei Gromyko told the Central Committee which elected him. This became evident as he rapidly removed from the Politburo Grigori Romanov, formerly regarded as his main rival for the leadership. By the end of the year he had also replaced one-third of the government ministers and 40 out of 157 of the party first secretaries.

In achieving political dominance, Gorbachev has also modified the rules of Soviet politics as practised under Brezhnev. This became evident when the new leader flew to Leningrad in May and at a meeting in the Smolny Institute, the Bolshevik headquarters in the 1917 Revolution, heavily criticised the way in which the Soviet economy is run. "Try to get your flat repaired: you will definitely have to find a moonlighter to do it for you—and he will have to steal the materials from a building site," he told the audience. This was not usual fare for Soviet television viewers, and there was a surprising delay before radio and newspapers reported the speech in full. Over the summer, in a series of trips to the main regions of the Soviet Union, Gorbachev outlined his plans for economic change in a way not heard since the 1920s. He told one group of workers: "You can understand the consumer who wonders why we know how to make spaceships and atomic-powered ships, but often produce defective modern household gadgets, shoes and clothes."

This openness is new for the Soviet Union. The personality cult which surrounded the General Secretary under President Brezhnev has also been limited. When a senior trade union official described Gorbachev as "a banner of peace" during a meeting of the Supreme Soviet after the Geneva summit, the new leader threatened to leave the hall if such compliments continued.

Gorbachev needs this popular appeal because in the immediate future the public will not see many economic benefits from the new regime. There are tight limits on consumption in the plan for 1986, in which investment is to grow by 7.6 per cent and real income by 2.5 per cent. The re-equipment of existing plant, machine tools, high technology and energy are given priority. Given that the plan for 1986, unlike the five-year plan published earlier in the year, was devised by men of Gorbachev's own choosing, the emphasis on economic renewal rather than satisfying the consumer will probably be the main feature of Gorbachev's economic policy until at least 1990.

The men whom Gorbachev has appointed to run the economy in the past three months are not radicals. They are administrators in their fifties like Nikolai Ryzhkov, the new Prime Minister, and Nikolai Talyzin, the new head of planning. Their emphasis is on increasing the efficiency with which the existing economic structure is run. They are, however, to be taken seriously because they come primarily from the ruling Communist Party and not, like the economic reformers of the 1960s, from the state administration. In the short term, the new generation of economic leaders have little choice but to seek results using present methods of organisation. Soviet society and the economic structure of the country are not as malleable as they were thirty years ago. The pressure for structural economic change might be greater if the Kremlin faced an economic crisis or a fall in output. In fact, despite ossification of parts of the economic structure and the failure to modernise, it faces neither.

The real change in Gorbachev's first year in power is political. Far more quickly than expected he has ended the leadership crisis in the Kremlin which had gone on for a decade and become almost an accepted part of international politics. This fact alone has led to an immediate increase in the Soviet Union's power and influence in the world.

The boast of the Brezhnev leadership was that it had achieved military parity with the USA. This was true, but the siege mentality born of fifty years of revolution and war prevented it turning this parity into visible political equality with the West. Only in the past nine months have Gorbachev and the men he appointed sought, and to a degree obtained, the equality which so long eluded their predecessors.

28 December 1985

The Switch from Economic to Political Reform

Mikhail Gorbachev goes to the Reykjavik summit at a moment when his efforts to reform the political and economic management of the Soviet Union have reached a critical stage.

The target of his reform plan has changed. The emphasis over the last three months has no longer been on reorganising the economy but on restructuring the Communist Party. The extent to which Gorbachev wants to see the Communist Party democratised is unclear, but he has said enough to cause disquiet among officials who fear they will lose their jobs or that the institutions for which they work will lose power.

While the Western media has concentrated almost exclusively on the Daniloff affair and US–Soviet relations over the last six weeks, Soviet citizens have watched their television sets and read *Pravda* with astonishment as Gorbachev, in tours of the country, has attacked the Soviet political establishment as undemocratic, exclusive and incompetent, and accused it of secretly sabotaging reform. During a tour of the north Caucasus area he made a speech in the city of Krasnodar in which he said the restructuring of the economy could not succeed unless there was "a democratisation of our society at all levels".

Gorbachev's criticism of the way the political system is run is now very radical indeed, much more so than most middle-ranking party and state officials expected or wanted when he became leader. "We must not have individuals who cannot be touched, we must not have circles beyond our control," he said. He has repeatedly returned to the theme that many of those making formal obeisance to economic reform, democracy and decentralisation have not changed at all. Taking a specific example, he said that the top Communist Party official in Kurgan province in Siberia had delivered a sharply critical speech on the local state of affairs. When it was published in the local press, however, thirty major cuts had been made in the speech, leaving it bland and uncritical. "So it turned out in Kurgan that there existed two types of information—one for the narrow circle, and the other for everyone else. One set of laws for some and another set of laws for others," said Gorbachev.

This pledge to change the relationship between the ruling Communist Party and Soviet society has created a mood of edginess and unease in Moscow. Nobody knows how far Gorbachev's rhetoric will be transformed into reality. He himself pointed out that heavily publicised experiments in new decentralised management methods introduced three years ago at the Ministry of Heavy Machine Building had remained a dead letter.

In his attack on party privilege and commitment to greater democracy, Gorbachev has the Politburo and Central Committee secretariat behind him—but it is not clear how close behind. No other full member of the Politburo has been as radical as Gorbachev. Yegor Ligachev, his number two, makes speeches on economic change which are far more conservative in tone. A problem is that Gorbachev has raised political and economic expectations. The economy is not doing badly—the growth rate in the first eight months of the year was 5.2 per cent against a target for 1986 of 4.3 per cent—but the campaign for greater openness has made people more conscious of the failings of Soviet society.

Gorbachev's leadership is not in danger, but he has had some bad luck over the last six months: the disaster at the Chernobyl nuclear power plant in April, the death of 398 people aboard the *Admiral Nakhimov* cruise ship in the Black Sea in August and now the sinking of a nuclear submarine in the Atlantic. A demonstrable achievement such as a successful outcome of the Reykjavik summit would therefore be useful to him at home, but this is unlikely to affect the Soviet stance during the negotiations. The divisive issues within the Soviet leadership are the proposed reform of the party and the management of the economy. On foreign policy there is a large measure of consensus.

The economic benefits of a curtailment of the arms race, often mentioned as a central motive for Gorbachev's campaign to reduce the development of nuclear weapons, would also take a long time to make themselves felt. In any case, the aim of the talks with President Reagan is to limit nuclear arsenals, and these are cheap compared with the conventional weapons which dominate both US and Soviet defence budgets.

What institutional pressures from within the Soviet government are acting on Gorbachev as he goes to Iceland? The Foreign Ministry under Eduard Shevardnadze and the Communist Party Central Committee secretariat looking after foreign affairs under Anatoly Dobrynin, former Soviet ambassador to Washington, have both functioned very smoothly to resolve the Daniloff affair and to arrange the pre-summit summit. The Foreign Ministry has been one of the quickest Soviet institutions (perhaps because it is small) to remould itself in Gorbachev's image.

The Soviet military may be less happy, but this is impossible to know. Marshal Sergei Akhromeyev, the Chief of Staff, has said there is a military cost to be paid for the unilateral Soviet nuclear test ban, but that it is outweighed by the political gains. The military also has a stake in the success of Gorbachev's economic reforms. Marshal Nikolai Ogarkov, the former Chief of Staff, argued that nuclear weapons were now so diverse and powerful that a first strike was not militarily feasible. He said that what was really changing in modern warfare was high-technology conventional weapons. He urged the Soviet Union to keep up.

The agreement most likely to be reached in Reykjavik or at a full summit in Washington would cover intermediate nuclear weapons in Europe. The Pershing 2 and cruise missiles in Western Europe and the SS-20 Soviet missiles are all peripheral to the main nuclear arsenals on both sides. Gorbachev is therefore likely to face much less opposition from the Soviet military to their reduction or elimination than he would to cuts in the Soviet ICBM force, the backbone of the Soviet deterrent.

Gorbachev's position at Reykjavik is much less inhibited by special interest groups than President Reagan's but it will be influenced by a general Soviet fear, at both official and popular levels, of appearing weak. "We speak softly to people abroad. Do we perhaps speak to them too softly?" asked a man in the crowd when Gorbachev was in Krasnodar.

Belief that Gorbachev was being too conciliatory to the USA would certainly damage his position at home much more than failure to agree a full summit meeting in Washington later this year or next.

9 October 1986

The Fall of Yeltsin

Mikhail Gorbachev goes to the Washington summit with President Ronald Reagan with his plans to rejuvenate the Communist Party as the Soviet Union's instrument of change dented but still intact after the sacking of Boris Yeltsin, the radical leader of the party in Moscow.

The setback for reform at home is unlikely to have any immediate effect on Gorbachev's freedom to negotiate with Reagan. The record of his two-and-a-half years in power is that there is a general consensus on foreign policy within the Soviet leadership, a measure of agreement on economic reform— but deep and lasting divisions on political change.

Yeltsin succeeded in detonating the long-expected conservative reaction within the top and middle ranks of the party on 21 October, when he accused many of the 300 leading Soviet officials belonging to the Central Committee of covertly sabotaging reform. If this conservative backlash prevails, it will have a serious impact because it will destroy the political basis for Gorbachev's diplomacy, which is to be a more flexible partner in the international arena. This is in contrast to the concentration under previous leaders purely on state-to-state relations.

One of the main successes of Gorbachev's leadership has been the change in foreign perceptions of the Soviet Union away from the demonology of the "evil empire". But the consequence of this is that the Kremlin knows that domestic political events such as the fate of Yeltsin, which three years ago would have been considered nobody's business but its own, now take on a different aspect affecting its dealings abroad.

Yeltsin's critics at the meeting on 11 November, which dismissed him, recognised this. One party official said: "Tomorrow we shall probably hear political speculation abroad and from our own people about the crisis in restructuring, and we shall see people trying to make Boris Nikolayevich Yeltsin into a Jesus Christ figure who has suffered for revolutionary commitment to social renewal and democracy."

The Yeltsin affair therefore illustrates three new, but somewhat contradictory, developments in Soviet politics. The first is a conservative reaction to reform which has gathered strength since the summer, the second a more active public opinion at home. The third is the need— important if presenting a more open face to the world is to form a key part of foreign policy—to take seriously what the outside world thinks about the way the Soviet Union runs its society.

At present the first of these points is the most important. Up to the time of Yeltsin's outburst, Gorbachev had made extraordinarily success- ful use of a single tactic to defuse opposition to radical change within a largely conservative Central Committee. This tactic was always to criti- cise conservatism as an attitude of mind and never to identify factions within the party as opponents of reform. The reason for this approach is that Gorbachev needs simultaneously to pursue two conflicting aims: to preserve the unity of the party, which is the only effective lever for change in the Soviet Union, and to transform it internally without fright- ening conservative leaders into open revolt.

This policy has been under strain since the summer as conservative forces within the party realign. The old common front of the mid 1980s, between radical reformers and leaders who want a little modest house- cleaning in the wake of the Brezhnev era, is breaking up, with the latter moving back towards the conservatives. There is, in any case, always a greater consensus within the party on the necessity for economic reform than there is for political change. Gorbachev therefore wants to hold a special party conference next June to change membership of the all- important Central Committee to strengthen the ranks of political reformers.

The prospect of this move may have added steam and urgency to the conservative reaction. Throughout the spring and summer, Yegor Liga- chev swung to the right, attacking the excesses of perestroika. The seven weeks in August and September which Gorbachev spent writing a book created a vacuum in Moscow which was filled by the conservatives. But it was Yeltsin's ferocious attack on the party establishment, which Gorb- achev now says the Moscow leader had promised to postpone, that undermined Gorbachev's tactic of avoiding outright confrontation between radicals and conservatives.

When the Moscow party committee met on 11 November, Yeltsin was not only dismissed but became the object of an extraordinary display of hatred by middle-ranking party and state officials. Again and again, men whose cosy bureaucratic world was threatened by the peres- troika restructuring programme accused him of being a would-be Bona- parte consumed by ambition, using terms seldom heard since Stalin's show trials of the 1930s. For instance, Kozryev-dal, chairman of the

Moscow agro-industrial committee, said Yeltsin's speech to the Central Committee was "far from being a mistake, but a calculated and well-timed stab in the back for the party Central Committee and its Polit-buro".

Giving a remarkable glimpse of the detestation which had grown up between Yeltsin and the city administration, a district party official claimed: "Even police inspectors were given the right to shadow us. They were told: see if those sons of bitches are getting up to anything."

The surprise is not only that these speeches were made but that they were published in *Pravda*, presumably in a bid to discredit Yeltsin. In fact, the lynch-mob atmosphere of the 11 November meeting created a wave of public sympathy for him. Students at Moscow University held a rally, informal clubs collected signatures in favour of the Moscow leader, and there were reports of short strikes in Moscow and Yeltsin's home city of Sverdlovsk.

One target of public hostility was Professor Protapopov of the Economics Faculty of Moscow University, who had criticised Yeltsin. When he went to deliver his next university lecture he found his audience numbered about 150, well above the normal figure of thirty, but as he started to speak they all rose to their feet and walked out. Such incidents should not surprise Gorbachev and other leaders since they have repeatedly said that they favour more democracy. It is ironic, however, that the first time the Politburo's call for more public involvement in Soviet politics is answered, it is on an issue—a split in the leadership—which is the last topic Gorbachev and the Politburo want to see debated.

As it was, the news of Yeltsin's offer to resign leaked first to the foreign press and was confirmed by senior Soviet officials, but not a word was allowed to appear in the Soviet media until much later. To find out about a crisis in the leadership of their own city, Muscovites had to listen to foreign radios just as they had under Brezhnev. The authorities clearly recognised that glasnost and greater freedom of expression mean that Soviet politics can no longer be confined to the high bureaucracy. If the publication of details of the Moscow party meeting which sacked Yeltsin was an effort to discredit him, then it backfired.

A more successful official effort to calm the political mood was Yeltsin's sudden appointment on 18 November, in contrast to his complete disgrace of a week before, to be the first deputy chairman of the State Construction Committee. "The leadership underestimated the reaction of the party apparatus against Yeltsin and of the people against the apparatus," says one Soviet political commentator. "The problem is there is no tradition of political crisis management in the party leadership."

Most senior Soviet officials have risen to their present positions in a bureaucratic hierarchy organised on semi-military lines, in which all commands come from the top down. Few have political skills in the sense of an ability to persuade large numbers of people to act in a particular direction. A similar lack of experience of public criticism and debate explains the extreme sensitivity of party officials to Yeltsin's populist style. One Moscow official pointed an accusatory finger at his former leader and said: "You wallow in struggle, pressure and aggression all the time. You are constantly exposing someone so you can parade on your charger in front of ordinary people."

These accusations are important because they are typical of feelings of many middle-ranking Soviet officials affected by perestroika. Furthermore, few of them will have missed the fact that the most common complaint made against Yeltsin was of publicly criticising or firing officials, and this charge could be equally made against Gorbachev. There is no question that the fall of Yeltsin is a blow to Gorbachev's political prestige. His failure to support a man so closely identified with reform in the face of bureaucratic attack, whether justified or not, is seen as a sign of weakness.

At a time when nobody quite knows the new rules of Soviet politics— political fluidity is probably greater now than at any time since the 1920s—these perceptions are important. But the promotion of Lev Zaikov, a close ally of Gorbachev, to take Yeltsin's place in Moscow shows that there has been no major shift yet in the balance of power in the Politburo in favour of conservatives.

But has Gorbachev become more conservative? In the edgy political atmosphere of Moscow after the Yeltsin affair, some supporters of reform fear he is reverting to the mould of past Soviet leaders. Political jokes, the stock-in-trade of Moscow cynicism but out of fashion in the past year, are popular again. A recent one, referring to the Soviet habit of naming places after deceased leaders, catches the political mood: a man goes to the railway station to buy tickets for the cities of Brezhnev, Andropov, Chernenko and Gorbachev. The ticket-seller, after giving him the first three tickets, looks surprised and says: "But there is no city of Gorbachev." "Not yet," replies the other. "But I would still like to make an advance booking."

Such cynicism may be as facile as the official line that the Yeltsin affair was an accident which will have no lasting impact. Conservatives within the party would find it difficult to get rid of Gorbachev, and they are weakened by the lack of alternative policies to the reforms. Gorbachev's attitude is that the only way to remove the dead weight of eighteen million Soviet officials and administrators (out of a total population of 280 million) is to end the day-to-day administration of the economy from above. This will automatically limit both their authority and their numbers. This sounds good as grand strategy, but does not explain why Gorbachev played such a prominent role in getting rid of Yeltsin. When Gorbachev returns from Washington, supporters of perestroika still look for some gesture to show that reform has suffered a short-term setback rather than a serious defeat.

The Yeltsin affair is probably only the first of a series of political crises likely to punctuate the process of reform, as conservative and radical currents come into conflict. Gorbachev clearly believed that he had to maintain party unity, even at the cost of the political head of a man close to him. He can do this once and get away with it, but a repeat performance would probably destroy the credibility of his reform programme and at the same time cast a cloud over what he can achieve in external policy.

4 December 1987

PART III

Ethnic Politics

Gorbachev and the Soviet Nationalities

Nationalist unrest emerged in 1988 as the greatest threat to democratic reform in the Soviet Union. Its impact is so serious because it undermines Mikhail Gorbachev's fundamental thesis that there is sufficient consensus about the way Soviet society runs itself to allow a less authoritarian rule. He has repeatedly defended greater diversity of opinion by arguing that the views expressed do not question or contest the basic political framework of the country: greater individual liberty is compatible with stable government.

Escalating violence in the southern republics of Armenia and Azerbaijan throughout 1988 seemed to prove Gorbachev wrong. Hundreds of thousands of Armenians repeatedly demonstrated and went on strike to support the return of the Armenian enclave of Nagorno-Karabakh, which was incorporated into the neighbouring republic of Azerbaijan in 1921. Sporadic incidents of violence culminated in the massacre of thirty-two people, mainly Armenians, in the Azerbaijani town of Sumgait on 28 February. By November at least 50,000 refugees had taken to the roads to flee a recurrence of sectarian killings, the mounting ethnic conflict being overshadowed in Armenia only by an earthquake in December which left at least 25,000 dead.

Nor is the Caucasus, the region between the Black and Caspian seas, the only scene of ethnic violence and dispute. The 1986 dismissal of Dinmukhamed Kunaev, the long-serving party leader of the Soviet Central Asian republic of Kazakhstan, provoked two days of rioting. Groups of Crimean Tatars, exiled from their homeland since World War II, have staged marches and demonstrations demanding the right to return. And in the three Baltic republics of Estonia, Latvia and Lithuania, mass demonstrations supported by the local Communist Parties called for a greater measure of political and economic autonomy within the Soviet Union. On 16 November the Estonian Parliament even demanded the right to veto any law passed in Moscow.

It is not that the Kremlin lacks the strength to maintain its authority: Armenia has a population of only 3 million and Estonia 1.5 million out of a total of over 280 million for the whole country. But the necessity to deploy troops means that in this instance authoritarian methods of governing worked and democratic methods did not. This would have mattered little under Leonid Brezhnev, but Gorbachev, after all, is trying not just to maintain law and order but to mobilise public opinion behind his reforms. In this sense, a sullen and resentful—if pacified— Armenian population is a political defeat.

The picture is not all black. Resurgent nationalism is an opportunity as well as a threat to reform. In the Baltic republics local leaders demand the very political and economic decentralisation which the Kremlin says it wants to extend to the whole country. Here Mikhail Gorbachev's revolution from above is finally producing the mass political participation which he says is essential to the success of perestroika. The danger is that the testing ground for the success of democratic reform in the Soviet Union as a whole is located where the demand for greater civil liberty is most likely to combine with a nationalist challenge to the integrity of the state itself.

Armenia and Lithuania are small, but what happens there—and the way the Kremlin reacts to it—sets an important precedent for other nationalities because the Soviet Union is a multi-ethnic state. Relations between the 102 nationalities listed in the 1979 census is at the centre of Soviet politics. The multiplicity of small ethnic groups, from the Paleo-Siberians to the Chechen-Ingush in the Caucasus, makes the country an ethnologist's paradise, but the nationalities which matter are the twenty-two which number more than one million, fifteen of which have their own republic. Another twenty nationalities have the lesser status of an autonomus republic, and eighteen live in national districts.

Gorbachev himself has come to see the seriousness of the implications of the ethnic conflict in the Caucasus. he told a special meeting of the Supreme Soviet on Nationalities on 18 July 1988 that his whole reform programme was in danger: "Restructuring requires very great cohesion among the people, but what is offered is strife and national distrust." Instead of freedom of expression producing a spirit of conciliation, it had revived ancient grievances on which no Armenian or Azerbaijani was willing to compromise. Sounding aghast as his plans for the future were endangered by the old hatreds of the peoples of the Caucasus, the Soviet leader said ruefully: "These are not just machine-gun bursts but complete artillery salvoes from the past."

Party conservatives were quick to take advantage of the breakdown of government in the southern republics by portraying it as the outcome of changes at once too radical and too rapid. Vladimir Shcherbitsky, Ukrainian party leader and a member of the Politburo since 1971, said that people were asking why the outbursts were not suppressed, adding:

"Nobody whatsoever must be allowed to equate our democracy with permissiveness. Otherwise situations like this will arise again and again." A few days later, Yegor Ligachev blamed the crisis on lack of discipline and disregard for traditional methods of dealing with nationality problems. On 28 July a stringent new decree was passed increasing penalties for illegal public meetings and strengthening the powers of the police.

A problem for Gorbachev is that he is introducing political and economic reforms at a moment when Soviet ethnic politics are changing, and with them the relationship between Russians and non-Russians. This is a fundamental fault line in Soviet society today, as it has been since 1917, but it is far more complicated than the essentially colonial relationship of some Western commentary in which Moscow continually manoeuvres to avoid "the break-up of the Soviet empire". Indeed, if separatist movements were the only national problem facing Gorbachev, he would be in a far stronger position.

In reality the threat he faces is rather different, and is frequently obscured from view in Moscow and Washington for exactly the same reason. Both see the dynamic for change as springing from the most traditional parts of society least touched by the consequences of the Bolshevik revolution. A number of studies in the late seventies and early eighties claimed that the threat to the Kremlin would come from a resurgence of Islam in Central Asia and the Caucasus making converts among a traditionally Moslem population. At the opposite end of the political spectrum, Soviet party and academic specialists also focused on survivals from the past in upcountry villages or dissident religious sects. Where anti-Soviet beliefs or practices were detected, they prescribed the traditional remedies of more and better education and propaganda. In one case, local officials were reprimanded for not seeing that the falling turnover of local catering enterprises during the Moslem fast of Ramadan must mean that more people were adhering to Islamic belief.

Few events during the 1980s confirm this analysis. Both Soviet and Western experts on nationality problems appear to have been looking in the wrong direction. The new ingredient which creates the dynamism for change among non-Russians comes not from the traditionalist fringes but from the educated urban elite who are often the beneficiaries, not the victims, of Soviet rule. For instance, in the aftermath of the riots in Alma-Ata, the capital of Kazakhstan, in 1986, the authorities singled out for criticism the elite Alma-Ata Institute of Energy as the establishment where many of the rioters were being educated.

This is in keeping with the history of nationalist movements elsewhere in the world. An invigorated sense of ethnic identity comes not from peasants in the villages protecting their traditional way of life but from highly literate students and intelligentsia in the cities. Today a young educated Kazakh or Moldavian probably has far more in common culturally and socially with his Russian counterpart than did his parents, but by the same token he is now much better placed to compete with Russians for jobs and power.

Yet these social and economic changes, profound though they are, would not of themselves have detonated the nationalist unrest of the past two years. On the contrary, in the changing political relationship between Russians and non-Russians, it is important to realise that it is the Russians who have taken the initiative in attacking the status quo. At the time of Leonid Brezhnev's death in 1982, three years before Gorbachev became General Secretary, Moscow was already embarking on moves which have the effect of altering the balance between Russians and the rest of the country.

The problem for the Russians is that the old nationalities policy was successful in raising economic and social development of the poorer republics, but did so at the expense of the Russian heartlands. The three non-Russian republics in the Caucasus and the five Central Asian republics received the right to divert into their own budgets 100 per cent of the turnover tax—the main source of Soviet revenue. In the 1988 budget the Central Asian republics of Uzbekistan, Kazakhstan and Kirghizia will receive a subsidy of 5 billion roubles and even Lithuania, which is relatively well developed, has begun to rely on subsidies from the centre. "As a result, the condition of the social infrastructure in all major Russian republic cities is considerably worse than it is in other republics' capitals. Sadly, even Moscow, our capital and Russia's foremost city, ranks only somewhere between seventieth and eightieth among the country's cities in terms of development of its social and cultural infrastructure," one Soviet specialist told a conference last year.

Certainly the non-Russian republican capitals often look better built and maintained than Moscow. Theatres, museums and major government offices in the centre of Frunze, the capital of the Kirghiz republic close to the Chinese border, are all faced in white marble—adornments expressly criticised when the republic's first secretary was dismissed. Russians also resent the fact that villages in the deserts of Turkmenistan or the mountains of Tajikistan should be linked by blacktop roads when Russian villages have only tracks that become impassable in winter.

At times popular resentment is misdirected—people in Estonia and Latvia in turn see themselves as being hindered by Russian backwardness—but there is no doubt that it is deeply felt. The feeling that everybody does well in the Soviet Union apart from the Russians is neatly expressed in one of many anti-Georgian jokes. President Ronald Reagan is boasting to Eduard Shevardnadze, Soviet Foreign Minister

and former leader of Georgia, that in America every family has a house
and a car. "So do we in Georgia," responds Shevardnadze. "But how
about Russia?" asks Reagan. "Look," replies Shevardnadze, "I didn't
ask you about the Negroes in America, so don't you ask me about the
Russians in the Soviet Union."

Affirmative action in favour of members of local nationalities also
created frustration among the Slav minority working in non-Slav
republics. A Russian worker in Tashkent, the capital of Uzbekistan, was
quoted as saying: "We taught them everything they know and now all
you hear is 'Hire more Uzbeks! Hire more Uzbeks!' Even if a place is
one hundred per cent Uzbek, you still hear them yelling it." Another
said: "I've lived here all my life. My parents lived here and my grand-
parents lived here. It's my home too." Reverse discrimination had major
benefits for native citizens of the less developed republics, but it largely
failed in its original intention of creating a social mirror-image of the
Russian heartlands of the Revolution in every part of the country. The
aim was to build factories in which an indigenous working class would
seek employment, but in Central Asia and the Caucasus the tendency
has remained for Slavs to take jobs in the factories and the local
nationality to concentrate on agriculture, service and administrative
jobs.

In pursuit of employment in these sectors the number of Kazakhs or
Uzbeks in republic capitals such as Alma-Ata or Tashkent has risen
sharply in the postwar period. In Ashkhabad, the capital of Turkmenistan, the streets today are increasingly filled with Turkoman women in
flowery local dress. In Tallinn, the capital of Estonia, on the contrary, it
is the Russians attracted by industrial jobs who are increasing in number
and now amount to almost half the city's 750,000 population. In the
industrial northeast of the little republic only 20 to 25 per cent of the
population today is still Estonian.

Despite many successes in raising the overall social and economic
level of the republics, the country remains very diverse. This point is of
particular importance at the moment because it makes it extraordinarily
difficult for glasnost and perestroika to be introduced across the country
without igniting some local grievance. In other words, to a Moscow
intellectual glasnost may mean publishing the works of Pasternak, but in
Armenia it turns out to have meant publicising the Nagorno-Karabakh
issue, of which the same intellectual had probably never heard before
February 1988.

Economic reform also affects different nationalities in different ways.
For instance, ever since 1985 Gorbachev and Soviet economists in
favour of reform have said that investments should be made where they
bring the greatest return. This sounds politically anodyne, but if it is put

into practice—and so far it has not been—this means investing in a new plant in Estonia or Latvia and not in Uzbekistan or Tajikistan. Nor do the ethnic implications of such a decision end there. If the new factory is built in the Baltic republics, it will need workers, and this in turn means a fresh influx of Russian immigrants, the growth in whose numbers is deeply resented by Estonians and Latvians.

No doubt Moscow expected some friction among the nationalities as glasnost and perestroika were introduced, but it is evidently surprised by the degree of heat generated. Its explanation for the unrest is to emphasise past neglect. Asked about the increase in inter-ethnic tensions and nationalist movements, Gennadi Kolbin, the Russian Party Secretary for Kazakhstan, said in June: "The revival of archaic views has been helped by the atmosphere of an authoritarian regime and individual power in which the masses found themselves without rights and without a voice." Other Soviet leaders and academic specialists on relations between nationalities have echoed the same explanation, blaming Stalin and Brezhnev for present unrest—a view that has much to be said for it. Gorbachev has inherited, and must now grapple with, a series of unresolved problems and grievances, from the future of Nagorno-Karabakh to the construction of a vast and hugely unpopular nuclear power station at Ignalina in Lithuania.

But the weakness of the approach of blaming everything on the years of neglect is that it fails to see how the reformers themselves have played an important role in destabilising ethnic relations. Above all it does not take into account the fact that since 1982 the Soviet leadership has pursued a set of policies which have centralised power in Moscow. This was not their conscious aim. Gorbachev and Ligachev believed that they were offering clean government in place of the corrupt oligarchies of the Brezhnev era, but the consequence was a transfer of power from the republics to the centre. This shift was all the more serious because it reached its peak in 1986–87 just as censorship was being relaxed and the ability to complain had increased.

Under Brezhnev the political weight of the republics and their leaders within the system had increased. Republic leaders like Sharif Rashidov of Uzbekistan were often in power for fifteen or twenty years. They were able to build political machines whose immense patronage was reminiscent of the Cook County machine of Mayor Daly of Chicago. So long as their political loyalty was unquestioned they enjoyed a fair measure of autonomy. By the time of the 1981 Party Congress six republican party leaders were members of the Politburo, though non-Russians were less well represented in the government ministries or party secretariat.

For the non-Russian republics the Brezhnev system represented a form of devolution, but it was devolution by default and politically vulnerable because it was never institutionalised. Rather, it was the result of Brezhnev's policy of keeping the same men in power for long periods and meeting the needs of the interest groups they represented. It was also extraordinarily corrupt. Scandals in Uzbekistan, even by the standards of the Brezhnev era, were in a class of their own. Investigators discovered that part of the Uzbekistan's cotton crop had simply been invented and the money for the non-existent cotton stolen. Yuri Churbanov, Brezhnev's son-in-law and former Deputy Interior Minister, went on trial in September 1988 for accepting bribes worth one million dollars from Uzbek police officials.

Radical and moderate reformers in the Politburo were united in attacking the great party barons who had flourished under Brezhnev. Four of the leaders of the five Central Asian republics were sacked and the fifth died, possibly as a result of suicide, just as investigations into his rule got under way. Only three out of fourteen of the men who were republican leaders under Brezhnev still hold their posts, and of these only Shcherbitsky of the Ukraine is a full Politburo member. It is probably a mistake and certainly an exaggeration, to see the new generation of Soviet leaders as conscious Russian nationalists, although Russian chauvinism inside and outside the party became stronger in the seventies. Anti-Semitic nationalist organisations such as Pamyat generate more publicity than their position on the political fringe really merits. Frustration at the way in which Brezhnev ran the country, which Gorbachev calls the years of stagnation, may have been greatest in the Russian heartlands, but it did not articulate itself primarily as Russian nationalism.

But the very fact that modernisers and reformers in the top ranks of the party such as Gorbachev, Ligachev and Nikolai Ryzhkov, the Prime Minister, all come from parts of the country which are overwhelmingly Russian makes them insensitive to the political situation in the non-Russian republics. Worse, this insensitivity can appear to non-Russians as indistinguishable from Russian chauvinism. Certainly, in purging the regional party leadership of the political barons who had flourished under Brezhnev in the sixties and seventies they saw no political difference between getting rid of Viktor Grishin, the party boss of Moscow, and Dinmukhamed Kunaev, the long-serving leader of Kazakhstan. The fact that there was a difference became apparent only on 17–18 December 1986, when there was serious rioting in Alma-Ata after news spread that Kunaev was being replaced by Kolbin, a Russian. The nationality of the new party leader indicates the priority Moscow gives to clean government over ethnic sensibilities. Troops had to be brought in to restore order after two days of riots by Kazakh students from elite educational institutions whom the government has since attacked as members of families who owed their privileges to the ruling clique which Kunaev had created.

In the eighteen months since the riots Kolbin appears to have had a fair measure of success in isolating the rioters from the rest of the Kazakh population. The full force of government propaganda has been used against the old ruling elite, blaming them for shortages of food and housing and portraying the demonstrations as the reaction of a class under threat rather than Kazakh nationalists defending their rights. At the same time the media has tried to reassure Slavs, the majority in Alma-Ata, that they are not threatened by Kazakh insurgency.

It is also interesting to note what did not happen in Kazakhstan in 1986: there was no suggestion that resurgent Islam was playing a role in fomenting anti-Soviet feeling. The authorities clamped down on higher-education institutes and members of the old ruling elite, not on the village mullahs. The point is of some importance in the light of publicity given to theories popular in the 1970s—and boosted by the Iranian revolution and the Soviet invasion of Afghanistan—that Islamic fundamentalism was on the increase in Soviet Central Asia and on the other side of the Caspian Sea and was the key element in unrest.

Religious practice is increasing—though this is difficult to assess, given that open worship became easier under Brezhnev—but without having much political impact. There is no evidence that the Iranian revolution is attracting Soviet Central Asians who are, except in Tajikistan, traditionally Sunni Moslems speaking Turkic languages, in contrast to the Shiah faith of Ayatollah Khomeini. The main outside influence in Azerbaijan comes from Turkey, and local people say that they watch Iranian television less since it replaced Western feature films with religious sermons.

The Alma-Ata riots came as a shock to Moscow, but they were not politically damaging for Gorbachev and reformers. The student rioters did not attract mass support among Kazakhs. Their actions tended rather to discredit the old leadership around Kunaev, which was seen as resorting to violence in defence of its power and privileges. The events confirmed studies by Soviet ethnologists that the trend is for friction between different nationalities to be the greatest among well-educated members of the elite living in cities.

What happened in Armenia and Azerbaijan just over a year later was much more serious. Suddenly the Politburo was confronted with a genuine nationalist mass movement over which the party had no influence unless it was prepared to use coercion on a mass scale. Tass admitted that government authority had crumbled:

Taking advantage of the fact that the former leaders of the Central Committee of the Communist Party of Armenia let the initiative slip from their hands and retreated step by step, members of the [Karabakh] committee created ramified organisational and political structures. Karabakh branches operate at almost every industrial enterprise, organisational and educational establishment.

Yet Moscow itself was partially responsible for the initiative slipping from the hands of the local party. For sixty-seven years it had ignored Armenian protests at the inclusion of Nagorno-Karabakh in the neighbouring republic of Azerbaijan. Then, from 1986, Gorbachev said that local leaders must be responsive to the demands of public opinion as well as to orders from above. The party leadership in Armenia and Azerbaijan were heavily criticised in the central press as corrupt, incompetent and undemocratic. Geydar Aleiev, the former Azerbaijani party chief, was retired from the Politburo on 21 October and a few weeks later Dr Abel Agenbegyan, a senior adviser to Gorbachev, said during a visit to London—remarks immediately relayed to the Caucasus by Western radio—that Moscow had decided to change the relationship between Nagorno-Karabakh and Armenia. The vacuum of authority following the purge of the Brezhnevite old guard and the greater freedom of expression flowing from glasnost had combined to create an explosive mixture.

Will it do so elsewhere? Many of the problems Gorbachev faces in Armenia exist in the rest of the country. A less authoritarian party means one more responsive to public opinion and better able to achieve its ends by persuasion rather than coercion. The difficulty is that where the party is politically moribund, the attempt to shift to a more democratic approach may leave it unable either to coerce or to persuade. This danger exists throughout the Soviet Union, but it is at its greatest in republics like Armenia and Lithuania which have a strong sense of national identity. Here the party will have to compete with nationalist movements, informal groups and the Church to prevent them becoming the vehicle for social, economic and political discontents which Gorbachev admits but sees it as the task of his reformed Communist Party to resolve.

To prevent this, republican parties need to be effective advocates of local requirements without losing the confidence of Moscow. They need to steal a lot of the political clothes of informal clubs and pressure groups which are beginning to emerge. Above all they must avoid the fate of the Armenian party, which ultimately failed to satisfy either the Politburo or its own people. Events in Estonia, Latvia and Lithuania this year show that this is a difficult balancing act to perform. Here, in the most developed part of the Soviet Union, there were stirrings among radicals in the party even in February. They wanted greater political and economic autonomy, claiming that they could carry out perestroika more effectively without interference from Moscow. In Estonia, for instance, 90 per cent of enterprises are fully controlled by ministries in Moscow, complained Vaino Valyas, the Estonian party leader, to the party conference.

On 13 April a discussion programme on Estonian television generated such public response that a political pressure group called the Popular Front was established. Its aims include autonomy (but not independence), increased use of the Estonian language, safeguards against Russian immigration and solutions to ecological problems. Events moved quickly. On 16 June Karl Vaino, Estonian party leader for ten years, was replaced and the following day a meeting of 150,000 people in Tallinn, organised by the Popular Front with the support of the party, sent off delegates to the party conference in Moscow, armed with a programme of radical reform. A Popular Front leader said: "Before, there had been a crisis of trust between the population and the leadership. The meeting was a turning point. It gave the people back the feeling that they are the real force."

In Lithuania the authorities have also sought to co-opt and defuse nationalist sentiment by *rapprochement* with the Roman Catholic Church, a powerful force in the republic. A cathedral, built in the 1960s but confiscated by the state, was handed back. As a result "word went out in churches round the republic to pray for Gorbachev", according to one Lithuanian. Sentiments like these must be music to the ears of party leaders. Vaino Valyas said: "The only sure guarantee of perestroika— the reform of Soviety society—is the widest participation of the masses. Many members of the Communist Party also participate in the Popular Front." But in the long term co-operation between party and non-party will become more difficult once it moves beyond support for vaguely worded programmes and begins to affect the distribution of power. Both sides are riding the tiger, with no very clear idea of who will end up inside.

Yet the party in the Baltic republics, presumably with the approval of Moscow, is prepared to go a long way to broaden its political base. On 23 August it even participated in demonstrations commemorating the Nazi–Soviet non-aggression pact, the signing of which forty-nine years ago was the signal for the end of the independence of the Baltic states. These meetings questioned the legitimacy of Soviet authority. "It is not enough to recognise the Soviet occupation of 1940," one Estonian militant told the meeting. "We have to restore our independence." Such expressions of militancy will frighten conservatives in the party, but they may be more tolerant towards nationalist sentiments in Estonia—with a population of only 1.5 million, of whom 40 per cent are Russian—than in the Ukraine, with 50 million. If the worst comes to the worst, as it did in Armenia, it would be easy enough for Moscow to restore order by force.

More immediately, the lesson drawn from the Armenian crisis by the leadership is that there can be no boundary changes in the Caucasus or anywhere else because the Kremlin cannot give to one nationality without offending another. The promotion of Nagorno-Karabakh from the status of a national district to an autonomous republic was ruled out, presumably on the grounds that it was a compromise which would satisfy nobody. "Restructuring not recarving" is the slogan which sums up the new approach to nationality problems.

The real test of the party's ability to broaden its appeal is not over independence, which is not on the agenda, but on issues where the interests of Moscow and individual republics are opposed. For instance, the leader of the Lithuanian Communist Party called at the party conference in July for a halt to construction at the Ignalina nuclear power plant. This would be a popular move in Lithuania but would provoke a flood of demands from other cities and republics to stop work on nuclear power plants in their own area, leading to a shortage of electric power for the country as a whole. Decisions like this, indicating real devolution of power, will determine the success of the party's new popular front tactics.

Nationalist unrest has emerged as the single most potent, but also most misunderstood, threat to Gorbachev and reform. The misunderstanding is rooted in the diversity of the Soviet Union's ethnic mosaic, which provides some evidence for every theory and has spawned a rich mythology about the future of its nationality problems. Western commentators tend to see difficulties as insoluble crises in the making and underestimate the effect of government countermeasures. It is therefore important to describe what, on the evidence of the last two years, is either not happening or fails to explain what is new in Soviet ethnic politics.

There is, for instance, little evidence for "the break-up of the Soviet empire" in which constituent republics and nationalities break away to form independent states. Nationalism is strongest in the Baltic republics, but both Estonia and Latvia have large Russian minorities. In Armenia, the scene of the most intense nationalist unrest, separatism was never a real issue. There have been major outbreaks of violence in two of the six traditionally Moslem republics, Kazakhstan and Azerbaijan, over the past two years, but very little sign of resurgent Islam playing any important role. It is now very difficult to take seriously the idea, much touted over the past decade, that growing Moslem belief and practice together form a threat to Soviet authority.

Some theories are not so much untrue as irrelevant. Thus the relationship between Russians and non-Russians is changing, but there is no reason to suppose that a fall in the number of Russians below half the population will have a significant impact on the distribution of political power. Obviously a growing number of recruits from Central Asia entering an army with an almost entirely Slav officer corps causes tension but little, going by Soviet literature on the topic, which the authorities cannot handle.

Another fallacy is to see every Soviet republic as a potential Estonia or Armenia. National self-consciousness varies enormously and it does not necessarily follow that a nationality like the Ukrainians, very conscious of their own identity, feel alienated from the Soviet Union as a whole. In the Ukraine nationalism is strongest in the six western provinces incorporated into the republic after the war, but this is an area which has only 10 per cent of the Ukrainian population. In other words, if the diversity of the Soviet Union causes problems for the introduction of reform, it also rules out any uniform nationalist opposition.

The threat to Gorbachev and reform lies in a different direction. His vulnerability in the fourteen non-Russian republics is largely because he faces here, in an acute form, problems which also exist in the Russian heartlands. To take one example: reformers in Moscow have always argued that conservative strength is concentrated in the middle ranks of the party—the provincial first secretary level—and the top ranks of the state bureaucracy—ministers and the heads of state organisations in Moscow. But as Gorbachev has found out to his cost, the removal of a powerful first secretary in a Russian city like Krasnodar creates no reaction, while sacking the leader of Kazakhstan does.

Many of these difficulties were predictable, and it is a measure of the lack of men in the Politburo experienced in dealing with national problems that they were caught by surprise. Glasnost was bound to bring to the surface demands for the redress of grievances which had existed since the 1920s. In Armenia they surfaced, moreover, when the party was extremely vulnerable as it sought, under pressure from Moscow, to make the transition from coercion to persuasion as its instrument for achieving its aims.

But there is more to the Soviet nationalities problem than the re-emergence of ancient grievances. The common factor in the otherwise wholly diverse incidents of national unrest in Central Asia, Armenia and the Baltic states between 1986 and 1988 is the growing involvement in politics of a new educated urban elite which has developed since World War II. The problem for the Kremlin is not that it is unable to repress such groups but that it needs to welcome and harness their radical potential if it is to broaden its political base.

In a sense Gorbachev has got *what* he wanted, but not *where* he wanted it. Ever since 1986 he has said that economic reform from above could succeed only if accompanied by the active involvement of masses of people in politics. This has now happened. In 1988, for the first time in the Soviet Union since the 1920s, people voluntarily attended vast public meetings, but they did so in the national capitals of Yerevan, Tallinn and Vilnius. And here, unlike Russia, the danger for Moscow is that the Communist Party is not the only potential instrument of change. As has already happened in Armenia, local organisations may contest the party's authority.

It is not a contest they are likely to win. Moscow may cede a measure of self-government but not self-determination, and it still has an over-whelming preponderance of political and military force. The Politburo will clamp down if it feels the party is losing control in a non-Russian republic and accept the political cost of an alienated public opinion and a return to political apathy. This is why nationalism is such a dangerous threat to democratic reform: the demand for civil liberty escalates into an attack on the framework of the state itself, which is not likely to succeed but is sufficient to provoke repression.

This is what happened in Armenia, and if the Soviet government is to become less authoritarian, Gorbachev cannot afford to let it happen elsewhere. He needs to take the initiative by adopting as his own poten-tial and actual nationalist demands for political, economic and cultural autonomy. Local parties must become an effective vehicle for the expression of national feelings and frustrations in republics like Estonia, Latvia and Lithuania. Failure to achieve this does not necessarily mean that Gorbachev will be overthrown or glasnost and perestroika become a dead letter. This could happen, but a more likely outcome is that persist-ent nationalist tension will tip the balance towards a more authoritarian state and distort the development of civil liberty. In Russia the effect of Gorbachev's reforms on the exercise of power remains hazy. It is the non-Russian republics, where reform has elicited a mass response, which will show in the immediate future the degree to which democratic centralism will become more democratic and less centralist.

The Last Wilderness

At a temperature of minus 30 degrees centigrade, a light mist forms in the vast opencast mine at Neryungri in Eastern Siberia, making it difficult to see clearly the mechanical grabs and 180-ton trucks extracting coal at the bottom of the pit. Standing on the rim of the excavation it is possible, nevertheless, to watch the bucket shovels move along enormous terraces on the other side of the pit. On the higher terraces they are removing the 350 metres of hard rock which lies above the coal seam from which dumper trucks roll backwards and forwards as they are rapidly filled by the bucket shovels.

In the eight-month winter, work never stops. At these temperatures it is easy to understand why the truck and bucket shovel drivers earn up to 800 roubles a month, four times the average Soviet wage.

On their success at extracting 13 million tons of coal this year depends both the Neryungri mine and the town of the same name, built from nothing over the past ten years as a test case or laboratory for the development of the far eastern parts of Siberia. The mineral wealth of the Yakutia, an area six times the size of France with a population of just one million, has always tempted Soviet planners, but they have never decided on the way to obtain the best return from the vast investments needed to exploit it. The investment is so heavy because the climate is among the worst in the world. Everything is built from scratch on the frozen earth.

Pyotr Fyodorov, the mayor of Neryungri, says that when he arrived in 1975 the site of the city was only pine forest inhabited by hardy wild life. Neryungri now has a population of 60,000 and South Yakutia as a whole 112,000. Throughout the town cranes are working to build new tower blocks from building materials made in a local factory. There is a three-year waiting list for apartments. Shops are well stocked, and there are no queues.

To attract labour, salaries rise by annual increments to two-and-a-half times the average of the rest of the country. A truck driver named Volodya in his late twenties, delivering building panels to a construction site, said he earned 800 roubles a month. "Far more than I earned in the Urals where I used to work." This is a good wage even for Neryungri. The average salary is between 400 and 500 roubles, with pay going up for each extra year a worker stays in the town. Rent for a three-room flat is only 25 roubles a month, and other incentives include the right to buy a car after three years. In the truck depot, the noticeboard offers inclusive tours to Cuba for 640 roubles.

The aim of the planners is to establish a city with a permanent population of 150,000 which can be used as a base for exploiting the region.

This is preferred to a miners' camp with minimum facilities and a shifting population of workers attracted by the high wages at the mine. Neryungri is already linked to the Baikal–Amur mainline (BAM) railway by a spur line, and this is to be extended to Yakutsk, 830 kilometres to the north, by 1995.

In the short term, coal cannot be expected to pay for the high costs of these plans. Last year 3.75 million tons of enriched coking coal was produced, but of this 3.2 million tons is earmarked for Japan in repayment for a $450 million credit facility for Japanese plant and equipment arranged in 1974. Another 600,000 tons was sold to North Korea.

Yuri Zakharov, chief engineer of the Yakuti Coal Administration, admits that the coal produced at Neryungri is expensive. He cites three reasons: 7 cubic metres of rock have to be moved for every ton of coal extracted at Neryungri, much higher than other Soviet opencast mines; the cost of imported equipment is five to six times the cost of their Soviet equipment; salaries are higher than in other mining areas.

Officials in Neryungri say that good apartments are as important as high salaries in keeping workers. V. Balduyev, Communist Party First Secretary for Neryungri, quotes a survey: "Twenty-five per cent of those questioned say they will stay with us for good, while fifty-five per cent say they will stay for fifteen to twenty years."

For those who stay, the rewards are high. Yuri Mekin, a forty-five-year-old foreman at the truck depot, and his wife Nina arrived nine years ago from Irkutsk. They live in a well-heated, three-room apartment and say that after the first year new arrivals get used to the cold. Every two years the couple holiday in the Crimea and they also own a holiday bungalow outside Neryungri. Nina Mekin says they will stay another five years. Their ambition in life is to "buy or build a yacht to sail on Lake Baikal".

Neryungri is the first of eleven territorial production centres to be built along the BAM railroad, opening up the resources of Eastern Siberia and the Far East. Although local workers refer to the rest of the Soviet Union as "the mainland", decisions on local investment remain largely with the ministries in Moscow. This lack of a local development authority with real power hampers co-ordination of planning and decision-making, say some local officials. It also makes it more difficult to answer the question always facing the builders of Neryungri.

Will the town and its industries, impressive achievements though they are, ever be worth the money and effort they have cost to construct in the barren hills of Eastern Siberia?

6 February 1986

An End to the Cavalry Charge

When Mikhail Gorbachev recently visited the Soviet Union's main oil province of West Siberia—in which he plans to spend 82 billion roubles in the next five years—he said he was "astonished to see how much had been done any old how, on the principle of 'we'll muddle through somehow'".

"But we're not muddling through, comrades," Gorbachev told the men who run the oilfields, and he warned that the Soviet Union could not afford to see big investments "become frozen into the soil of Siberia". He made it clear that he was not only criticising the oil industry: the Kremlin needs a better return on the money swallowed by the development of Siberia as a whole.

The future of this vast region—Yakutsk is as far to the east of Moscow as Jamaica is to the west—poses a dilemma for Gorbachev. He must decide how long the Soviet Union will continue to pour funds into developing Siberia's raw materials, funds badly needed east of the Ural Mountains to re-equip plant with high technology in the old industrial areas.

The question is all the more pressing because of the fall in world commodity prices over the last year. Soviet foreign trade consists essentially in selling fuel and raw materials, mostly from Siberia, and buying manufactured goods and food. In 1984, 60 per cent of the Soviet Union's $34 billion* exports to the West came from oil, but the fall in prices from oil and other raw materials could cut this by up to 40 per cent unless oil sales are increased.

Today's prospects contrast sharply with expectations during the last ten years of President Leonid Brezhnev. Then successful exploitation of the Siberian wilderness appeared a short-cut method of boosting the economy as the annual growth rate lagged during the 1970s. The opportunities in Siberia seemed endless: the area east of the Urals to the Pacific Ocean contains at least 10 per cent of the world's oil reserves, 20 per cent of its gas, 40 per cent of proven and probable coal reserves and 15 per cent of its timber.

Impressive results were achieved. Geologists and prospectors moved away from developed areas along the old trans-Siberian railway, where most of the 29 million population of Siberia lives, into areas where the ground is permanently frozen and exposed skin freezes in thirty seconds. In the 1970s the Soviet Union developed the world's largest oil and gas field in the swamplands of Western Siberia. The 3,100-kilometre

---

*For the purposes of this book, there are 1.6 dollars to £1.

Baikal–Amur Mainline railway was cut through mountains to open up Eastern Siberia.

"In Western Siberia today we recover 60 per cent of our oil and more than half our gas: what would our lives be like if we had not performed this great endeavour in Siberia?" asked Boris Shcherbina, one of the men behind the development, recently. But the expense has been vast. Too often the engineers' dream of opening up Siberia turned out an accountant's nightmare. Worse, the area diverts capital funds which the Politburo wants to spend on its four priority sectors—machine tools, machine building, computers and electronics—in the European part of the country.

What Gorbachev wants to do is only now becoming clear. Big new projects, essential or already under way, are to be completed but new schemes will be cancelled or shelved. Casualties among the latter so far include:

- A plan, recently shelved by the Politburo, to divert water from the rivers running north through Siberia southwards via a canal to the parched plains of central Asia.

- Out of four big $1 billion-plus petrochemical plants put out to international tender for construction during this five-year plan, one on Lake Baikal has been cancelled and another shelved.

- In the Far East, Japanese companies have told Soviet officials that they are not interested in buying gas from Sakhalin Island. This means that the scheme to develop gas for export and build a liquid natural gas plant in the Far East is dead.

Joint ventures with Western companies to develop Siberian raw materials or credits secured against long-term contracts to supply commodities such as coal or ore no longer look as attractive as they did in the 1970s. Meanwhile, every fall of $1 in the price of oil costs the Soviet Union $550 million over a year.

In these circumstances it is not surprising that Gorbachev wants to retrench in Siberia, but this is easier said than done. Last summer he wanted to hold steady the proportion of investment absorbed by energy, but in the face of the mounting problems besetting Western Siberian oil fields, investment in oil rose 31 per cent in this year's budget. The problem is that the Western Siberian fields were exploited too fast in the late 1970s and early 1980s. Brezhnev's energy policy was devised on the assumption that Western Siberian oil could supply more as the old European oil fields declined. Five years ago there was even talk of raising Western Siberian production to 500 million tonnes by 1985. "A realistic outlook on the requirements of tomorrow was eclipsed by the dictates of today: pump, pump, pump," recalls one observer. In fact production peaked at 365 million tonnes.

To achieve this, exploration drilling was neglected despite the warnings of Western Siberian officials. Social and engineering infrastructures were neglected and underfunded in the rush to produce. Gorbachev says that the Kremlin and its planners were misled by their experts: "The geologists were saying that everything up to the year 2000 was provided for, everything that was needed was there."

But if the Politburo believed that Western Siberia had limitless oil, it was because it listened only to what it wanted to hear. The real mistake was Moscow's strategic decision in the mid 1970s to invest largely in increasing oil output rather than trying to reduce consumption. Conservation and substitution of gas for oil got under way ten years later than in Western Europe.

As exploration drilling is stepped up in Western Siberia, production can probably be stabilised not far below the 595 million tonnes of crude produced last year. Even if production drops further, it will not produce a crisis so long as gas-fired power stations and nuclear power plants, which should produce 20 per cent of Soviet electricity by 1990, are brought on stream.

Investment in reducing the amount of fuel and raw materials used is twice or three times as effective as investment in increasing their output, according to Gorbachev—ominous mathematics for many high-spending schemes in Siberia. He made it clear, nevertheless, that heavy investment will continue in the cost-efficient exploitation of projects already built.

However, local officials along the BAM railway were gloomy last month about the prospects for many of the new territorial production complexes—industrial towns centred on a local energy source—being built soon. There are too many calls on resources. Long-developed industries are also in chronic need of investment. The Kuznetsk coalfields, for instance, are Siberia's biggest and they produced 147 million tonnes of coal in 1984, but "no one has begun the construction of a single new mine in the basin in the past twenty-five years" according to *Pravda*. The newspaper blames the ministry for the coal industry of increasing output mindlessly and neglecting development.

But the drive to develop Siberia has always been more than an attempt to wrest raw materials from a barren wasteland. The population of 29 million is already 3 million more than Canada's and a central aim of current planning is to settle areas previously inhabited only by fur-trappers, prisoners and exiles. Wages are high. In Yakutsk, where temperatures this winter often dropped to below minus 50 degrees centigrade or three times colder than the interior of an average domestic freezer, pay is two and a half times that in the rest of the Soviet Union.

Wages of between 800 and 900 roubles a month are not uncommon, and there are well-stocked shops in which to spend the money.

Other newly developed areas have less to recommend them and there is a rapid turnover of labour. A trade-union official recently wrote that a couple he knew were leaving the BAM, where they had lived since 1976: "They have two small children and all huddle together in a small railway carriage."

Gorbachev conceded that in Western Siberia it was "awkward— embarassing even—to talk about millions of tonnes of oil and cubic metres of gas when a drilling foreman says that the greatest incentive in Nizhnevartovsk is to be given a ticket to see a film. Nizhnevartovsk is a town of 200,000 inhabitants and yet it does not have a single cinema."

Solving the problem involves more money and better management of the way it is spent. In the past central planners in Moscow never really got a grip on costs in Siberia. They could never distinguish between projects likely to produce a reasonable return on investment and those which would not. The so-called "cavalry charge" method of Soviet econ-omic management—hurling resources at a problem until it cracks— proved wholly inadequate as costs spiralled in the swamps and mountains of the Siberian interior.

The lack of central control over costs was exacerbated because Soviet ministries often behave like feudal baronies. Neryungri, for instance, is a generally well-run little town divided between areas built by their respective ministries for coal miners, transport and energy workers. In summer, the road turns to mud between the different sectors and is known to local drivers as "the interministerial no-man's land".

But for all that, the development of Siberia's wasteland in an appalling climate over the past fifteen years is an engineering achieve-ment which matches the construction of the Panama Canal in scale and difficulty. The problem is that under Brezhnev, Siberian raw materials, and the foreign trade they underpin, became a substitute for economic reform in the Soviet industrial heartland. The result was that Siberia's resources were exploited too quickly.

Investment in the region became a costly game of double or quits, and Gorbachev wants to end it. Over the last year the leader's attitude towards change in the management of the Soviet economy has become clearer: greater central control of investment and strategic planning combined with more managerial autonomy at local level. The way Gorbachev copes with the problems and opportunities of Siberia will provide the first chance to see how far these attitudes translate into policies.

18 February 1986

Siberian Tigers

Tigers in Siberia have killed dozens of people over the past ten years in increasingly frequent attacks, according to the Soviet daily newspaper *Izvestia.*

The number of Siberian tigers has risen since hunting them was prohibited forty years ago at a time when they were almost extinct, but it is only in recent years that tigers have moved closer to human settlements. This is because they are finding it more and more difficult to live on wild boar and deer, their natural prey, which it is still legal for people to hunt, compelling the tigers to kill the village cattle.

Soviet specialists say that villagers in Siberia are often killed by tigers which they have unwittingly provoked. On meeting a tiger, the first thing to do is "let him know you have no claims on his hunting ground and are not afraid of him," advises V. Zhivotachenko, a leading expert.

How this explanation is to be made he does not elaborate, but he adds that "critical situations often arise when people run away or try to climb up trees—tigers can lie in wait for a very long time."

In one case a tiger found a dead animal in a village and was dragging it back to the forest when it saw two villagers in pursuit. "It is common knowledge that a tiger does not like to be followed," says *Izvestia.* It rounded on the villagers, knocked one over and sat on him. Instead of lying quietly he poked the tiger in the eye and the animal, thus provoked, bit him to the bone. The man survived but, the newspaper notes with regret, the tiger was shot dead.

16 July 1985

Kazakhstan: The Virgin Lands

The grain crop in the northern plains of the Central Asian republic of Kazakhstan had reached a critical stage last week. A year ago a prolonged drought here led to a poor harvest and helped push Soviet grain imports up to 53 million tons at a cost of $8 billion.

The vast open fields which stretch to the horizon have received limited rain since the middle of June. As a result, the US Department of Agriculture has lowered its estimate of Soviet grain production for this year by 5 million tons to 190 million tons. "This is a vital month for us," said Mehlis Soleiman, an agricultural specialist. He expects Kazakhstan to produce an average crop of about 27 million tons this year, well above the 21 million tons grown in 1984.

The steppelands of Kazhakhstan have never quite come up to expectations. They were first ploughed in the 1950s in the so-called "virgin lands" campaign started by Nikita Khrushchev in an attempt to produce a great leap forward in Soviet grain output.

Train loads of temporary and permanent immigrants from the European parts of the Soviet Union were exhorted to plough up 25 million hectares (62 million acres) of grassland formerly grazed by the cattle and horses of the Kazakh nomads. Khrushchev hoped that the new lands would be the country's granary, a Soviet version of the American Midwest.

At first the sod-breaking campaign produced impressive output, but variable weather, lack of fertilisers and the need for specialised machinery have led to disappointing results since 1976. The problem is that the southern steppes of the Soviet Union receive overall only two-thirds of the rainfall needed to grow wheat. They are regularly ravaged by drought which, in the words of one specialist, "occurs one year in ten in the wooded steppes of the Ukraine, one in three or four in the Volga provinces, one in every two in Kazakhstan".

Every year, farmers around the city of Tselinograd, the region's administrative centre, as well as the planners in Moscow, wait to see if sufficient rain will fall. It can do so with spectacular violence. As I drove back from a state farm three hours from Tselinograd last week, the rolling black clouds opened to produce a sudden rain storm, illuminated by forked lightning, which turned the dirt track road into a brown stream.

Scientists at the Grain Institute in Shortandy have produced high-yielding grains and specialised machinery geared to the needs of the region. Conservation tillage with special ploughs has reduced soil erosion and many fields are now kept fallow. A. Barayev, the present head of the institute, was dismissed by Khrushchev in 1964 for arguing that fallow and conservation were essential in the region. The change in the leadership that year saved him, but even the scientific farming methods the institute has developed are slow to show results.

North Kazakhstan remains highly vulnerable to drought. According to one economist: "It suffers from a short growing season, and the winter snow cover is insufficient to permit autumn sowing as frost would kill the plant." New technology helps productivity: in winter ploughs now heap snow into ridges to ensure that the seeds get more moisture in the early spring. The melting snow would otherwise flow into the numerous gullies and streams without penetrating the frozen ground. More fertiliser is also needed. Arable land in Kazakhstan receives 18 kilograms of active ingredient of fertiliser per hectare, only a third of what is needed according to foreign agricultural experts.

Kazakhstan planners are confident that agricultural productivity can be raised with more machinery and fertiliser. This is true, though the capital investment needed may be high. Certainly the hopes that spectacular results in raising agricultural output at low cost could be quickly achieved were dashed long ago.

20 July 1985

Alma-Ata Before the Riots

Across the vast gorge which leads down from the mountains to Alma-Ata, capital of the Soviet republic of Kazakhstan, a dam has been built to stop avalanches sweeping down on the city when the summer sun melts the glaciers.

The earth and concrete barrier built in the late 1960s protects the city of one million people immediately below the Tien Shan mountains from sudden inundation. Guides show photographs of Alma-Ata the last time it was devastated by an avalanche of water, mud and boulders torn from the mountainside.

Today the city looks prosperous, its streets lined with Lombardy poplars and elms. Tall modern buildings rise around Leonid Brezhnev Square, commemorating the time when the former Soviet leader was the Communist Party chief in Kazakhstan in charge of Nikita Khruschchev's campaign to plough up the "virgin lands".

Alma-Ata, like the rest of Kazakhstan, has benefited from heavy investment in the development of its natural resources and from its former association with Brezhnev. The present Communist Party chief for Kazakhstan is Kunaev, aged seventy-three, who has held the job since 1964 and was a close Brezhnev supporter. He was in a strong position to secure investment for Kazakhstan, but given his age, past associations and the new leadership in Moscow, Kunaev's authority now looks less secure. A number of senior party leaders from Kazakhstan have recently been dismissed and there is persistent press criticism of the way in which the republic is run.

Despite this, the state shops in Alma-Ata look well stocked with clothes compared with cities further north. The peasant free market, filled with fruit and vegetables in the summer, has lower prices than Moscow. But most of the people buying water melons and vegetables in the market are of distinctly Russian rather than Central Asian appearance. Here in the capital, and to a lesser degree in the rest of Kazakhstan, Russians are the largest of the hundred nationalities who live in the vast republic. Kazakhstan is four times the size of Texas and stretches from the Caspian Sea to the Chinese border.

Russians now make up 41 per cent of the republic's 15 million population: Kazakhs, the titular nationality, make up only 36 per cent. Other national groups include Koreans (deported from Sakhalin Island near Japan after the Second World War), Germans who came as settlers at the turn of the century or were deported from the Volga region by Stalin, and Central Asians descended from the nomads who once grazed their flocks across the plains. Russian settlers from the other side of the Ural Mountains have been attracted by the unploughed grasslands since serfdom ended in the last century. After the 1917 Revolution, the Soviet government began to develop the republic's natural wealth: agricultural land in the north, coal in the centre and oil in the west close to the Caspian Sea.

The cities stand like symbols of different periods in the country's economic development. When Karaganda was founded in 1934 it was a cluster of miners' settlements in the semi-desert. It was rapidly developed in the first surge of industrialisation, and now 30,000 people work in the city's iron and steel plant. It looks like a typical example of the big old industrial enterprises which Mikhail Gorbachev says must be re-equipped.

Apart from the blazing sun, the industrial landscape looks like parts of South Wales. Slag heaps, pit wheels and tall factory chimneys stand, somewhat incongruously, on the shores of a large artificial lake fringed with reeds. A plant manager, when asked about plans to reduce pollution, said that on 320 days of the year the prevailing wind is from the west and blows smoke away from Karaganda. He did not explain how the 600,000 people in the city cope during the remaining forty-five days.

None of the new Kremlin leaders has any experience of Kazakhstan and they are unlikely to pour investment into the republic, but the old industrial base, once crucial to the Soviet war effort, will presumably be improved and the political leadership which has run the country since the mid 1950s will be replaced.

1 August 1985

On the Iranian Border

The border between the Soviet Union and Iran is marked by a snow-covered mountain range running just to the south of the city of Ashkabad, capital of the Soviet republic of Turkmenistan. Soviet guards armed with Kalashnikov machine guns search cars driving into the foothills below the mountains, but few people cross the border itself.

For almost everybody in Ashkabad, apart from a few with relatives in Iran, the Kopetdag mountains form an uncrossable barrier between Soviet Central Asia and the Iran of Ayatollah Khomeini. The two worlds could not be more different. Although the holy city of Mashhad lies not far away on the other side of the border there is not a single mosque in Ashkabad (population 400,000) and only four in the whole of Turkmenistan.

Evidence is slight that Islamic belief survives among the 3 million people of Turkmenistan, most of whom were Moslems before the 1917 Revolution. In front of a twelfth-century Islamic shrine in the semi-desert outside the city of Mari recently a Turkoman with a grey beard was praying fervently, but a mile away a working mosque was empty. A well-educated local woman said that religion was a matter for women and the old.

However, a Soviet handbook for spreading atheism in Turkoman villages published last year says that in country areas, as opposed to the cities, religious sentiment and old customs make a strong contribution. "Selling girls, taking bride money and keeping the bride at her parents' home for a certain period of time, and people working as quacks and sorcerers to lead a life of ease, are still seen among the population." But there is little sign, apart from such sporadic indications of official Soviet nervousness, to support the theory that the Islamic revolution which overthrew the Shah in 1979 or the Soviet intervention in Afghanistan in 1980 has had much influence on the 44 million inhabitants of Soviet Central Asia.

Nevertheless Turkmenistan and the other four Central Asian republics remain different from the rest of the Soviet Union. When Moscow was under deep snow in mid February it was warm enough to walk about without a coat in Ashkabad and Mari, the second biggest city of the republic. Fresh grass was growing in the pasture land between the mountains and the vast Kara Kum desert which makes up 80 per cent of Turkmenistan.

Ashkabad itself is a new city, rebuilt entirely since in 1948 it was completely destroyed by an earthquake in which as many as 60,000 people were killed. "I have to live at home to look after my mother whose legs were crippled in the earthquake," said one woman. The massive supporting columns of the new earthquake-resistant buildings give them a squat appearance, but the people in the street look prosperous.

The warm climate of Turkmenistan—nearly 300 days of sunshine a year—has always made it appear to be the land of agricultural opportunity to planners in Moscow. There are few rivers or streams, but starting in 1954 the Kara Kum canal has been extended 1,100 kilometres west towards the Caspian Sea, making it one of the longest canals in the world, carrying water from the Amu Darya river to the irrigation ditches in the cotton fields on either side.

It is cotton and the size of the cotton crop, not Iran, Afghanistan or resurgent Islam, which has been a key factor behind the recent purge of Communist Party leadership in Turkmenistan and the rest of Central Asia. Between 1980 and 1985 Turkmenistan supplied the USSR with 6 million tonnes of cotton, but yields are low and investment high. Irrigation with inadequate drainage has increased the amount of salt, known locally as "white poison", in the fields, reducing annual cotton output by some 400,000 tonnes.

An attack on the way in which Turkmenistan agriculture is run in *Pravda* last August was a signal that Mukhamednazar Gapurov, Communist Party First Secretary for Turkmenistan since 1969, would not long survive. "Many fields which at first were quite fruitful are empty today, and look as if they were covered in snow but in fact it's salt," wrote *Pravda*. Why, it asked, given sunshine, warmth and land, did Turkmenistan eat more than it produced?

Gapurov was pensioned off at the Turkmen party congress in December. "Under him cadres were often promoted to leading posts on grounds of personal loyalty, family ties or birth place," reads a report of the congress. He had created "a breeding ground for nepotism, flattery and careerism, created an atmosphere of laxity and back-scratching, and gave rise to servility and irresponsibility".

Harsh words, but the local leadership cannot be blamed for everything. Moscow's insistence on judging everything in Turkmenia by the cotton statistics is also responsible for the troubles of local agriculture. "The republic supplies the country with cotton—that is its chief duty and concern—but it has no strength left for anything else," say local party officials in charge of food and agriculture.

Too much was expected from the reclaimed desert watered by the Kara Kum canal, exploitation was too rapid and local leaders tried to cover up the failings that inevitably ensued.

27 March 1986

Corruption in Georgia

Russians envy the prosperity of the 5 million inhabitants of the southern republic of Georgia stretching from the Black Sea into the southern

folds of the Caucasus mountains. This envy is caused by the belief that
Georgians, warmed by a Mediterranean climate at this time of year,
have access to all the luxuries other Soviet citizens lack. Russians express
this jealousy in numerous anti-Georgian jokes.

Envy of Georgia is exacerbated by the conviction that much of its
wealth is dishonestly acquired. There are stories of whole Aeroflot
aircraft being chartered to fly mimosa blossom to Moscow to be sold for
vast profits. Soon after he became Georgian leader in 1972, Shevardnadze himself said: "We Georgians, a people of farmers, heroes and
poets, have become thieves, cheats and black-marketeers."

Despite all his efforts to root out dishonesty, Georgia has retained its
reputation for corruption. Periodic scandals surface in the press.
Dzhumber Patiashvili, who succeeded Shevardnadze, gave a list at the
Georgian Communist Party congress in February of past leaders who
have been dismissed. "Bribery and careerism are closely interwoven and
merge with toadying, servility, flattery and hypocrisy," he warned delegates.

This is rough stuff even by the standards of the clean-up campaign
launched by Yuri Andropov after the death of Brezhnev in 1982 and
continued by Mikhail Gorbachev.

Presumably, Mr Patiashvili's denunciation is deserved, but it is doubtful if Georgia is quite the thieves' kitchen most people in Moscow
imagine. Rather it is an illustration of an important theme in present-day
Soviet politics: the resentment felt by Russians about the prosperity of
the republics on the periphery of the Soviet Union. The three Baltic
republics, the Caucasian republics of Georgia, Azerbaijan and Armenia
and the five in Central Asia have all sucked in investment since the
Second World War, while people in the industrial belts in the provinces
around Moscow feel left behind.

Georgia has become a popular symbol of this resentment. Spring
comes in Tblisi, the capital, when the streets of Moscow and Leningrad
are still lined with snow. The republic is an important producer of
tobacco and tea, and most farmers have a small vineyard for making
their own wine. Car ownership, while not as extensive as Muscovites
imagine, is 55 per 1,000 inhabitants, compared to an average of 40 per
1,000 for the country as a whole.

Georgian wine-growing has come under pressure because of the
clampdown on drinking under Gorbachev. A senior Georgian official in
Tblisi said last week that there would be no rooting up of vineyards.
"There is a slight shift from making brandy and distilled spirits to fruit
juices," he said, but "We have always drunk, and will continue to drink,
natural wines."

This is likely to be popular with tourists from the rest of the Soviet

Union who flood south to sit amid palm trees and oleanders in the Georgian Black Sea towns of Batumi and Sakhumi. Tblisi, a narrow city of 1 million, winding along the banks of the Kura river, attracts large numbers of foreign and Soviet visitors each summer.

Part of the prosperity is due to Eduard Shevardnadze, under whom Georgia pioneered economic experiments now advocated for the whole country. As early as 1979, he started an experiment at the town of Ababha in Western Georgia grouping all agricultural institutions under one management, while farmers were given increased incentives. Production rose and the experiment was later expanded.

Georgia has had high growth rates—last year output was up by 7 per cent on 1984—but it also has many of the problems of under-investment and low technology with which Gorbachev is now trying to cope. Typical of this is the Rustavi metallurgy plant not far from Tblisi. It is important because it produces much of the pipe for the Soviet oil and gas industry. Couram Kashakashvili, the managing director, said his plant employed fewer men that similar ones in the Ukraine "because of the high level of mechanisation". The reject rate for the 1 million tonnes of finished products a year is low.

But the plant itself, although efficient given the technology employed, uses equipment of 1960s vintage. There is no continuous casting, although electric arc furnaces are to be introduced by 1992. In the control room, men and women turn levers to control the movement of the steel billets from the furnace, but the lack of microprocessors means that quality control can never become guaranteed quality.

11 June 1986

Backlash as the Barons Fall

On 16 December, a meeting of the Communist Party of the Soviet Republic of Kazakhstan, in the city of Alma-Ata, decided to retire Dinmukhamed Kunaev, leader since 1964 and a long-serving member of the ruling Politburo, and replace him with Gennadi Kolbin, a Russian. The retirement of Kunaev, an old-guard supporter of Leonid Brezhnev, had been expected. It is what happened next which caused astonishment in the rest of the Soviet Union.

Soon after news of the party decision spread through Alma-Ata, a city of 1 million, Kazakh students began to riot in protest against the replacement of Kunaev, a Kazakh, by a Russian. Even more surprisingly, the riots were immediately reported by Tass, in keeping with the policy of greater openness introduced by Mikhail Gorbachev. This is the first time immediate publicity has been given to such a sensitive subject as violence between two Soviet nationalities.

Egged on by nationalist elements and joined by what Tass described as "hooligans and parasites", the students attacked the police, burned down a food shop and shouted insults. Some police and rioters were seriously injured, according to unofficial reports, and a member of the Politburo was sent to investigate the unrest.

After the first admission of rioting, information has been scanty, but it is evident that the riot had an anti-Russian motive. This is surprising since Kazakhstan has more Russians than Kazakhs among its 16 million population. In Alma-Ata Russians are in an overwhelming majority. It is already clear, however, that the riots in Alma-Ata are only the latest episode in a series of dramatic events which, in the past four years, have led to sweeping changes throughout the five Soviet Central Asian republics (with a total population of 46 million). Moscow has sacked four of the Communist Party leaders of the republics and fear of a similar fate may have led to the sudden death, possibly through suicide, of the fifth.

Kunaev first became leader of Kazakhstan in 1960, was briefly demoted by Nikita Khrushchev and then restored in 1964 by Brezhnev. He is the last of the five to go; his departure appears to end the clean-out which began in 1983 when Sharaf Rashidov, ruler of Uzbekistan for twenty-four years and a non-voting member of Moscow Politburo for twenty-two, died suddenly, just before the exposure of a swindle which had systematically exaggerated cotton production by up to 900,000 tonnes a year.

The purge, accompanied by accounts of political and economic corruption on a grand scale, is the result of three trends in Soviet politics over the past four years: a purge of leaders appointed or supported by Brezhnev, a reassertion of central authority over the local party apparatus, and more careful control by Moscow of government spending and the return on investment. These trends have had the greatest impact in Central Asia because the region has the same political relationship to Moscow as the American Deep South to Washington. Local leaders of great longevity have built up political machines dependent on patronage and their ability to extract funds from the centre. "Self-styled noblemen with party tickets infiltrated the leading posts on a large scale and built up a personality cult around the local leader," confessed the local party newspaper in Uzbekistan.

It is Moscow's attack on these great baronies, and the break-up of the political machines which supported them, which has been the force for change, rather than a sudden upsurge in local nationalism or Islamic fundamentalism.

The scene of the rise and fall of the great bosses of Soviet Central Asia is the area bordered to the north by Siberia and to the south by Iran and Afghanistan, conquered by the Russian Tsars in the nineteenth century. The new Communist government in the 1920s split the region into five republics, each with a different ethnic mix.

Although the area originally taken by the Russians was Moslem, Russian emigrants quickly moved south along new railways to found cities and plough up grazing lands. The result is a mosaic of nationalities and an ethnologist's paradise. Ethnic Kazakhs form only 36 per cent of the population of the republic. Uzbekistan is more homogeneous, but Uzbeks make up only a bare majority of the 2 million population of the capital, Tashkent.

Industry developed under Stalin, and in the 1950s Khrushchev started his campaign to plough up the "virgin lands" of North Kazakhstan in a bid to boost Soviet grain production. Oil and gas were discovered. Investment was poured in by Moscow to exploit Central Asia's resources of raw materials, labour and land. The result was a surge in growth, which raised the standard of living of Soviet Central Asia well above that of Iran. The capitals of the five republics look better built than much of Moscow.

Some of the reasons for the rapid development are obvious. The area is the Soviet Union's sunbelt. The Central Asian plateau can be freezing cold at this time of year, but the winter is much shorter than in the rest of the country. Turkmenistan receives 300 days' sunlight a year and sees the first signs of spring in February.

One result of the warm climate is that Central Asia produces almost all the Soviet Union's cotton crop, which totalled nearly 8 million tonnes this year. In Uzbekistan, where two-thirds of the Soviet cotton crop is grown, the difficulties in increasing output led to the greatest swindle in Soviet history—details of which have come out in a trial just ended.

Between 1978 and 1983, it emerged that no less than 4.5 million tonnes of raw cotton were conjured up by Vakhobzhan Usmanov, Uzbekistan cotton industry Minister. Hundreds of millions of roubles were paid by Moscow for cotton which never existed. He was able to carry out the swindle by a system of bribery. Children were once kept in the cotton fields when all the cotton was picked to give the impression that the harvest was continuing. Usmanov, sentenced to death, was arrested in 1984. Before then he had ceased even to open envelopes containing bribes which were handed to him in his office. He tossed one envelope containing 40,000 roubles into a corner of his office, where the police found it lying unopened two years later.

The cotton fraud showed that the local party machine was saturated by corruption. It also underlined how central and local leaders in the last years of Brezhnev refused to believe that the boom years in Central Asia were over. They still thought big investment in its resources would produce massive returns. Just before he died, possibly by his own hand, Rashidov was close to getting Moscow to agree to an enormous investment in a canal to bring water from the north-flowing Siberian rivers to irrigate the cotton fields and orchards of Central Asia.

With the death of Brezhnev in 1982, the party leaders in Moscow started a sustained campaign to retrieve economic control for the centre and to break political machines, often dominated by extended families, which had flourished for twenty years. Cuts have gone deep. Two-thirds of Kunaev's Kazakh party Central Committee were removed last February. In Uzbekistan, ten of the thirteen party first secretaries have been fired. The new party leader in Kirghizia says that in the last five years between 82 and 87 per cent of local party leaders have been sacked. The replacement of this number of officials is clearly causing serious problems. In the past the local leader usually came from the indigenous nationality and his deputy was a Slav. Over the last three years men like Gennadi Kolbin have suddenly been parachuted in to reassert central control, but—as the riots in Alma-Ata show—at the cost of local resentment.

It is difficult to judge how costly. Soviet reports of the Alma-Ata riots hint darkly at the students being the cat's paws of the Kunaev regime, but the violence confirms other evidence of growing self-assertiveness among Kazakhs, Uzbeks and other local nationalities.

Local people say there is greater attendance at mosques and prayer meetings. More people abide by the month-long Moslem fast of Ramadan—catering companies complain of an increasing loss of business during this period. There is more press and party criticism of local authorities' failure to combat the growth of religion. Increased education, as elsewhere in the Middle East, has led to greater consciousness of national differences. A good indicator of relations between nationalities is intermarriage—the rate of marriages between Russians and Uzbeks fell in the 1970s.

Not only is the indigenous population better educated, but its high birth rate (average family size in Russia is 3.3 compared to 6.0 in Tajikistan and 5.8 in Uzbekistan) means that Russians are a falling proportion of the population. Tashkent now has a native majority, and native dress is increasingly seen in other capitals.

However, signs of Islamic revivalism are still few and the border with Iran is sealed tight. All but one of the five republics speak Turkic languages and adhere to the Sunni branch of Islam, rather than the Shiah Moslem faith of Ayatollah Khomeini. Fears of Iran or nationalist revolt have not, in any case, been Moscow's main concern during its attack on the political bosses of Central Asia. The Alma-Ata riots do show, however, that tightening central control can produce a backlash among an educated and urban native population, increasingly conscious of its national and religious identity.

6 January 1987

Digging up Rashidov

The body of Sharaf Rashidov, for twenty-four years leader of Uzbekistan, the largest of the five Soviet Central Asian republics, has been removed from its prominent burial place as a sign of his final disgrace.

Rashidov died in 1983, just before the exposure of widespread corruption in Uzbekistan, including fraudulent exaggeration of the cotton crop, led to an extensive purge of party and state officials which is still going on. The party last year posthumously stripped Rashidov, who was a non-voting member of the Politburo, of all honours after he was denounced for corruption, servility, fraud and nepotism. His body is now to be removed from its tomb in the centre of Tashkent.

"The time has come to call things by their real names. It was necessary to rebury the remains of the so-called Leninist," *Literaturnaya Gazeta* said yesterday. The heads of all the other Central Asian republics have been sacked since 1983, the removal of the last, Dinmukhamed Kunaev, leader of Kazakhstan, provoking riots in Alma-Ata last December.

Some 2,600 officials in Uzbekistan have been sacked, fined or otherwise disciplined in the drive against corruption and incompetence, *Pravda* said. Among those expelled from the party last year was Narmakhonmadi Khudaiberdyev, Prime Minister of Uzbekistan between 1971 and 1984, the most important Soviet official after Rashidov. The local party leadership said that together the two men falsified the figures for cotton, of which Uzbekistan is the Soviet Union's largest producer.

"This gave rise to a system of padding of results, deception of the state, whitewashing, bribery, embezzlement of state funds on a particularly large scale, and other self-serving abuses," according to a report by the new Uzbek leadership.

11 June 1987

Furs and Films in Leningrad

As the temperature in Central Leningrad dropped to below minus 20 degrees centigrade last week, 250 fur traders gathered for the Soviet Union's biggest fur auction in Moskovskii Shosse. The protective white coats worn by all gave the gathering a medical flavour, an impression reinforced as the fur experts bent over what look like operating tables to examine the sable, mink, silver fox or karakul.

Conversation among the fur men was gloomy. They said that mink, some 70 per cent of the world fur trade, was overproduced and foresaw tumbling prices. Already the Soviets, responsible for over a third of 33 million mink in the world, had marked prices down to around $38 a pelt. "It costs us about $18–19 just to feed a mink, so at this price they cannot be making much money," said a thoughtful Finnish fur trader as he examined white mink.

The different floors of the Leningrad headquarters of Soyuzpushnina, the Soviet fur-trading company, were stacked with 2.5 million pelts, including 1.7 million mink. On the top storey the grey Persian lamb pelts look like stacks of enormous kippers, while on a lower floor experts examined samples of the 60,000 sable offered for sale.

It is the sable, 90 per cent trapped wild and produced only in the Soviet Union, which gives the auction its distinction, and it is not surprising that two bronze S-shaped sables are the handles to the main doors of Soyuzpushnina's building. The sable is also the subject of heavy publicity from Neiman-Marcus, the Dallas retailers, who made an advertising video about the fur during the auction. The star of the video was a shy but poised twenty-year-old ash-blonde student from Leningrad called Marina, who was wrapped in a series of $75,000 ankle-length sable coats. David Wolfe, Neiman-Marcus senior vice-president, himself swathed in a sable coat, directed as Marina modelled the coat on a corner of Nevski Prospekt before an audience of perplexed Leningraders.

As the temperature dropped further, Wolfe, Marina and the Neiman-Marcus party drove out of the city to Petrodvorets, the eighteenth-century Christmas cake palace overlooking the Gulf of Finland. In the throne room, before an enormous portrait of Catherine the Great on horseback, the video was completed, the participants somewhat impeded by the flip-flop slippers which the fierce old woman guarding the room insisted everybody wear to protect the floor.

Back in Leningrad, nobody could think of anything except the cold. Soviet buildings are usually well heated by central boiler systems, but in the antique Astoria Hotel the radiators had fought a feeble battle with the falling temperature, and lost. In the restaurant, a cavernous hall with palm trees and marble statues of nymphs, diners not wearing overcoats shuddered as they waited to eat.

Contrary to popular belief in the West, the main difficulty in Soviet restaurants is not getting a table, slow service or quality of food. The difficulty is in hearing a word anybody says, because the noise of the band drowns all conversation with a medley of sixties Western rock music and sentimental Soviet songs. The other hazard of eating out in the Soviet Union is that in addition to the band, every restaurant has a table occupied by very drunk men from the southern republic of Georgia. The five obligatory Georgians in the Astoria restaurant were typical: every few minutes they sprang to their feet, kissed each other and began to accompany the band which, after brief financial negotiations, they had induced to confine its repertoire to songs of the Georgian mountains.

Other Soviet nationalities staying in Leningrad show less *savoir-faire*, but are also keen to socialise. One of a party of Tajiks, from the republic of Tajikistan on the Chinese border, eager to demonstrate his English, prodded me gently in the upper ribs and said: "Margaret Thatcher ... Sherlock Holmes ... Scotland Yard." He then retreated, still beaming, back to his fellow Tajiks.

Leningrad has made an effort to improve its entertainment. The Literary Café, once famous as the place from which the poet Pushkin set out for his fatal duel, has been reconditioned on the corner of Nevski Prospekt and the Moika Canal. Small chamber orchestras play as customers drink champagne and eat caviar. The attraction of Leningrad comes from the combination of baroque buildings and the water of the canals. The Neva River is crossed by numerous elegant bridges. Peter the Great, who founded the city in the marshes of the Neva estuary in 1703, originally wanted no bridges at all, on the grounds that this would encourage seamanship among the inhabitants thus compelled to row themselves about. He was dissuaded only by heavy casualties among civil servants, who drowned by the score.

The city today is beautiful but melancholy. Since the 900-day siege in the last war, in which 650,000 people died, all old buildings are preserved and, where necessary, reconditioned or rebuilt. Estimable in principle, the preservation of the city as it was before 1917 gives it the appearance of an enormous doll's house. Neiman-Marcus are right in seeing its virtues as a film set.

25 January 1986

Stalingrad Revisited

"The older people would like to go back to calling the city Stalingrad, but the young are happy to call it by its new name," said a woman in Volgograd, the city which was the site of the battle which marked the turning point of the Second World War on the eastern front.

Volgograd, its name changed by Nikita Khrushchev, now has a population of almost a million and stretches forty-five miles along the right bank of the Volga River, more than half a mile wide at this point. Tank turrets mark the former front line, at places only 200 yards from the Volga, where the Soviet troops managed to cling on to their positions against repeated German attacks in 1942. Otherwise there are surprisingly few memorials to the war, apart from a vast statue of a woman with a drawn sword on top of the hill of Mamayev Kurgan, where the fiercest fighting took place. The main department store, in the cellars of which Field Marshal Von Paulus, the German commander at Stalingrad, surrendered his force of 90,000 men in 1943, has only a simple plaque to commemorate the fact.

The old city of Stalingrad was entirely destroyed in the war. Its replacement is important because it is in industrial cities like Volgograd, with dated but by no means archaic plant and equipment and a good infrastructure, that the fate of Mikhail Gorbachev's efforts to restructure and update the Soviet economy will be decided over the next five years.

Regions of the Soviet Union like Estonia on the Baltic or Georgia in the Caucasus, most often mentioned as being at the forefront of modernisation, are atypical of the Soviet Union. Volgograd, at the centre of a region the size of Czechoslovakia and with a population of 2.5 million, is a much better guide to developments in the Russian heartlands.

The city's industrial production comes mainly from its large tractor, steel, aluminium and chemical plants. Electric power is generated by the nearby hydroelectric power plant, whose dam across the Volga marks the northern end of the city. At the southern end, overlooked by a vast statue of Lenin which has replaced one of Stalin, a canal links the Volga to the Don River to the west and to the so-called Donbass industrial region. The canal, scarcely large enough to take more than a big trawler, is too narrow to bring the coal Volgograd needs to expand its aluminium and steel mills. V.I. Kalashnikov, the Communist Party leader for Volgograd, has pressed to get the canal widened, though without evident signs of success.

Yet the overall infrastructure of the city is of good quality. The housing, all built since the war, is 40 per cent in private hands and there is a five-year waiting list—not long by Soviet standards—for people wanting to live in the state-owned blocks of apartments. In a new departure the city is now planning to build a limited number of houses for sale, with a price range of between 35,000 and 45,000 roubles. The transport system also appears more efficient than it is in Moscow or cities of similar size to Volgograd. A fast tram system on which tickets cost 3 kopecks carries passengers underground to bypass the city centre and acts as a substitute for an underground railway. The cost of a car, as always in the USSR, is high at about 7,000 roubles, but two makes, the Niva and the black Moskvitch, can be bought here—but not in Moscow—on two years' credit with a 30 per cent deposit.

Kalashnikov, a former Minister of Irrigation in the Russian republic, appointed Communist Party leader for the Volgograd region in 1984, called in a speech to the Communist Party Congress in Moscow in February this year for a better pricing system—in other words higher prices—to make farms profitable. Retail prices of basic foodstuffs—meat in a state shop costs 1.90 roubles a kilogram—have not been increased since 1962, while incomes have almost doubled. More realistic retail prices would make it possible to narrow the gap between supply and demand and to abolish ration coupons and other forms of distribution, Kalashnikov told the Congress, which meets every five years. He added that the present state procurement and retail price system prevented farms making a profit.

Since then, food supplies in Volgograd have improved. In the huge central market, where peasants come to sell their produce at high prices—a kilogram of mandarin oranges from Central Asia costs 6 roubles—bright orange booths were erected this spring for state and collective farms to sell the permitted 30 per cent of their vegetables and fruit direct to the customer. "We now have four different prices for goods: state, co-operative, state and collective farm and free-market," said a shopper. The co-operative meat price, for instance, is 3.50 roubles, compared with a state price of 1.90 roubles and a free-market price of up to 5 roubles. The tendency in Volgograd is for an increasing proportion of produce to be sold midway between state and free-market prices.

The importance of Volgograd and cities like it is that they were sufficiently well run during the 1970s and early 1980s to enable changes to be carried through quickly now. This requires competent local political and managerial leaders, adequate infrastructure and industrial plant in need of upgrading rather than replacement. If Gorbachev's economic reforms do not succeed in Volgograd, where these conditions are met, they are unlikely to succeed elsewhere.

4 December 1986

The Army's Role in Armenia

Mikhail Gorbachev told the United Nations on 7 December that the Soviet Union was considering the problems of converting its military plant and expertise—soon to be redundant because of the proposed cutback in the Soviet armed forces—to civilian use. On the same day an earthquake devastated Armenia. The disaster may have provided an opportunity—far more immediate and horrific than Gorbachev would have liked—to use the army to meet civilian needs, by placing the Soviet armed forces in charge of the reconstruction of Armenia over the next two years. This has important advantages for Armenia, for the Soviet armed forces and for Gorbachev himself.

The Armenians would benefit because the Soviet military has the best construction organisation in the Soviet Union—far superior, in skills and equipment, to its civilian counterparts. Instead of switching scarce resources from other parts of the Soviet economy to meet the needs of reconstruction, the military could use equipment, materials and personnel it already has. For example, Gorbachev told the UN that "assault crossing units with their weapons and combat equipment" would be withdrawn from Soviet forces in Eastern Europe. This means that the Soviet military has surplus bridging equipment which could be used in Armenia.

The army's political standing has been reduced under Gorbachev, and it is blamed for absorbing resources needed by consumers. Successful reconstruction of Armenia would increase army prestige in the country as a whole and would make its presence much more acceptable in Armenia itself.

In the two weeks before the earthquake at least twenty-eight people were killed in Armenia and Azerbaijan, and some 170,000 had taken to the roads as refugees. Baku and Yerevan are almost under martial law; continued heavy military presence is necessary to protect people against sectarian attacks.

It is plain, however, that the troops on the streets are an irritant—blamed by both Armenians and Azerbaijanis for partiality towards the other side. This might change if the Soviet army were to undertake projects such as construction of a highway linking Armenia to the Armenian enclave of Nagorno-Karabakh in Azerbaijan, the return of which has been the aim of Armenian agitation. The point would be not just to build a road, but to provide enough military protection to ensure that Armenians could travel safely between the enclave and Armenia proper. Such palliatives are the more necessary because long before the earthquake it had become clear that any shift in Nagorno-Karabakh's status would provoke a furious reaction in Azerbaijan (and set a dangerous precedent for some thirty-five similar enclaves, scattered around the Soviet Union, which want to change their relationship with the republic in which they are included). Gorbachev made a serious mistake a year ago in failing to rule out any change in territorial boundaries: he raised hopes he was in no position to satisfy.

Does the earthquake offer the Soviet leader a new opportunity to break out from this impasse? In the past Gorbachev has been adept at turning to his political advantage disasters or mistakes such as Chernobyl in 1986, or Mathias Rust's flight to Red Square in 1987. In Armenia and Azerbaijan both the political crisis and the natural disaster are on a much larger scale. Gorbachev needs to produce a creative solution to the problems of the area if it is not to become a Soviet version of Lebanon or Northern Ireland.

Handing over reconstruction to the armed forces has the advantage of simultaneously meeting the material needs of Armenians, providing security so long as sectarian tensions persist, and initiating an alternative and useful role for Soviet soldiers at a moment when their prestige and numbers are under attack.

22 December 1986

PART IV

Glasnost, Corruption and Chernobyl

In 1986 Yegor Ligachev, Gorbachev's number two in the Politburo, quoted Lenin as saying that the greatest dangers to Communist officials were self-satisfaction, drunkenness and corruption. He saw all three as typical of the Brezhnev era. The attack on corruption had begun under Yuri Andropov in 1982, but the first action by Mikhail Gorbachev to affect the whole population was the clampdown on alcohol. A year later glasnost became a central theme of the new generation of political leaders in the Kremlin. Openness, along with sobriety and honesty, was seen as essential to the mobilisation of society in favour of reform. The nuclear disaster at Chernobyl was the critical test for this new policy.

Glasnost

Soviet Censorship: The Beginnings of Glasnost

The Soviet leadership has always had an ambiguous attitude towards the intelligentsia. Calling on the party to respect culture and those who possessed it, Lenin once issued the injunction to "command less, or rather not to command at all". At another moment, however, he said of the intelligentsia: "they must be given work but they must be carefully watched, commissars should be placed over them and their counter-revolutionary schemes suppressed."

Since Mikhail Gorbachev became Soviet leader, the first attitude has started to predominate over the second. In the last month the authority of the main censorship body has been reduced and both the Minister of Culture and the head of the Writers' Union have been shifted to cere-monial posts.

The extent and radicalism of the new policy of glasnost are endlessly debated by intellectuals in Moscow. Censorship is not abolished, but criticism is much freer than under Brezhnev. "The nation wants glas-nost," Andrei Voznesyensky, a distinguished poet, told the Writers' Union Congress in June. "It knows the monstrous strength of evil, lawlessness, corruption, bribe-taking, deception and double dealing." But instead of books dealing with such topics, Voznesyensky continued, readers were offered works from which all hint of controversy had been removed by editorial censors: "Sometimes a writer spends 10 per cent of his life writing books and 90 per cent trying to get them printed." He said that even then the censor sometimes so manicured works of liter-ature submitted to him as to reduce them to the level of vaudeville.

Significantly, Voznesyensky's speech, and others equally critical, were fully reported in the press. Editors and publishers are increasingly confi-dent that "openness" as a policy is here to stay. They are less worried that publication of critical material today might, if the present trend towards liberalisation were reversed, be used as evidence against them in future.

The problem for editors, theatre directors, film-makers and the censors themselves is that over the last eighteen months the party line on

105

glasnost has maintained Lenin's tradition of ambiguity. Gorbachev and the Central Committee commended the change in general, but it was not clear what this meant in specific instances. Many officials did not want to be the first to find the limits of the new policy by putting their foot on the wrong side of the party line. Even so, the Soviet press has become progressively more interesting since Brezhnev's death. Recent corruption scandals have been heavily publicised. There are many more articles about what is wrong with the economy.

Other, more esoteric questions have also been covered in the press. Why, asked *Izvestia* early last year, do Soviet citizens often have bad teeth? The reason, it explained, was that for twenty years Soviet dentistry was dominated by Dr Anatoly Ivanovich Rybakov, head of the Central Dentistry Research Institute. Deciding that what mattered was not teeth but gums, Dr Rybakov stopped Soviet dentists using for fillings the type of amalgam employed elsewhere. "Our dentists have had to use fillings made of rather flimsy plastics, which are destroyed in six months or a year. If you're lucky they may last a year and a half," *Izvestia* continued. Specialists who disagreed with Dr Rybakov were forced to resign and the Ministry of Health ignored all protests and criticism. Dental disease was reduced in other countries, but not in the Soviet Union. A later issue of *Izvestia* reported Dr Rybakov's dismissal.

The press is powerful in the Soviet Union because it is an instrument of the government and newspapers have enormous circulations. *Izvestia* sells six million copies a day, as do three other daily newspapers in Moscow. Their influence is also great because of the lack of any real forum for debate in the Soviet Union (the Supreme Soviet is a rubber-stamp parliament). Debate, controversy and criticism—as in the case of Dr Rybakov—surface in the newspapers because they have nowhere else to go.

There are limits to this criticism. Key institutions of power are seldom attacked. For instance, there are many detailed and interesting articles on the failure of the oil industry in Western Siberia to produce enough crude because of lack of exploration, technology and infrastructure. There is almost nothing, however, on the failure of the state planning organisation, Gosplan, to cut consumption in the 1970s and early 1980s.

The Soviet leadership also appears genuinely divided on the extent of glasnost it will allow. The press played a significant role during the 1982–85 leadership crisis, which ended with Gorbachev taking charge, in undermining the position of the Brezhnev old guard. In the lead-up to the party congress this February, local party leaders and officials often came under attack in the central press for incompetence or corruption. Yet it was never clear if the new leadership in the Kremlin would be quite so interested in washing dirty linen in public once it was in control.

Gorbachev was forthright during the party congress in his call for less secrecy and greater freedom of expression. But Yegor Ligachev went out of his way to attack *Pravda* for publishing letters criticising privileges for Communist Party members.

So it is not surprising that many in Moscow suspect that more openness might be the flavour of the year rather than a new policy. Some editors have contented themselves with issuing a call for greater criticism and debate, but have avoided doing anything about it themselves. "Lead editorials on the need for freshness of thought and language are often written in a language so dry that you involuntarily yawn," Yevgeny Yevtushenko, another prominent poet, noted last December.

In the past three months, however, two key events have forced the party leadership to determine its attitude to secrecy and freedom of expression.

The first was the nuclear disaster at Chernobyl. For the first three days after the fire at the atomic power station the Soviet authorities said nothing. It was ten days after the catastrophe that the Ukrainian Health Minister appeared on television in Kiev to tell people to take precautions against radiation.

Since about 6 June there has been a complete change. Stories have been detailed and often critical. This is illustrated by one recent Soviet anecdote: two men, one from Chernobyl and the other from Kiev, meet in heaven. "What did you die of?" asks the man from Kiev. "Too much radiation," says the man from Chernobyl; "and you?" "Too much information," replies the man from Kiev.

The Writers' Union Congress at the end of June may prove to be a similar watershed for Soviet writers and intellectuals. Just before it started, Petr Demichev, the Culture Minister since 1974 and a chemical engineer by training, was given the ceremonial post of vice-president. At the congress itself the head of the Writers' Union for the past fifteen years, Georgy Markov, was also kicked upstairs.

Given that membership of the 10,000-strong Writers' Union guarantees a Soviet writer employment and ability to get published, the departure of the old guard significantly changes the cultural atmosphere. Demichev has presided over an extraordinary haemorrhage of talent out of the Soviet Union including the exiling of Alexander Solzhenitsyn and Yuri Lyubimov, Moscow's most prominent theatre director. Markov is believed to have been behind the award of the Lenin Prize for Literature to President Brezhnev for his three-volume war memoirs.

The departure of such men was almost universally welcomed by the intelligentsia, but some of them point out that many of the old taboos remain and the fundamentals of Soviet society are still unquestioned. This is true, but Gorbachev apparently sees greater openness, less

secrecy and more intellectual freedom at all levels as an essential part of
the economic changes he wants to introduce. He directly links economic
mismanagement with intellectual repression, and it is this perception
which is the real basis for glasnost.

Yevtushenko made the same connection last December when he said:
"Intellectual stagnation stopped short the economic prosperity deserved
by our people and reached such depths that in our rich and beautiful
land forty years after the war there still exists in a number of cities the
rationing of butter and meat. This is morally impermissible."

9 July 1986

Gorbachev, the Press and Glasnost

Last Saturday Nicholas Daniloff, Moscow correspondent for the magazine *US News and World Report*, was telephoned by a friend whom he
had met four years before in Soviet Central Asia. The friend, a teacher,
suggested they meet.

Daniloff, due to leave Moscow this week after five-and-a-half years
as correspondent, gave the friend several books by Stephen King, the
American horror-story writer, as a goodbye present. In return the
teacher gave him an envelope, saying it contained clippings from his
local newspapers in the republic of Kirghizia—a useful present for a
journalist based in Moscow, where the provincial press is often impossible to obtain. Gifts exchanged, the friend declined to accompany him
further, and as he walked home Daniloff was arrested by half-a-dozen
KGB security police. The envelope, opened in Daniloff's presence in
prison, turned out to contain not clippings but two maps marked secret
and photographs of Soviet military bases.

The arrest of Daniloff, probably the most distinguished American
correspondent in Moscow, appears to be in retaliation for the arrest in
very similar circumstances in New York of Gennady Zakharov, a Soviet
physicist working at the UN. Neither has diplomatic immunity.

At first sight the arrest of an American journalist appears contrary to
Gorbachev's efforts over the past eighteen months to improve the Soviet
Union's image in the world and to cultivate the Western media. It will
obviously sour US-Soviet relations just before Eduard Shevardnadze,
the Soviet Foreign Minister, and George Shultz, his US counterpart,
meet in New York to discuss the prospects for a summit this year.

The arrest of Daniloff as a spy after a week in which Soviet scientists
in Vienna had revealed more about the Chernobyl nuclear power

accident than anybody had expected demonstrates the contradictory elements in the Soviet attitude towards the outside world. This does not mean that the new openness is insincere but that some, if not all, in the Kremlin, feel it necessary periodically to demonstrate their toughness.

In the first year after Gorbachev was elected, many diplomats in Moscow believed that the new openness at home and abroad would diminish as the new leadership established itself. In fact the reverse has happened, and the handling of Chernobyl was the crucial test.

For a week after the world's worst nuclear accident on 26 April, Moscow's behaviour was a caricature of the Soviet obsession with secrecy. Roy Medvedev, the dissident Soviet historian, has said that at a Politburo meeting two days after the disaster, Gorbachev himself argued that government should reveal what had happened but was overruled by his colleagues. Only as the extent of the disaster, and the impossibility of hushing it up, became evident was Gorbachev able to get his views accepted. Extensive reports began to appear in the press and briefings were arranged for foreign journalists.

Since then Soviet newspaper editors seem to have become confident that openness is here to stay. Gorbachev has already changed the rules of the Soviet political system by making direct appeals to national public opinion in a way which has not happened since the 1920s. Without this change in Soviet politics it would be impossible for him to appeal to international public opinion as he has done since he first visited London in December 1984.

This is all very different from the early 1970s when Brezhnev and Gromyko, the Foreign Minister, preferred to handle détente through secret negotiations with President Nixon and Dr Kissinger. This eighteenth-century-style diplomacy was clearly vulnerable to shifts in Western public opinion which Moscow made little attempt to influence at any level. It is this aspect of Soviet foreign policy which Gorbachev and the men around him have changed. Three changes are notable:

• Gorbachev looks good on television. He is the first Soviet leader to do so (Brezhnev is not a hard act to follow) and this is largely responsible for the better Soviet public image in Western Europe and beyond.

• By taking the initiative in nuclear arms control in a way Brezhnev never did, Gorbachev has been able to present the Soviet Union as more accommodating and flexible than in the past.

• By holding press conferences, appointing official spokesmen and giving briefings, the Soviets have put themselves in a stronger position to present their case.

Too much can be made of the latter point. "Remember," a Soviet diplomat warned me in May 1984, just before I came to Moscow, "no Soviet official ever lost his job because he refused to talk to a foreign correspondent." This grim little piece of advice still holds largely true, but senior decision-makers now give briefings to the foreign press as they never did before. This is useful, but much the most important source of information for a foreign correspondent in Moscow is the Soviet press. The fundamental changes which have taken place here are of far greater significance than the cultivation of public relations techniques by the Soviet Foreign Ministry.

"We spend all our time reading the newspapers," says a Muscovite woman in a tone of surprise and excitement. She points to an article in *Pravda* made up of critical letters from Chernobyl refugees. Such articles in a paper like *Pravda* tarnish the gloss of official accounts of an orderly evacuation and resettlement of refugees from the Chernobyl area. Even more surprising was the publication earlier in August of a series of articles in an Estonian newspaper which described how a group of Estonian military reservists clearing up at Chernobyl had gone on strike in June, when their tour of duty was suddenly extended from two to six months.

Other recent articles in the Soviet press have included:

• A piece in *Moskovsky Komsomolets* describing how Smolensk Square, the small triangle of parkland in central Moscow immediately in front of the Foreign Ministry and close to the Belgrade Hotel, had become a centre for black-marketeers and prostitutes. The main reason for this, explained the newspaper, was that Smolensk Square is at the intersection of two police districts, both of which disclaim responsibility for it, leaving black-marketeers "to feel absolutely safe".

• In recent months, many newspapers have carried articles on drugs, a topic previously never mentioned. There are interviews with policemen who discuss the difficulties of cutting off drug supplies when enormous amounts of wild hemp grow in the east of the country.

Many of these topics would not have been discussed in the press a year ago. Articles give fascinating little insights into Soviet life. For instance, about 30,000 people are diagnosed as having appendicitis in Moscow every year—some 10,000 find out after the operation that there was nothing wrong with their appendix.

Not only do newspapers tackle subjects previously off limits but there are increasing signs that broad political issues are being fought out in the press. These include a massive scheme to divert water from lakes and rivers in the north of the country into the Volga—a project which the

Politburo cancelled last month, citing public opposition. At the same time the Politburo abandoned a project, already under way, to build a vast monument in Moscow to commemorate the 1945 Soviet victory over Germany. To this end a 330-acre park had been appropriated and the hill where Napoleon waited in vain in 1812 to receive the surrender of the city flattened. At the centre of the park, a 230-foot-high statue was to have been erected, an object described by Andrei Voznesyensky as "one of the most cheerless and talentless monuments in the world". It is now being redesigned.

The Soviet press was always slightly more revealing than it was given credit for in the West. The fact that the Supreme Soviet and other nominally representative institutions have only rubber-stamp authority has always meant that debate is displaced sideways into newspapers which have enormous circulations and power. But the campaign for more openness under Gorbachev has done more than just limit secrecy. Access to knowledge has ceased to be an attribute of leadership and is increasingly seen as the right of a citizen. This in turn is changing the relationship between the state and Soviet society from the mould which was set in the early 1930s.

3 September 1986

The Admiral Nakhimov Sinks

Almost 400 people are dead or missing, feared drowned, after a Soviet cruise liner sank in the Black Sea on Sunday. The cruise liner *Admiral Nakhimov*, carrying 1,234 passengers and crew, collided with a Soviet grain freighter and sank almost immediately, a Soviet spokesman said yesterday.

Leonid Nedyak, Deputy Merchant Marine Minister, told a news conference that 79 people died and another 319 were missing, most of whom he believed had gone down with the ship, which sank fifteen minutes after its hull was ripped open by the freighter.

The announcement of the casualty figures and full information about the accident—the worst in Soviet maritime history since the Second World War—less than forty-eight hours after it occurred late on Sunday night marks a significant change in the way disasters are reported in the Soviet Union. In the past they have either not been reported at all or with limited details. In the aftermath of the Chernobyl nuclear accident the Politburo has evidently decided that in line with the new policy of "openness", details of such accidents are to be made available immediately to the foreign and domestic media.

Nedyak said that the *Admiral Nakhimov*, a 17,000-deadweight cruise liner built in 1925, had just left the Black Sea port of Novorossiysk with 846 passengers and some 346 crew when it was struck by the grain freighter *Pyotr Vasev*. The freighter hit it between the engine room and the boiler room and "ripped the ship open". The high casualties are explained by the speed with which the *Admiral Nakhimov* sank, giving no time to launch the lifeboats. Survivors clung to rafts and fifty Soviet ships, assisted by helicopters, are still searching the area. Nobody was aboard the freighter, which is still afloat.

In an interview with *Izvestia*, the helmsman of the cruise liner said his ship had just left port. "We saw the bulk carrier far ahead. The duty officer started calling by radio—we took its bearings and realised that the ship was to cross our path—and after a moment the answer came from the *Pyotr Vasev*: 'Don't worry, we shall steer clear of each other.' A few minutes later we repeated the call since the bulk carrier continued on its course. Then I saw it cutting into our side. It went astern, but it was too late."

Nedyak said yesterday that it was too early to attribute blame for the accident. A commission of inquiry under Geidar Aleyev, a Politburo member, had been appointed on Monday to investigate its cause. The captains of both ships survived the accident. He said that there were no foreigners aboard the *Admiral Nakhimov* and that many of the passengers came from the Ukraine. In addition to the dead and missing, twenty-nine people had been injured and were in hospital.

Holidays on board cruise ships in the Black Sea, the Baltic and on the major river systems have remained popular in the Soviet Union as passenger cruises have declined in popularity in the West. The worst accident in recent Soviet maritime history occurred in 1983, when 100 people were killed when the passenger ship *Alexander Suvurov* ran into a bridge on the Volga. Earlier this year another cruise ship sank off New Zealand after striking a rock, but only one crew member died.

3 September 1986

The Release of Sakharov

The Soviet authorities will free many more political prisoners in the next few months following the release from external exile of Dr Andrei Sakharov, the Soviet physicist, according to Roy Medvedev. "In the first place Sakharov himself will be entering into their defence, and apart from that many were convicted under the same law as he was," he said.

Dr Medvedev, himself one of the most prominent opponents of Brezhnev's government and the historian of Stalinism in the Soviet Union, said in an interview at the weekend that while he believed there would be many releases, he did not expect a general amnesty of political prisoners, whom he estimated to total between 2,000 and 2,500. Other reports citing Soviet officials said yesterday that the government had set up a special commission to examine the cases of prisoners held for political reasons and this was likely to be followed by the release of many.

Dr Medvedev said the release of Dr Sakharov was primarily motivated by two considerations: the authorities' fear that he or Yelena Bonner, his wife, could die in Gorki, combined with the Kremlin's consciousness of the damage that holding Dr Sakharov did to the Soviet Union's reputation abroad. The immediate step leading to the release of Sakharov from his seven years of exile in Gorki, according to Dr Medvedev, was the death of Anatoly Marchenko in prison on 8 December. Marchenko was the first name on a list of fifteen whose release Dr Sakharov demanded in a letter to Mr Gorbachev this spring.

The government in Moscow feared that Dr Sakharov, who is sixty-five, would start another hunger strike, his fourth since he was exiled in 1980. He and his wife have both refused medical attention since they were secretly filmed receiving treatment; therefore "the authorities had no way of knowing what condition Sakharov and Bonner were in".

"The death of Sakharov in Gorki or the death of his wife there could have become an indelible stain on the reputation of the Soviet government, and this is the main reason which prompted Sakharov's release at this time," Dr Medvedev said. Moreover, he continued, government was conscious that despite more democracy and liberalism at home, its reputation was still tarnished "because everyone said: 'You are holding hostage the most outstanding scientist in the country'." Sakharov's detention also prevented the Soviet Union taking the offensive, as it wished to do, on human rights, and did it particular damage among scientists in the West at a time when Moscow wanted to accelerate its scientific progress.

Dr Medvedev said that another important reason for releasing Dr Sakharov was the Kremlin's realisation that his views on nuclear weapons were very similar to Gorbachev's arguments against President Ronald Reagan's Strategic Defence Initiative (SDI) and in favour of a moratorium on nuclear testing. He said that in the 1960s Dr Sakharov, one of the creators of the Soviet hydrogen bomb, had opposed the creation of a Soviet anti-ballistic missile system because it is efficient only "when the country has been hit by a first strike and is already weakened and therefore it is not the one who wants to defend who creates the anti-missile system, but the potential aggressor."

Dr Sakharov's criticism of Soviet intervention in Afghanistan and of human rights violations "will, of course, create a certain problem for Gorbachev, but for him what is far more important is Sakharov's quality as an ally in the struggle against the new American arms programme". The Kremlin, said Dr Medvedev, was conscious that Dr Sakharov's reputation as an honest scientist independent of the Soviet government "can act in their favour as well as against it".

29 December 1986

Second Chance for Soviet Media

"It used to be very easy for an editor to have a liberal reputation in the Soviet Union. You could always say to a writer: 'Of course I'd like to publish your stuff', and then add that the censor or your boss had stopped publication."

These days editors publish what they want, says Vitali Korotich, editor of the popular Soviet weekly news and cultural colour magazine *Ogonyok* and one of a new breed of Soviet editors willing and able to take advantage of the end of near-total censorship to publish what they like. In six months as editor he has already transformed the fusty product he took over into the most interesting and widely read magazine in the country.

This greater freedom of speech that *Ogonyok* represents is for most Soviets probably the most important change in the two years since Gorbachev became leader. He promised political and economic change in his speech to the Communist Party Central Committee in Moscow this week, but in much of the press glasnost has actually arrived. The change is all the more important because the Soviet press, even when Brezhnev was leader, functioned as a limited forum for debate. People will take a grievance to a newspaper office but never think of going to the representative they have voted for in single-candidate elections.

Korotich points out that many ordinary Soviet citizens are still unwilling to take glasnost at face value, fearing a return of censorship and the rigidly enforced uniformity of the past. But "people become braver, more open, less afraid", he says, adding that the main objective is not to commit the same blunders which occurred after 1956 when Khrushchev denounced Stalin only to lose power to Brezhnev in 1964. He refers to an article in the current issue of *Ogonyok* by the playwright Mikhail

Shatrov, comparing 1956 with 1985 and noting that Gorbachev's selection as Soviet leader was opposed.

In a scarcely veiled attack on Viktor Grishin—one of the Brezhnev old guard and for long party boss for Moscow, who stood for the party leadership in 1985—Shatrov says there was a danger that the self-laudatory and mendacious slogans which used to appear in Moscow could have been on every wall in the Soviet Union. Conflict with the ruling Politburo is never normally referred to in the Soviet press, so Shatrov's article has been the talking point of Moscow over the past week. The message is that the lost opportunity of 1956 to break with authoritarianism has not been lost. "History is giving us a second chance," concludes Shatrov.

Deeply researched articles on corruption scandals also appear in the magazine. Earlier this year it carried an exposé on corruption in the organisation supplying food to Moscow. Its head was sent to jail for fifteen years and his deputy for twelve years.

Writing such pieces has changed the working habits of Soviet journalists. "It is easier to publish soporific articles about great victories and new tractors which can't move but look beautiful," says Korotich, whose own career reflects the ups and downs of Soviet writers over the past twenty years. Trained as a surgeon, elected an official of the Writers' Union in 1965, when the liberalism of the Khrushchev era was only just beginning to ebb, he was sacked in 1969 and worked as a freelance journalist editing small magazines before taking over *Ogonyok* last year.

Korotich's magazine is important because it is symptomatic of the change in the Soviet media and arts over the past two years which is having a deep effect on the political system. The Soviet Union is a society which relies heavily on the printed word. Newspapers and magazines have enormous circulations: the trade-union daily, *Trud,* has a print run of 18.5 million, the daily youth paper, *Komsomolskaya Pravda*, 15 million, the Communist Party daily, *Pravda,* itself 11.5 million and the evening paper, *Izvestia,* 7 million. City and local papers number 3,600 and have a combined daily circulation of 36 million.

In the battles between Gorbachev and the Brezhnev old guard, the press has played an important and at times critical role. In many—if not most—cases, the attack on political machines created by former retainers of Brezhnev in Moscow, Kazakhstan or the Ukraine has been led by local or national papers. But the freedom of expression of new magazines like *Ogonyok* plays another important function: it breaks down the nervousness and apathy of ordinary Soviet citizens who suspect that Gorbachev's calls for greater democracy are simply another campaign, whose end will eventually come as it did after Khrushchev's years in power. Confidence has been very slow to return, and only in the past six months have those who believe glasnost is here to stay outnumbered the sceptics.

Korotich himself feels it is now or never: "If we fail to rebuild now we'll lose everything. We must destroy all these stone and concrete people and do something more human, more democratic. That is the only way to live in the modern world."

29 January 1987

Life and Fate

A Soviet magazine is to start publishing the long-banned novel *Life and Fate* by Vasily Grossman in what one Soviet literary critic has described as "the most significant cultural event in the Soviet Union for years". The novel, which takes place during the Battle of Stalingrad, deals extensively with Stalin's purges, torture in prison, anti-Semitism and other topics previously censored. Some Soviet critics regard Grossman's work as superior in quality to Solzhenitsyn's, though it deals with similar themes. They say its publication in full will have much greater impact within the Soviet Union than anything published since censorship was relaxed in 1986.

Grossman was a war correspondent for the military daily *Krasnaya Zvezda* (Red Star) in the war, during which he covered the Battle of Stalingrad. The monthly magazine *Oktyabr* has now signed a contract to start the publication of *Life and Fate* next year. Grossman died in 1964 after his novel had been rejected for publication and almost all manuscripts of his work confiscated, though one survived to be published in translation in the West.

There is now strong competition among Soviet publishers and magazines for works on "hot" political and social themes previously banned by the censor. For instance, novels such as Anatoly Rybakov's *Children of the Arbat*, dealing with Stalin's terror and Moscow society in the 1930s, was written during the 1960s but published only this year.

Grossman's life and work are described sympathetically and at length in the latest issue of the weekly *Ogonyok*, one of the flagships of the radical intelligentsia. After the confiscation of *Life and Fate*, Grossman had little money and earned his living by translating novels from Armenian into Russian. He also wrote short stories for *Novy Mir*, the main liberal literary journal under Khrushchev, but refused to make changes demanded by the editor, so they remained unpublished.

Publication of Grossman's last book, uncut, will be taken by Soviet

intelligentsia as an indication that greater freedom of expression introduced by Gorbachev and Alexander Yakovlev, the Party Secretary for
Propaganda and a member of the Politburo, is continuing undiminished.
Their mood has changed since 1985, when Gorbachev took over,
according to Boris Kagarlitsky, one of a new generation of social and
literary critics who have become vocal over the last year. The grip of
conservatives and censorship on the main cultural unions—writers, film
and theatre—into which full-time Soviet intellectuals are organised has
been broken or much reduced. However, Kagarlitsky also says: "the
trouble with the liberal intelligentsia was that it showed itself quite
incapable of any constructive initiative of its own, preferring just to
applaud Gorbachev's decisions."

In this sense events keenly awaited by the intelligentsia such as the
rehabilitation of Bukharin, the most prominent of the Old Bolshevik leaders executed by Stalin in 1938, or even the publication of *Life and
Fate*—may be a somewhat dated barometer of the state of Soviet intellectual life.

The critical point for intellectuals is becoming not just the need for
freedom of expression about the present and the past, but what to do
with that freedom once it is acquired. Many writers in Moscow fear
that the present thaw will be followed by a renewed freeze, but there is
little evidence of this. Gorbachev and Yakovlev have said they see most
of the present critical literature as a perfectly acceptable sign of intellectual vitality rather than an undermining of the Soviet system.

7 October 1987

Vital Statistics Revealed

The Soviet Union has started to publish more statistics about health,
economy and population in a shift of policy away from the concealment
of figures which showed Soviet performance lagging behind other
countries.

Moscow recently published figures for its grain output which had
been kept secret since 1980, ostensibly for commercial reasons but
almost certainly because of embarrassment at a succession of poor
harvests. The secrecy over grain production was in any case largely
nominal, since the estimates of the US Department of Agriculture
(USDA) turned out to be very accurate. The USDA estimate for 1985
was 190 million tonnes compared to a Soviet figure of 191.6 million
revealed last month. Yesterday Moscow announced a near-record 1986

harvest of 210 million tonnes.

Moscow also decided to reveal infant mortality rates for the first time in twelve years. These had been the subject of academic studies in the West showing a dramatic increase in the death rate among children under the age of one. In fact, the Soviet figures show that infant deaths rose from 24.7 per 1,000 births in 1970 to 27.9 per cent in 1974, and then fell back to 26 per cent last year. One explanation for the deterioration in the 1970s is that the figures were either fraudulent then or figures from Central Asia and outlying parts of the country only started being scientifically collected at that time.

The greater openness on adverse statistics is connected to a government campaign against fraudulent figures produced by factories, ministries and whole republics. Semyon Grossu, the Communist Party leader in Moldavia, was admonished for fiddling figures last month. The party in Moscow said that at one in every five enterprises in Moldavia inspected this year the production figures had been falsified. The extent to which fraud was previously practised was underlined in the Soviet cotton-growing republic of Uzbekistan, where the raw cotton production was systematically exaggerated over a five-year period by between 500,000 and 900,000 tonnes up to 1983. The Uzbek Cotton Minister at the time has been sentenced to death.

7 November 1986

Political and Social Clubs

In the next few weeks the Soviet authorities will decide their attitude to the many independent political and cultural clubs—1,200 in Moscow alone—which have sprung up over the last year. The development of the clubs, and the authorities' reaction to them, is a test of the degree to which independent public opinion in the Soviet Union can develop its own institutions and take advantage of the greater freedom of expression allowed since Gorbachev became leader.

Current official attitudes are in sharp contrast to previous policy, which saw all independent groups as actually or potentially dissident. Even small organisations with such apolitical aims as help for the handicapped were systematically stamped out by harassment and arrests. The very idea of a club voluntarily set up by its members is foreign to recent Soviet experience. In the Russian school edition of *The Pickwick Papers*, the editors go out of their way in a footnote to explain to the reader that Mr Pickwick is not, as they might assume, a paid employee of the Pickwick Club.

People set up clubs for various reasons. Gleb Pavlovsky, a member of the Club for Social Initiative set up in September last year, says that many are established by the young. There are numerous environmental groups in Leningrad, and about thirty or forty clubs in Moscow with distinct social or political policies. They represent a wide variety of views: the Club for Social Initiative, many of whose members are sociologists, was set up to discuss the present and future shape of Soviet society. Another club, Perestroika, draws its membership primarily from the Moscow intelligentsia but includes a strong contingent of economists.

Environmental groups are also becoming common outside Leningrad and Moscow. "We're tired of being the slaves to the architectural bureaucracy," say members of the Ecopolis Club in the town of Kosino, east of Moscow, which has just stopped a construction project that threatened unique fauna in a local lake. Another club is restoring the Belopesotsky Monastery on the Oka River. They will use the monastery as a culture centre, using local crafts to help revive decayed villages whose inhabitants have moved to the cities.

In Moscow an impressive sign of concern about the environment came when residents of Vorovsky Street in the centre of the capital stopped building workers cutting down elms at the site of a new Turkish Embassy building. A demonstration this week outside the National Hotel led to the Council of Ministers reversing a decision to move some museums to the outskirts of Moscow.

Yet strong inhibitions about unofficial action remain. Commenting on this lack of local initiative, Tatyana Zaslavskaya, a leading Soviet sociologist and adviser to Gorbachev, told the CSI: "They say we've let the genie out of the bottle, but look at the poor thing! He can hardly stand up. Intensive care is what the genie needs." Nor is the official attitude towards the new clubs clear. A conference of fifty-three clubs under semi-official auspices met in August and another is planned at the end of January or beginning of February when university students, who make up much of the membership, are on holiday.

Official sympathy came last week when the news agency Novosti organised a press conference for the clubs to explain their views. Given that the Perestroika Club is planning to build a monument to victims of Stalin, this seems a daring move. The difficulty from the official point of view is that the existence of independent clubs dilutes the monopoly of the Communist Party over political life. It has the advantage, however, that almost all the clubs support perestroika.

With some significant exceptions the clubs are, if anything, on the left rather than the right. Fifteen of those attending the August conference have formed a Federation of Socialist Clubs, whose ideas have much in common with the New Left in Western Europe in the 1960s. They also tend to be strongly opposed to the chauvinist and anti-Semitic populism of clubs such as Pamyat (memory). Grigory Pelman, leader of the Club for Social Initiative, argues that while nobody in the Soviet Union dares come out publicly against perestroika, there are seeds of a right-wing backlash with strong political appeal for parts of the bureaucracy and in the backward provinces of central Russia.

Because the clubs are such a recent phenomenon, the extent of their development outside Moscow is unclear. According to Pavlovsky there are 200 to 400 in Leningrad; others spread across the country from Odessa on the Black Sea to Novosibirsk in Siberia. They tend to be small, based on a few enthusiasts, and for the most part their interests are cultural rather than political. The clubs are also important because of the seriousness of the generation gap in the Soviet Union. Youth may sympathise with the aims of Gorbachev's revolution from above, but Komsomol, the 42-million-strong Communist youth organisation, has become a moribund bureaucracy. Old orthodoxies are being questioned by the young, particularly students, and this gives the clubs an influence out of all proportion to their size. Those doing the questioning over the last year have often produced bizarre, contradictory or incoherent ideas, but the incoherence is evidence of intellectual vitality.

Cultural and social life in the Soviet Union is very fluid at the moment. Old orthodoxies and dogmas are being questioned in an atmosphere in many ways similar to Western Europe and the USA during the 1960s.

The existence of the clubs means that some—but not necessarily all—Soviet leaders see diversity of opinion outside the party as no threat, and probably as a source of strength. The clubs are evidently nervous, either of being labelled dissident or of being absorbed by the system, but neither they nor the government really knows what the new rules are.

14 October 1987

Soviet Intelligentsia and Glasnost

In the Soviet Union today, a new and highly educated generation is looking for fresh ideas on how they and their society should live. Unfortunately, despite the opportunities given by glasnost, the old intelligentsia have proved largely incapable of providing new ideas to cope with present problems. The central reason for this is that many Soviet intellectuals remain as rooted in the 1950s as the former leadership. Writers debate how long the present thaw will last and how many victims of the purges will be rehabilitated.

But for the younger generation—and the Soviet generation gap is much greater than in the West in the 1960s—de-Stalinisation is not enough. Reflecting on the impact of the current historical debate on Soviet youth, Mikhail Gefter, one of the Soviet Union's most perceptive historians, asks: "Should we carry the picture of Khrushchev and trample on that of Stalin? They will never believe us, they will refuse to listen to us." Such sentiments are in keeping with the present mood of social, historical and political self-appraisal. Historical archives previously under lock and key are being opened up. Sociologists examine the way Soviet society actually works, as opposed to how it is meant to work. Opinion polls show what people actually believe rather than what the government would like them to believe.

Some of the conversions of previous upholders of orthodoxy to the new way of thinking have been too fast to be convincing. Nothing, said a Soviet commentator on television last year, is more repulsive than "collective recovery of eyesight". Overall, however, the current intellectual changes run far deeper than those under Khrushchev. There are three main reasons: a much wider range of publications are involved; almost every Soviet household has a television, so changes in the media have far greater impact on public opinion; above all, the spread of higher education means that there is a much more active and well-informed public opinion looking for new ideas.

Again in contrast to the thaw under Khrushchev, it is journalists catering for a mass audience, not novelists and poets writing for an elite, who are now in the vanguard of intellectual change. "Now literature seems to have stepped aside," wrote Sergei Baruzhdin, editor of a literary magazine, recently, "with the exception of journalists attacking the current and potential opponents of perestroika rather than past shortcomings."

Western observers of the Soviet Union have tended to concentrate on changes in the press as the central feature in glasnost; but for most of the 280 million Soviet citizens, new discussion programmes, documentaries and phone-ins on television have had a greater impact than articles in the press. A youth programme such as "The Twelfth Floor" has an audience of up to 100 million according to official figures. Last Monday, for instance, a large part of the adult population watched a documentary called "Risk", on the development of nuclear weapons, including criticism of Stalin and footage of Khrushchev. Gorbachev is the first Soviet leader who knows how to use television.

Underpinning these changes in the intelligentsia and the media is an enormous shift in educational levels and the social composition of the USSR. Stalin and Khrushchev ruled a land still dominated by the village. Higher education has produced a much larger and more sophisticated mass audience for magazines such as *Ogonyok*, newspapers such as *Izvestia* (much more avant-garde than *Pravda*) and television programmes such as "The Twelfth Floor". To win readers and viewers the Soviet media now have to compete hard, while before they did not.

This social revolution is the real basis for Gorbachev reforms. According to Dr Vilen Ivanov, director of the Sociological Institute in Moscow, the main feature of this revolution is a rapid increase in the number of people with higher education, professional and managerial groups who now make up 22 per cent of the population. As this group has grown, the number of peasants has dropped sharply and the working class has remained static as a proportion of the population.

These social changes have also had an impact on the position of Soviet intellectuals. They are no longer the preservers of culture in a semi-literate country. Ironically, their influence is therefore likely to diminish at the very moment when they have largely obtained the freedom of expression denied them for so long.

Largely, but not entirely. There are, for instance, still no wholly independent publishing houses. When Josip Brodsky, exiled Soviet poet, won the Nobel prize for Literature this month, poets in the capital were still noticeably glancing over their shoulder to discover the party line on the award before welcoming it. On the other hand, there is no sign of Russians losing their appetite for large doses of culture. In one packed Moscow theatre last month the audience watched a four-hour performance of Chekhov's *Uncle Vanya* in Lithuanian (with simultaneous translation into Russian), at the end of which the director invited the audience to join in a discussion of the play.

But the most interesting intellectual changes in the Soviet Union today are in mass rather than elite culture: the transformation of the mass media, the creation of informal groups and societies, and the development of a public opinion with its own institutions.

In the past intellectuals in Moscow owed some of their influence to the degree to which the rest of Soviet society, including most of the Communist Party, had become not just muzzled but depoliticised. Talk in the West about conflict between opponents and protagonists of Gorbachev's reforms often misses the significance of the dog which does not bark in the night: that too often perestroika provokes neither conflict nor debate, but apathy.

Society is now becoming politicised again, but nobody knows how far the process will go, or the future political shape of the country. Grigory

Pelman says: "The question is not of people opposing perestroika but of workers and peasants remaining passive observers."

As this passivity ends—assuming it does end—it will reduce the role of the Communist Party and, ironically, of the intellectual elite, both of which in the past have owed part of their influence to substituting themselves for the rest of society.

3 November 1987

Corruption

The Clampdown on Alcohol

High above Mayakovsky Square, near the centre of Moscow, a flashing electric sign shines through the falling snow. It reads: "A glass of mandarin juice a day contains all the vitamin C an adult needs." One hundred yards away, outside a drink store, a long queue, unimpressed by the virtues of mandarin juice, waits patiently in the cold to buy vodka when the shop opens at 2 p.m.

The crackdown on drink and drunkenness has affected the Soviet people more than any other measure since Mikhail Gorbachev became leader. The new regulations introduced on 1 June fall short of total prohibition, but 749 plants making alcoholic drinks have closed or are being converted to alternative production. Buying a bottle of vodka today usually means two hours in a queue, because the number of shops selling it have been drastically reduced. Drunkenness at work or in the street leads to fines and possible dismissal.

These are drastic measures in a hard-drinking country. A recent survey concluded: "Drinking has become a virtually inseparable part of leisure time." But Soviets differ from drinkers in Southern or Western Europe in consuming most of their alcohol in the form of spirits rather than beer or wine. Celebrations lead to spectacular consumption, which the crackdown has not prevented. Under the new regulations, for instance, the Soviet Union's Pacific fishing fleet has gone dry. But when inspectors visited one trawler they found, in a single cabin, 576 bottles of vodka, intended for the second navigator's wedding.

In some country villages every house has its own still to make *samogon* (moonshine). In one region 5,115 stills were recently handed in from 6,000 homes, and another 400 were found discarded in the nearby orchards and ravines. A Soviet journalist who visited the area wrote: "I was told that at the height of the moonshine brewing season some villages reeked so strongly that even the hens were staggering around drunk." Nor is entertainment the only reason for buying *samogon.* It is also used as payment: "Virtually nothing will be done without a bottle changing hands. You cannot get your private plot ploughed, transport logs from the forest, or stock up with coal or kerosene without half a litre of drink."

Consumption of alcohol on this scale has significant economic consequences. Productivity in industry and construction drops by between 15 and 30 per cent after pay day (twice a month in the Soviet Union), at weekends and at holiday times, according to research carried out by Soviet economists. One calculation shows that without alcohol factory productivity would rise immediately by 10 per cent. One in every six workers said they drank while at work. The social cost is also high: alcoholism is officially blamed for 90 per cent of murders, over half of thefts and robberies, a third of all road accidents and two-thirds of accidents at work. It is the reason given for half the divorces.

At first, the new regulations made it difficult to obtain any form of liquor, but the emphasis now is on making it time-consuming and expensive to buy spirits, generally vodka, but relatively easy to buy beer or wine. A bottle of the cheapest vodka today costs 6.20 roubles, an increase of 1.5 roubles since the campaign began, though *samogon* is available to some at 1.20 roubles a bottle. The average wage is 140 roubles per month.

A transport worker in Moscow summed up the results of the anti-alcohol campaign where he worked like this: "In my depot the heavy drinkers, leaving aside the alcoholics, drink as much as before, though more secretly. They are frightened of being fined or dismissed. People who didn't drink much, like me, have cut back because they can't be bothered to queue for two hours for vodka."

For very heavy drinkers and alcoholics it has been a bad year. Chemist shops now refuse to sell eau de Cologne or alcohol-based perfumes until after two o'clock in the afternoon, and shop assistants complain that customers who have bought hair tonic often gulp it down as soon as they are back on the street. On another occasion six workers at a Moscow chemical plant died and hundreds of others were hospitalised when they drank stolen methanol.

High prices do not deter the serious drinkers: "If you only drink beer—say ten bottles a day," said a man outside a drink store, "that would be 5 roubles a day, or 150 roubles a month, minus the payment for the return of bottles makes 90 roubles, but if you just drink a bottle of cheap port wine a day it would be only 70 to 80 roubles."

For moderate drinkers the situation has improved somewhat since 1 June. Beer and wine are now more freely available in the shops, though restaurants do not serve them before 2 p.m. Vodka is still hard to obtain. Scare stories that prohibition was to be introduced have died away, despite frequent demands for its introduction in letters to the press. Officials say it simply would not work. Other countries' experience shows that "dry laws inevitably give rise to illicit distilling on a mass scale, smuggling and illegal trading in spirits," says Vasily Trushin, the First Deputy Interior Minister.

The financial question is important: indirect taxes from vodka sales in the 1970s brought the state between 21 and 23 billion roubles in revenue each year. Drink sales are vital if shops are to meet their turnover targets. In Kaluga, for instance, the number of drink stores was reduced from 170 to 55 in June, but in succeeding months the amount of drink consumed in the town rose as the local authorities, eager for revenue, stopped enforcing the regulations.

To achieve a reduction in drinking in the Soviet Union would mean altering the shape of the country's social life. The boost in real incomes by 70 per cent since 1960 has stimulated consumption, but Russians have always drunk heavily. "In the whole of Europe I have seen no other people empty a tumbler at a gulp," said the writer Alexander Herzen 150 years ago. Such traditional habits cannot easily be modified. Official pronouncements acknowledge that if people drink less, they must be given something else. Gorbachev said that in one Siberian oil city he visited the most valuable possession was a ticket to the one cinema.

The majority of people in the Soviet Union lived in the countryside until 1962. Any provision for services and leisure lags behind the expansion of the cities. Similar conditions led to the growth of the Temperance Movement in Britain in the late nineteenth century and of Prohibition in the USA in the 1920s.

Changing the way people drink will be a slow matter, but the anti-alcohol campaign is the first serious test of the determination of the new Soviet leadership. Retreat now from the campaign against drunkenness would be a political defeat which would feed popular cynicism about the Kremlin's commitment to other changes in the economy and Soviet society. For this reason the long queues of vodka drinkers are unlikely to get any shorter.

18 January 1986

Penalising the Black Economy

Corruption in the Soviet Union can bring rewards. When police arrested one man for taking bribes this April they found his property included 12 cars, 47 tape-recorders and colour televisions, and 3,000 bottles of cognac and wine. This pales compared with property confiscated from another criminal sentenced at about the same time. He had three Volga cars, 23 dinner services with 380 settings, 74 suits and 149 pairs of shoes. "He had hidden some things away for emergencies," reported Moscow Radio, "including 735,000 roubles in cash, 18,300 roubles' worth of 3 per cent loan bonds, 450 gold coins and 39 gold wrist watches."

In stepping up the anti-corruption campaign which started in the last years of Brezhnev, the government has drafted a law which compels anybody spending 10,000 roubles on an article to fill in a special form registering the deal and giving details of the purchaser's source of income. Only when buying houses or dachas (country cottages) is the threshold higher, at 20,000 roubles.

The aim of the new rules is to make it more difficult to spend unearned income from bribery or the black market. At the same time, penalties for minor kickbacks—use of state property for private use and petty corruption—are all increased. This is in keeping with the campaign launched shortly before Brezhnev died. Accusations of corruption undermined the political position of the Brezhnev old guard throughout the 1982–85 leadership crisis. Periodic scandals erupted: the Deputy Minister of Fisheries was executed in 1982 because of his involvement in a swindle whereby caviar was exported from the Soviet Union in tins labelled as containing salted herring. In 1984 the manager of Gastronom Number One in Gorki Street, Moscow's best-known food shop, was shot for systematic corruption and theft. When police dug up his garden they discovered bundles of rotting roubles he had not found time to spend.

Systematic corruption at the top worries the new leadership. The difficulty in fighting corruption at the top is that it is linked to the vast number of ways in which ordinary Soviet citizens can supplement their income. The number of people with second jobs greatly increased between 1964 and 1982 as real incomes soared but the supply of services and goods failed to keep pace. Surveys by Soviet economists show that the average Soviet citizen spends only 10 per cent of his income on services, but if demand were met this would jump to 20 per cent.

The size of the second economy in the Soviet Union is illustrated by a survey conducted between 1974 and 1979 of 1,936 former Soviet citizens who had emigrated to the USA. This showed that a family with husband and wife working would spend a third of their monthly salary of 304 roubles in the second economy—not counting food bought in the peasant markets. Outgoings ranged from 398 roubles spent on services, including construction, to 61 roubles in under-the-counter payments to shop assistants to keep goods.

The problem is that wholesale bribery at the top is linked to minor kickbacks by consumers across the counter. Last year a senior investigator from the Department for Struggle against Embezzlement of Socialist Property and Speculation (OBKHSS) involved in a crackdown against crime in the Moscow trade system said that since October 1983 he had dealt with over thirty cases involving the theft of 3 million roubles' worth of goods by some 100 management personnel from the capital's best-known shops.

He said officials received a million roubles in bribes "and paid three-quarters of this sum in bribes themselves". When OBKHSS inspectors carried out test purchases in shops across Moscow on a single day in 1982 they found that in 156 of 193 purchases they were cheated. The profits were then systematically passed up the line. The manager of one fruit and vegetable shop kept an account book noting all kickbacks over a ten-year period, including food hampers despatched to the responsible authorities across Moscow four times a year. None was ever returned.

The new law is unlikely to dent the second economy, which is an integral part of the Soviet economy overall. The compulsory registration of any large-scale transactions appears to be directly targeted against two forms of private property on which the better off or the corrupt spend money in the Soviet Union: cars and dachas.

The Soviet Union now has some 12 million private car owners, each of whom has paid at least 7,000 roubles to buy. Spares are in short supply. The Vaz plant at Togliatti which makes the Zhiguli, the most common car on the roads, satisfies only 40 to 45 per cent of the demand for spares, according to Soviet economists. The same is true of other car manufacturers, leading to a vast black market.

Moscow police recently arrested Mikhail Ryabkov, nominally a hotel worker earning 160 roubles a month. In fact, reported Soviet television, "Moscow speculators knew him well by the name of Dirty Misha, one of the very biggest speculators in spare parts for the Zaporozhets car." Although Ryabkov claimed to be a simple car enthusiast, a search of his department revealed 100 brake cylinder seals, 18 sets of brake cylinders, 10 sets of piston rings, 92 camshaft bearings and other spare parts. He was jailed for ten years.

Dachas can vary from a full-size country house to little more than a garden shed which costs 1,700 roubles bought prefabricated. Ownership is common. Leningrad, with a population of 5 million, is surrounded by 950,000 dachas, mostly for summer use only. Construction materials and garden equipment are often in short supply. A. Rekunkov, Procurator General of the USSR, said studies showed that 40 per cent of dachas are built with the illegal use of state equipment: "A crane or bull-dozer driver can make a profit of 50 roubles per hour."

It is almost impossible to quantify the size of the second economy. The survey of Soviet immigrants to the USA indicated annual expenditure in the second economy of 68 billion roubles a year, excluding money earned by peasants through their private plots of land.

Clearly some people do accumulate small fortunes. Total deposits in Soviet savings banks are 200 billion roubles, but in one region half the money in the savings bank is accounted for by about 3 per cent of depositors. The new law will make it more difficult to accumulate such capital sums publicly in future, but the overall level of unearned or privately earned income is unlikely to diminish.

2 July 1986

Gastronom Number One

The nine-month trial of senior officials in charge of Moscow's retail trade, which has just ended with heavy sentences has for the first time shown how a network of corruption has spread over twenty years.

The key figure in the scandal was Yuri Konstantinovich Sokolov, head of Gastronom Number One, who was executed for corruption in 1984. His trial provoked a wider investigation of theft and bribery in Moscow's retail trade which has now ended with a fifteen-year jail sentence for Nikolai Tregubov, head of the city's trade directorate for over twenty years.

The daily *Moskovskaya Pravda* has provided fascinating detail of how Sokolov, a taxi driver with a minor criminal record at the end of the 1950s, came to run Gastronom Number One. Built as the Moscow equivalent of Fortnum and Mason at the beginning of the century, its large hall is still dominated by enormous chandeliers, engraved pillars and stained glass.

Publication of the facts revealed at the trial of Tregubov and A. Petrikov, his deputy at the trade directorate, shows how corruption among trade officials in Moscow had reached saturation point by the early 1980s. The wide publicity given to their fate is clearly intended as a warning to others and is part of the campaign against corruption which started in 1982. At that time Sokolov and his friends were confident that they could protect themselves from any investigation. The newspaper describes how Sokolov gave a party to celebrate his daughter's wedding for over 100 guests in the Praga Restaurant in central Moscow. The guest list was carefully thought out: "Some were invited for prestige, some because of the jobs they held—they could help if anything went wrong."

As celebrations reached their peak in the Czechoslovak Room of the Praga, guests started hurling crystal glasses at the walls, a traditional Russian way of showing the party is going well. A waiter remonstrated with Sokolov, standing in the middle of the room: "Yuri Konstantino-vich," he asked, "what is going on?"

"Just get out of here," said Sokolov to the waiter, without looking at him. He sipped some champagne from his crystal glass and hurled it against the wall.

Sokolov had come a long way from his taxi driver's job, which he had to give up when charged with cheating passengers. He then became an inspector in the organisation in charge of supplying haberdashery in the capital. A few months later he joined the General Trade Organisation, where he met Petrikov, his partner for the next twenty years, who was sentenced to twelve years in jail last week. Through Petrikov he became deputy head of Gastronom Number One, universally known at "Yeliseyevsky" by Muscovites after its pre-revolutionary owner. He also observed that the chief director was often drunk. One day when his boss "could not walk straight", he rang the chief directorate of trade and said: "Just come and see what's happening here." His boss was fired and Sokolov again went to see Petrikov, now First Deputy Head of Glavtorg, the organisation controlling Moscow's trade. At his trial Petrikov explained what happened: "Sokolov came to see me and told me that if I helped him to become director of Yeliseyevsky Gastronom he would pay me 300 roubles monthly."

Where did the money come from? As soon as Sokolov took over, explained the head of the fish department in the store, "he invited me to his office and suggested that I pay him 50 roubles a week." And so on, down the scale.

Backhanders from customers at Gastronom Number One were supplemented by another simple swindle. The plan for Soviet stores allows for losses during storage and before sale. At Gastronom, fish, meat and sausage were written off under this heading—not difficult since the trade organisation was already in Sokolov's pocket—even though real losses were small. The profit made by Sokolov, the other managers at the store and their allies in the trade directorate was vast, far more than they could spend. Sokolov himself buried money, gold coins and jewellery near his dacha on the Moska River. Another official did not spend the heaps of 100-rouble bills in his house because he was afraid of attracting attention to himself.

The gang was finally caught in 1983 when the KGB security police, not the ordinary police, became curious about a man who worked in a special shop for foreigners who always had lots of foreign currency although he never went abroad. Then they started investigating his wife, who also worked at Gastronom Number One.

The sentences have been harsh: death for Sokolov, sentences of twelve and fifteen years for the head and deputy head of the Moscow trade organisation, along with lesser terms for five officials and eighteen trade workers.

Will it make a difference? The Soviet Supreme Court could find nobody approached by Sokolov who refused to be bribed. But the publicity given to the Gastronom Number One scandal, combined with the sentencing to death of the Cotton Minister of Uzbekistan for corruption last month and the revelation of other scandals, may make such blatant swindles more difficult to carry out.

The key to the problem is not just a lack of quality products but the fact that basic food prices in the Soviet Union are so low that they inevitably create excess demand, hence shortages. Given much increased purchasing power over the last twenty years, demand is met by vast secondary and black markets. While these conditions exist, Sokolov is bound to have successors.

23 September 1986

Siberian Gravediggers

Gravediggers in the Eastern Siberian city of Magadan refused to bury people unless their relatives bribed them with money and vodka. Their racket was exposed only when two gravediggers were shot dead by a drunken taxi driver in a quarrel over a gambling debt, according to *Izvestia*.

Details of the seamier side of Soviet life exposed in muck-raking articles like this are compulsive reading for many ordinary Soviet newspaper buyers. But even by the new standards of openness the events in Magadan, a city of 150,000 people on the Soviet Pacific coast, are bizarre. There was no way of getting buried in the city without first supplying vodka for the men to prepare the coffin and dig the grave, and then paying between 200 and 500 roubles, according to an on-the-spot means test conducted by the gravediggers.

When Yuri Khelev's adult son died suddenly, Zaitsev, the chief gravedigger, said he wanted 300 roubles in return for a good place in the cemetery. Even then, other members of the team refused to carry the coffin unless they received five bottles of vodka.

The undertakers of Magadan, known locally as "the Golden boys", also controlled the city's supply of illegal liquor, now scarce as a result of the anti-alcohol laws introduced across the country in 1985. A local nightwatchman said: "if it's already night time and you want a drink—the only place in Magadan you can get vodka at that time is the undertakers' office. The boys always have some supplies laid by."

They also liked to play cards, and this was the cause of their downfall. A former taxi driver named Baranov claimed to have won 2,000 roubles and when they refused to pay up he, in an advanced state of drunkenness, shot two of them dead.

Magadan's public prosecutor is gloomy about the standards of honesty in the local undertaking business: "Today's swindlers will be replaced by others tomorrow who will do exactly the same, except that being armed with the experience of their predecessors they will be more cunning about stealing from people."

His gloom is shared by the *Izvestia* correspondent, who writes that "this dreadful situation can also be seen in other cities and towns of the Magadan province." He singles out in particular a case in the town of Bilibino, where a drunken nightwatchman, in charge of a small morgue, sold it for 300 roubles. It is not clear why anybody should want to buy a morgue, but when doctors arrived next morning to conduct a post-mortem they found it had simply vanished.

27 January 1987

Fall in the Death Rate

The death rate among Soviet citizens of working age fell last year by 15 per cent compared to 1984 because of the crackdown on alcohol, according to figures published yesterday by the Central Statistics Board. The figures show that 799,000 people between eighteen and the age of retirement (fifty-five for women and sixty for men) died in 1984 compared to 680,000 deaths among this age group in 1986. This indicates a fall in the death rate from 510 to 432 per 100,000.

Tass says this was the first time for many years that the mortality rate in the Soviet Union had fallen and attributes the drop almost entirely to the anti-alcohol laws, which have cut hard liquor consumption by 38 per cent. In the past the increase in the mortality rate provoked official embarrassment and a clampdown on the publication of such statistics.

Western demographers have estimated that the life expectancy of a

Soviet male is a maximum of sixty to sixty-two years, possibly much less, compared to sixty-six in the USA. Life expectancy for American and Soviet women shows less disparity.

The new statistics for 1986 show that deaths from accidents at work are down by one-third, and demographers say that many of these fatalities are the result of drunkenness. Deaths from cardiovascular diseases, also often drink-related, fell from 143 to 125 per 100,000 between 1984 and 1986. Respiratory diseases were also down by one-third. Cancer is an increasing cause of death in the Soviet Union, rising fro 75 per 100,000 in 1970 to 93 in 1980 and 95 last year.

The Soviet authorities have been eager to prove that the tough laws on drink have produced immediate benefits. These include a 25 per cent drop in the crime rate, a 20 per cent fall in road accidents and a reduction in absenteeism at work by one-third. At the same time figures show that in the first eleven months of last year the 280 million Soviet citizens consumed 308 million gallons of vodka and other spirits. Cheap wine consumption, a favourite of Soviet heavy drinkers, was down by 75 per cent, but fruit juice production rose by 40 per cent.

11 February 1987

Mr and Mrs Shushkov Go to Jail

The jailing for thirteen years of Vladimir Shushkov, the former Soviet Deputy Foreign Trade Minister, and his wife Valentina for eleven years marks an escalation of the Kremlin's campaign against corruption, which is starting to affect senior officials. His month-long trial for corruption by the Soviet Supreme Court—details of which were recently published by the trade-union newspaper, *Trud*—is also significant because it is clearly intended as a warning to all Soviet officials who have commercial dealings with foreigners.

The revelations about the extent of Shushkov's corruption—on his return from business trips abroad, a minibus used to meet him at Moscow's Sheremetevo Airport because his official car was too small to carry all his purchases—is also proving damaging to the Foreign Trade Ministry at a time when it is fighting to retain control of Soviet imports and exports. This monopoly was formally ended at the beginning of this year, when twenty-one ministries and seventy-five enterprises were given the right to trade abroad. But between 1974 and 1985, when Shushkov was Deputy Minister, the Foreign Trade Ministry had total control of all Soviet commerce with other countries.

The case started at the end of 1985 when Customs at Sheremetevo Airport found jewellery and video equipment in the luggage of Yevgeny Kuzminykh as he returned with Shushkov from a short business trip abroad. Shushkov is said to have whispered to him: "Don't give away too much to the investigator. Don't name a single person or a single episode." The Minister then rushed to his country house in Barvikha, a prestigious area on the western fringe of Moscow where many senior officials have villas, where he began to bury coffee jars filled with jewellery and foreign currency in the garden.

There was a lot to hide. When Shushkov's town house was eventually searched, police found 1,565 gold brooches, diamond pendants and rings worth more than a million roubles, and other property worth 500,000 roubles. Other goods, which the couple had never bothered to look at, lay unopened. *Trud* says these goods had been accumulated over the years in the form of bribes from foreign businessmen looking for contracts in the Soviet Union, as well as systematic fiddling of expenses during the 120 trips Sushkov had taken abroad.

The revelations about corruption in foreign trade dealings are important because they are the first time systematic bribery of Soviet officials by foreign businessmen has been widely publicised in the Soviet media. *Trud* said there are officials who selflessly "fight for every kopeck of the people's money" in contract negotiations, but added that Shushkov was not among them.

The court heard details of how an Italian company supplying specialised chemical products had first made contact with Valentina Shushkov, a senior official of the State Committee for Science and Technology, who arranged meetings for the head of the company with the ministries handling chemicals and petrochemicals. The Italian businessmen nicknamed her "the golden sēnora" for her expensive tastes. Altogether Shushkov and his wife received 130,000 roubles from this company, whose head was quoted as testifying at their trial that "the activity of my company in the Soviet market depended on them. The goods and jewellery they received were not paid for out of my account but were bought with the company's money."

Sketching in Shushkov's background, the *Trud* correspondent says he came from an ordinary family. "At the start of the last war, although already aged twenty-one, he was fortunate to be sent for further education as an engineer rather than going into the armed forces. In the 1950s he headed the Soviet trade mission in Italy and then, for ten years up to 1974, he was in charge of the foreign trade organisation responsible for importing machinery and equipment from the West." How did he get away with it for so long? *Trud* says that the real reason was that the Foreign Trade Ministry was one of those organisations which occupied a zone within which criticism was forbidden. "Glasnost could not penetrate to their offices, where the curtains of their windows were always drawn," the newspaper says.

Despite efforts to extend the right to trade abroad to other Soviet organisations, the Foreign Trade Ministry still retains an effective monopoly over Soviet exports and imports. Nevertheless, the Shushkov case has badly dented the credibility of its claims to special expertise in foreign commerce.

7 March 1987

Chernobyl

The Kremlin Reacts to Chernobyl

In the year since he became Soviet leader Mikhail Gorbachev has advocated greater openness and less secrecy by Soviet officials, but in the five days since the Chernobyl reactor blew up his government has confined itself to three brief communiqués.

The first came on Monday night after mounting pressure from Sweden and other Scandinavian countries which had detected a cloud of radioactive dust spreading across the Baltic. Twenty-four hours later a second communiqué admitted that two people were dead. Last night the third statement said that radiation was decreasing and 197 people were injured, some of whom had already been released from hospital.

Foreign embassies in Moscow have had little more to go on in spite of repeated requests for more information from Soviet officials in the Ukrainian capital, Kiev. Diplomats and journalists, banned from entering the Ukraine, ceaselessly telephoned Kiev to try to find out the number of casualties and the extent of the contamination.

It has already become clear that Soviet handling of news about the crisis has inflicted the worst damage on the image of the Soviet Union abroad since the shooting down of a Korean airliner by a Soviet fighter in 1983. The Soviet press has confined itself to reprinting the official statements. Even local radio in Kiev and the parts of the Ukraine affected by the disaster has given no advice to the local population on whether or not to drink milk or how to cope with possible contamination.

Gorbachev faces no obvious domestic pressure to explain why or how the disaster occurred, but it is doubtful whether the government would have risked anything by providing more information. Why, then, did Moscow keep the disaster secret for as long as it could? It must have been evident to senior officials by last Sunday night that alarm bells would soon start ringing in Scandinavia.

The advantages of admitting what cannot be concealed have long been apparent to many Soviet officials, but by no means all. In a television discussion last month Valentin Zorin, a senior Soviet political commentator, said: "Self-criticism is used by enemy propaganda to cause harm to our country, for open slander against socialism."

This traditional view was immediately rebutted by Georgy Arbatov, the influential head of the US and Canada Institute, who replied: "When shortcomings exist, they are evident whether or not you criticise them." He said that secrecy was often self-defeating, and when "the ban on discussing the obvious was lifted" inside the Soviet Union, it often ceased to be a matter of speculation abroad.

The failure to tell the world about the Chernobyl disaster shows that under pressure Soviet officials almost invariably endorse Zorin's view that any admission of failure within the Soviet system hands ammunition to its enemies.

1 May 1986

May Day Dances

Tens of thousands of Muscovites waving red flags and carrying sprays of cherry blossom marched through Red Square to celebrate May Day yesterday, oblivious of the world's worst civil nuclear disaster at Chernobyl in the Ukraine. Meanwhile, foreign embassies in the capital are organising the evacuation of nationals, mainly students from Kiev, some eighty miles from Chernobyl, and from Minsk, which has been affected by the radioactive cloud carried north by the wind after Saturday's accident.

Some eighty-four British students, evacuated overnight by train from Kiev, were checked for radiation in Moscow before being taken to the airport for the flight home. All were given certificates saying they were "effectively healthy". Many appeared confused by the events of the past few days and angered by questions from correspondents and television crews. Some claimed that they had been evacuated unnecessarily as a result of Western press exaggeration of the danger. Mr Robert Walker, a twenty-two-year-old student from Bournemouth studying in Kiev, said he and the other students had stripped to the waist for their check-up and he had measured 20 on the Soviet Geiger counter calibrated up to 25. He said he knew nothing of the Chernobyl disaster until Monday, and it had then been difficult to decide whether to believe the official account of a limited accident or the more apocalyptic stories from abroad. However, some of his fellow students became rather frightened and stayed in their hotel rooms.

Nikola Mace and Robert Walker said that Russian students in Kiev apparently did not at first believe the news. However, by the time the Europeans left on Wednesday several of the Russians had become alarmed, particularly as no precautionary instructions had been issued.

The students underwent further radiation checks by British Airways at Moscow Airport before boarding a special flight for Heathrow. BA officials declined details of the results beyond saying that on average radiation levels were higher than normal—but not so high as to be dangerous.

As foreign embassies worked on evacuation plans, Soviet citizens have started the first day of the four-day May Day holiday and are showing no signs of alarm over the disaster. At the exhibition of Soviet economic achievements in north Moscow, people are visiting one hall devoted to nuclear power stations. Here, visitors can obtain a leaflet at the exhibition on the RBMK-1,000 reactor, and the first picture in it shows the white building of the Chernobyl plant, surrounded by electricity pylons and trees. The text of the leaflet is reassuring: in case of emergency the reactor's power is shut down "with a speed ensuring integrity of the fuel elements and structural units of the reactor. If necessary high-speed emergency protection of the reactor can bring it over to the sub-critical state."

The Soviet position is that Western media coverage of the disaster is wholly exaggerated, but there are signs in the past twenty-four hours of some official recognition that the failure to announce it until two days after the event has very seriously damaged the country's image abroad, particularly in Western Europe.

Since Wednesday night more information has been produced. Some Western ambassadors have been called to the Foreign Ministry to be told that the fire at the reactor is definitely out. Yesterday, the Canadian consul was given permission to go to Kiev to see Canadian students. He is the first diplomat allowed into the Ukraine since the reactor blew up.

2 May 1986

Boris Shcherbina

Four days after the Chernobyl nuclear power plant exploded, the Soviet government announced that Boris Shcherbina, the Deputy Prime Minister, was heading a commission to investigate the causes of the accident and was already at the disaster site in the Ukraine.

The appointment was one of the few events in Moscow over the last week which comes as no surprise. Shcherbina, a short, dark-haired man who looks younger than his sixty-six years, is not only the main trouble-shooter in the Soviet energy industry, but over the last twenty-five years has been largely responsible for creating out of nothing the world's largest oil and gas fields in the wastelands of Siberia.

Gorbachev had already recognised Shcherbina's talents as an organiser in March, when he put him in charge of a new energy bureau with offices in the Kremlin. This, he explained to a visitor a few days before the Chernobyl explosion, would fulfil a troubleshooting role—it would be a small organisation devoted to sorting out problems between the ministries. It also has power to switch between sectors the vast investment funds and resources which the Soviet Union has poured into energy.

Shcherbina owed his appointment to worry in the Kremlin that oil output in Western Siberia is stagnant while the old oil fields on the other side of the Urals are rapidly being depleted. The very success of Shcherbina in developing oil and gas in Western Siberia in the 1960s and 1970s has meant that the Soviet Union is ten years behind the West in conserving energy. The rush to make up for lost time by the development of nuclear power since 1982 may well turn out to be a major contributory factor to the explosion in Chernobyl's number four reactor, the relatively modern RBMK-1,000.

Although he made his reputation in energy in Siberia, Shcherbina was born in the Eastern Ukraine. The son of a railway worker in the industrialised Donetsk province, he was trained as a railway engineer in Kharkov, graduating in 1942 just before the city was captured by the German army. He spent the two years during which Kharkov was occupied and fought over (it was captured and recaptured four times) as a Komsomol organiser in Moscow, and when he returned to Kharkov it was as part of the Communist Party apparat. This combination of party background and technical expertise has clearly been useful in his career.

But the real key to Shcherbina's success was his move to Siberia in 1951: first to Irkutsk and then, ten years later, north to the province of Tyumen, a frozen wilderness inhabited only by hunters and trappers until oil was discovered the year before Shcherbina arrived. Over the next twelve years he developed new oil fields in a region where bare skin freezes in thirty seconds. "In Western Siberia today we recover 60 per cent of our oil and half our gas: what would our lives be like if we had not performed this great endeavour in Siberia?" Shcherbina said last year in reply to criticism that the pace of development was too rapid.

In his last months in the job, before being promoted to Moscow to head the Ministry of Construction for Oil and Gas Enterprises, Shcherbina himself sounded alarmed at the way in which the Kremlin—over-confident after the big oil discoveries in the late 1960s—was not looking for more oil.

As Minister, Shcherbina was primarily associated with the gas indus-try in Siberia and the construction of pipelines from the gas fields in the north of Tyumen to the European parts of the country to the west of the Urals. He was in charge of pipeline construction in the 1980–85 five-year plan, politically as well as economically a critical job. Shcherbina was also responsible for completing four large-diameter pipelines for domestic Soviet use before he left his ministry when the success of its efforts were rewarded by his appointment in 1984 as chairman of the USSR Council of Ministers (or Deputy Prime Minister). This did not necessarily place him in the first rank of Soviet politicians, although in practice he probably stands somewhere in the top thirty.

He had already, in 1976, become a full member of the Communist Party Central Committee, the 320-strong body which brings together all top office-holders in the Soviet Union. Gorbachev's accession to power also presented opportunities for the man who was only really associated with success. Many of the new men promoted by Gorbachev also made their names in Western Siberia and the Urals, which have turned out to be the fast lanes in Soviet politics. But few of these ministers and party officials can claim such a spectacular track record of economic success at a time when the Soviet economy was slowing down, with declining growth accompanied by a series of administrative and planning disasters.

Shcherbina has not, from his career record, had much to do with the nuclear power programme. This was moved to the centre of Soviet energy strategy in this five-year plan, in much the same way that gas dominated the early 1980s and oil the 1970s. In the event the "cavalry charge" methods of economic development applied to industrialise the Soviet Union over the past sixty years also seem to have been applied to the nuclear energy industry, with catastrophic results.

As head of the commission investigating the world's most serious and—despite all the efforts of the authorities—most public nuclear power station disaster, Shcherbina will now take a much higher political profile than he has done at any time over the past twenty-five years. It also probably means that his new energy bureau will take closer control of the vast Soviet energy industry than was expected when Shcherbina took up his job in the Kremlin two months ago.

3 May 1986

Useless Secrecy

"Don't eat the strawberries this summer—they come from the Ukraine," said a Muscovite woman this weekend. But by and large, Kremlin communiqués and attacks on the Western press have satisfied people in the capital that they are in no danger from radiation in the wake of the Chernobyl disaster.

This is scarcely surprising given the low level of knowledge about the impact of radioactivity among Soviets of almost all ranks: some of the more nervous arriving in Moscow by train from Kiev ask if they should boil their drinking water to avoid contamination by fallout. The main Soviet television news at nine in the evening repeatedly showed Ukrainian folk dancers whirling about, apparently under the impression that this would give the lie to Western slander that there is lots of radioactivity around.

The same misconception exists among senior Soviet officials. The destruction of the Chernobyl reactor has been treated as if it was a dam burst in which a finite number of people are killed or injured. There is no appreciation that a nuclear accident is different—and so is its political impact—because the effects of radiation are long delayed. Those Ukrainian folk dancers, however animate last week, may die of cancer in five, ten or fifteen years.

There is equally little sign in Moscow that the political implications of Chernobyl have sunk in on the Soviet leadership, as they return from the long May Day holiday. In his only communication since the disaster, a letter to six non-aligned Prime Ministers on an end to the Soviet test ban, Mikhail Gorbachev did not even mention it. There is no hint of appreciation that any Western European growth of trust in the intentions of the Soviet Union produced by Gorbachev in his year in office disappeared some time between Monday evening and Thursday.

The biggest mystery in Moscow is not the technical origin of the reactor disaster but how Gorbachev's new-look Politburo should have shot itself in its collective foot by saying nothing of the accident until a radioactive cloud was over Scandinavia. It then produced snippets of vague but alarming information sufficient to induce maximum hysteria in Western Europe. If Caspar Weinberger, the US Secretary of Defence, had been left in charge of Soviet public relations for the week he could not have inflicted more damage to the Soviet image in the world.

6 May 1986

Moscow Admits Chernobyl Underestimated

The explosion at the fourth 1,000-megawatt reactor at the Chernobyl power station took place at 1.23 a.m. on the morning of Saturday, 26 April, said Boris Shcherbina yesterday. The main course of events following the explosion is now becoming clear.

The explosion set light to the walls of the enormous machine hall where two of the reactors are housed. When the fire protection unit attached to the power station tried to put out the 100-foot-high flames, their boots sank into the molten bitumen. They found it difficult to breathe given the dense smoke and fumes, but eventually extinguished the blazing walls, thus saving the second reactor.

One man was killed by falling debris and another, with 80 per cent of his skin burnt away, died soon afterwards. Some 100 people were injured, eighteen of them seriously, and all were immediately flown to Moscow for special treatment.

One of the RBMK-1,000 reactors was damaged in the explosion and began to burn, according to two *Pravda* correspondents who visited Chernobyl this week. The firemen could not pump water or chemicals onto the fire because they were frightened of creating steam which would carry more radioactive debris into the air.

According to Shcherbina yesterday, the local authorities at the power station did not realise the seriousness of what had happened. "The first information we obtained was not the same as that which we obtained when we were in the area. There the local experts had not made a correct assessment of the accident," he told a crowded news conference in Moscow yesterday. He himself was in Kazakhstan when the commission was set up, so the underestimation of the seriousness of the crisis may have continued until Sunday.

Nevertheless, there was a rapid evacuation of the township at Chernobyl, on the banks of the Pripyat River, where the power station workers and their families lived. Shcherbina says it started at 2 p.m. on Sunday and was over by 4.20 p.m. *Pravda* says: "It took only four hours to get everything ready and to get the residents out of the township." Drivers at one garage in Kiev, eighty miles to the south, were lined up in the back yard of their depot and told that anybody who did not want to help the evacuation should take a step forward. None did so. They took eighty vehicles north to Chernobyl and nearby villages and farms, some 49,000 people eventually being moved to safety. Farmers in collective farms were moved to others in safer areas, while schools to which children have been evacuated are working two shifts.

The radiation increase after the explosion was immediately registered at the local weather station on Saturday morning. It reported to Kiev that radioactivity was increasing but, Shcherbina says, the peak of radioactivity was reached only on Sunday, the day after the accident.

At first, a small number of essential workers were left at Pripyat township next to Chernobyl, mainly communications workers, but as the situation worsened on Sunday they were also withdrawn. By the start of this week the town, which previously had a population of 50,000, was completely empty. Nothing moved, according to *Pravda*, except a special vehicle belonging to the radiation control service. Otherwise, a 33-kilometre zone around the plant is completely empty.

The original fire, presumably the one burning in the structure of the reactor hall, was put out within hours, according to Shcherbina, but it is not clear when the fire went out in the fourth reactor. This is now almost completely plugged, according to Boris Yeltsin, the Communist Party leader for Moscow city and a non-voting member of the Politburo who has been acting as a sort of *de facto* spokesman on the disaster. The other two reactors at Chernobyl, housed in a different building, are undamaged.

The Soviet government had moved fast to investigate the cause and eliminate the consequences of the disaster, Shcherbina said yesterday. But when the Swedish government started to make inquiries in Moscow on Sunday, more than forty-eight hours after the accident, it was met with a disclaimer that any disaster had taken place at a Soviet nuclear power station. Presumably, the Foreign Ministry did not know that wind had blown a radioactive cloud from Chernobyl across the Baltic.

Most radiation, say the Soviets, was in the immediate area of the plant and there was only limited danger beyond this. The increase in radioactivity was very limited in the cities of Kiev to the south and Gomel in Byelorussia to the north. In Minsk, there was almost no change in radiation levels. Nevertheless, the Ukraine Health Minister appeared on television on Monday night in Kiev to tell people not to eat vegetables or drink milk.

Yesterday's article in *Pravda* and Shcherbina's news conference explain much of what happened at Chernobyl, but leave a number of mysteries unresolved. The most important of these is how long the cover-up or miscalculation by local officials in the Ukraine continued, and the precise moment when Moscow realised the seriousness of what was happening.

7 May 1986

Chernobyl Disaster Leaves Three Vital Questions Unanswered

The immediate and long-term effects of the Chernobyl accident in the Soviet Union have become clearer over the last week, but there are still some mysteries. These mostly concern Soviet technical and political handling of the accident over the first critical week after the disaster.

Three important questions remain unanswered:

- The exact cause of the surge in power in the fourth 1,000-megawatt reactor at Chernobyl, which led to the explosion. This is important because it will show if there is a design flaw in the RBMK-1,000-type reactor, or if the accident was a one-off result of "human error". Soviet officials say the cause of the accident will be explained in a report to be handed to the International Atomic Energy Agency in Vienna in July.

- Who was responsible for the technical and political handling of the Chernobyl accident between 26 April and 2 May? Why did Moscow not tell Scandinavian countries that a radioactive cloud was heading in their direction, though officials here now say they monitored the cloud as it crossed the Soviet Union's Baltic coastline?

  There was a special Politburo meeting on 28 April to discuss Chernobyl and a commission of inquiry was appointed, but the gravity of the crisis continued to be underestimated until Nikolai Ryzhkov, the Prime Minister, and Yegor Ligachev visited Chernobyl on 2 May. People in Kiev were told to take precautions against radiation only on 5 May.

- The extent of radiation in North Ukraine, Byelorussia and Baltic states immediately after the accident.

Increased information from the Soviets now would enable many of the other questions asked in the first weeks of the crisis to be answered and a number of exaggerations about the long-term consequences of the disaster deflated.

Will Chernobyl significantly damage the economy? The damage is likely to be very slight. Only crops in the immediate 30-kilometre zone around the plant are likely to be contaminated. Soviets say that milk and other products regarded as suspect will be processed, stored for three months, checked and only then sold.

Gorbachev has been very lucky in the weather. A high-pressure zone over the European part of the Soviet Union has meant there has been little rain and no high wind in North Ukraine. This has limited the spread of radioactive contamination. Daily checks by embassies on produce in Moscow show no danger so far.

Will the Soviet nuclear programme go ahead as planned? Almost certainly. The Soviets have gone out of their way to stress that nothing is wrong with the undamaged RBMK-1,000 graphite-moderated reactors. Western diplomats say they were shut down for up to a week after Chernobyl, but Soviet officials deny it.

In this five-year plan (1976–80) nuclear energy plays a key role, with 40,000 megawatts to be added to 23,000 megawatts coming from forty-one nuclear reactors on the eve of Chernobyl. Greater safety measures may slow down the high-speed programme envisaged, but a move away from nuclear power is very unlikely given the size of investment already made.

Will the accident damage Gorbachev at home? Gorbachev's television broadcast last Wednesday, his first reference to the disaster, went down well. People in Kiev and North Ukraine were angered by the slowness with which they were warned of the danger. Less than a week after Soviet television mocked British students for leaving Kiev, the city's local authorities were advising parents to remove their children.

Gorbachev is benefiting from the switch from near-total secretiveness—treating Chernobyl as a minor accident exaggerated by the foreign press—for a week after the disaster to a policy of openness since May.

Will the accident affect US–Soviet relations? The failure to tell Western Europeans about the accident for almost three days and the provision of only minimal information for another week damages Gorbachev's image as the man who cares about the atom. He now says the summit with President Reagan needs "a better atmosphere". There is genuine Soviet resentment at what is seen as US exploitation of Chernobyl, but the Kremlin still wants a summit late this year or early next.

Immediate Soviet reaction to Chernobyl was almost a caricature of the Western view of Soviet foreign policy as blindly secretive and egocentric. Gorbachev is already busy restoring the Soviet Union's image by renewing his unilateral test moratorium until August. Other gestures can be expected. Long-term damage, however, may not be as bad as once appeared.

17 May 1986

The Results of Chernobyl

The most important long-term effect of Chernobyl on the Soviet Union is as a symbol of the disastrous consequences of economic mismanagement. Gorbachev has used it as an example of the bankruptcy of the rough-and-ready methods of the past, attacking the notion that the country can muddle through without too many radical changes.

Will it, however, affect Soviet plans to increase rapidly its total of atomic power stations? There are many more doubts post-Chernobyl, but the general thrust of the Soviet energy programme looks irreversible. The basic calculation, said Anatoly Mayorets, Minister of Power and Electrification (on the eve of Chernobyl), is that atomic power is cheap.

There is no sign that Soviet planners have changed their minds. They say every 1,000-megawatt reactor installed means 2 million tonnes of fossil fuel saved. Their strategy is to rely on atomic power stations in the European part of the country and on opencast coal mines in Siberia and Central Asia. Under the present five-year plan, the proportion of electricity generated through atomic power is to rise from 10 per cent now to 20 per cent by 1990 and to double again by the end of the century.

Nevertheless, conversations with Soviet officials and citizens reveal much greater anxiety about nuclear power, and this could have a long-term impact. Planning of nuclear power stations will not go through on the nod quite as it did before April 1986.

More immediately, Chernobyl has had an effect on reactor choice. Earlier this week Nikolai Lukonin, Minister of Civil Atomic Energy, said that of the eleven atomic power stations planned, only two where construction had already started would have Chernobyl-type graphite-moderated reactors. The government says that in future only pressurised-water reactors will be used.

Meanwhile, the loss of power from Chernobyl has had little effect on the Soviet economy. The plant produced only 4,000 megawatts out of total Soviet output of about 300,000. Even the additional loss of capacity when the other eleven RBMK-1,000 Chernobyl-type reactors were closed for the installation of safety devices, and the delay in bringing newly built plant on stream, had little impact because electricity consumption drops by 22 per cent during the summer.

Some small and uneconomic power stations, previously decommissioned, were resuscitated. The coal, oil and gas industries, boosted by more investment and better management, all met or surpassed their planned targets last year, helping to ensure that the general picture of the Soviet energy industry is healthier, despite Chernobyl, than at any time this decade. The fall in the world price of oil last spring had a far worse effect on the Soviet economy than Chernobyl.

25 April 1987

The Site of the Disaster

Soviet army reservists were at work last week sawing down a small pine wood contaminated by radiation, a mile from the Chernobyl nuclear power station. Once the trees and topsoil are gone, the area will be sanded over and seeded with grass. At the power station itself, an enormous steel and concrete shell — which looks like the bottom of an upturned ship and is known as the sarcophagus — contains the remains of the fourth reactor, which exploded in the world's worst nuclear accident last year.

There has been no danger of radiation from the plant for more than a year, but consequences of the original accident, which forced 135,000 people to flee their homes, are proving hard to eradicate. People have returned to only sixteen out of 179 villages and settlements abandoned in the first days after the disaster.

Throughout the uninhabited zone around the power plant, bands of clean-up workers, often wearing green military uniform and a white surgeon's mask, are monitoring soil, trees and plants. If these show signs of contamination on radiation meters, they are buried in vast pits. The largest of these is called the Lubianka, after the KGB's headquarters in Moscow. The Soviet authorities have heavily publicised these efforts by conducting parties of journalists on tours of the nuclear power plant and the abandoned zone in the past month. High priority is being given to reassuring Soviet citizens and the rest of the world that the Soviet nuclear industry is competent to pursue construction of nuclear power stations.

Since last October a new organisation called Kombinat has been in charge of the clean-up of the contaminated area, the operation of the two remaining reactors at the power plant, and reconstruction of a third by the end of 1987. It also needs to assure the safety of its own 7,500 workers.

The Soviet desire to prove that the errors which led to the disaster will never be repeated is understandable, but the main impression left by the shuttered villages and abandoned fields is the length of time necessary to eradicate the consequences of the original accident. Chernobyl itself is a large and prosperous village, twelve kilometres from the power station in the middle of rich water meadows and woodland. In past summers, people from Kiev would come to pick mushrooms and to fish in the streams. Now, visitors are informed "that going out in the forest, walking on the grass and using open water-pipes is strictly prohibited".

Workers at the power station were mainly housed in Pripyat, a town of 50,000 people only five kilometres from the plant. They were all evacuated in three hours by 1,200 buses and trucks, thirty-six hours after the accident, and the town is now desolate. Between the ugly blocks of prefabricated houses, the contaminated topsoil has been scraped away and replaced by sand in which grass and wild plants are beginning to sprout. On the outskirts there is a cemetery of cars, now mouldering in the summer rains, which were among the 2,000 contaminated vehicles handed over to the authorities, in return for compensation, after the accident.

Alexander Koralenko, an information official, says contamination levels have fallen sharply over the last year, and in theory people could return to fifty-five settlements. The problem is that not only must their homes and transport links be decontaminated, and there be no danger of radiation increasing, but they must be free to work in factories and fields.

About 70 per cent of the 4,000 men at the power station worked there before the accident, said Koralenko. Many of them now receive 1,000 roubles for a fifteen-day working month, compared to 400 before the accident. The average Soviet wage is 195 roubles a month. This kind of danger money is clearly attractive. A worker from Uzbekistan said he took a job in the area when he left the army in May.

The senior staff at the power station are new. Viktor Bryukanov, director of the plant at the time of the accident, and Nikolai Fomin, chief engineer, now in jail in Kiev, are to go on trial in the first week of July for gross negligence. Koralenko says he expects they will get sentences of up to twelve years.

The new managers, many of them in their thirties, look efficient and confident. On average, they are ten or fifteen years younger than the previous management — in sharp contrast to senior directors in most Soviet plants, where the average age is frequently well over fifty. Gennady Yaroslavtsev, the new chief engineer, says that his priorities are to produce electricity from the two 1,000-megawatt reactors and get a third going by the end of the year. Work has stopped on another two reactors — 80 per cent complete at the time of the accident — and they will probably never be built.

The Ukraine clearly needs electricity from Chernobyl, but this does not quite explain the decision to keep the plant going. With three reactors operating, it will produce just 1 per cent of the total Soviet output.

The more likely motive is fear of the damage to the prestige and credibility of the nuclear industry among Soviet citizens, if Chernobyl were completely abandoned.

22 June 1987

PART V

The Economy and the Impulse for Reform

The motor for reform in the Soviet Union throughout the 1980s is a consensus in the party that something must be done to improve the running of the economy. Gorbachev owed his election and continuing political strength largely to this belief, but paradoxically, he had no real economic programme. Instead, economic policy went through a number of stages: moderate perestroika or administrative reform in 1985–86; and a shift to more radical proposals in 1987–88. There were fundamental changes: an explosion in public expectations and the lack of inhibition in the radicalism of economic initiatives discussed. Joint ventures with foreign companies and co-operatives at home were introduced, but by the end of 1989 economic management was only slowly being transformed.

Radical Objectives

The Soviet Union must increase its national income at an annual rate of 4 per cent if living standards are to rise, Gorbachev has said in a keynote speech outlining his economic programme. National income has recently risen by 3 per cent a year. Members of the ruling Communist Party who do not go along with radical economic reform and "are an obstacle to the solution of these new tasks, simply must get out of the way and not be a hindrance", he said.

Gorbachev's speech, made to Communist Party activists in Leningrad on 17 May but only recently broadcast, is the most radical criticism of the way in which the Soviet economy is run delivered by a Soviet leader for twenty years. The reference to a 4 per cent growth rate in the national income being needed in the "present political circumstances" is possibly a reference to higher Soviet allocations for defence in the last year. Defence spending went up by only 2 per cent a year from 1976 to 1983, according to US estimates.

The increase in Soviet output is to come through greater labour productivity and better use of raw materials. The Soviet leader said that as long ago as 1966, during a visit to East Germany, he had been "tremendously impressed" by the East Germans' determination to make their products competitive on the world market. Gorbachev said the Soviet Union must do likewise. He singled out a number of enterprises in Leningrad making electric power generating equipment which, he said, "cannot stand competition on the world market".

The pungent style of Gorbachev's speech—delivered at the Smolny Institute in Leningrad, which was Lenin's headquarters during the 1917 Revolution—is in sharp contrast to the wearisome speeches delivered by his predecessors, Leonid Brezhnev and Konstantin Chernenko. Its broadcast has had a significant political impact.

Gorbachev underlined the cost to the Soviet Union of most of its natural resources being in Siberia. To reach them we must build towns and roads, he said. This is costly. "In some ten years, expenditure per tonne of additional petroleum has increased 70 per cent." Up to 22 million tonnes of oil could be saved if the older thermal power stations were brought up to modern standards. To increase labour productivity, machine tools in use had to be updated. According to one study, some 30–40 per cent of equipment in use in the Soviet Union has been operating for fifteen to twenty years.

Gorbachev's strong warning that leading party members who do not like the economic changes now envisaged must go is particularly significant since a new Central Committee, whose members dominate political life in the Soviet Union, will be selected this autumn before the next party congress in February 1986.

28 May 1985

Oil and Energy: The Exhaustion of Brezhnev's Economic Policy

At the end of last week Mikhail Gorbachev flew east from Moscow to the vast swamplands of Western Siberia, where most of the Soviet Union's oil and gas supplies can be found. The reason for his visit is that in the last eighteen months the output of oil has fallen for the first time since the Second World War. Massive investment and a wholescale purge of oil industry officials, including the dismissal of the Oil Minister in February, have not succeeded in reversing the trend in the world's largest oil-producing country.

Last year, oil output was marginally down at 613 million tonnes, and in the first seven months of this year it fell again by 4 per cent compared to the same period in 1984. Oil exports, which produce 60 per cent of Soviet hard currency earnings, had to be sharply cut back in the first quarter of 1985, leading to a trade deficit of $2 billion in contrast to a healthy surplus in the equivalent period last year.

Very cold weather last winter, well below minus 40 degrees centigrade, contributed to the drop in crude output. But the decline can be traced back to the over-rapid exploitation of the West Siberian oil reserves in the 1970s, which was regarded as the one great economic success of the later years of President Brezhnev. By 1981 there were plans to raise the output from Western Siberia alone to 500 million tonnes—but instead, the total has stuck at 365 million tonnes and this year is already 15 million tonnes behind target. A fifth of the wells in the area are not working because essential repairs are needed. The shortfall is all the more serious because the oil reserves of Western Siberia were intended to make up for the depletion of the oil deposits west of the Ural Mountains. The Siberian crude accounts for 7.6 million barrels a day compared to a total of 12.3 million barrels a day.

If the drop in output in the key oil province of Tyumen in Western Siberia continues, it will disrupt the Soviet energy programme, which absorbs a fifth of the country's total capital investment. This strategy, as set out in the official programme, involves "the maintenance of high levels of oil extraction, rapid increase in the amounts of Siberian gas extracted and transported to the European parts of the country and the accelerated development of nuclear power engineering". A shortfall in any one area throws the whole plan out of gear.

The problem today is that the oil industry is paying the price for the subordination of everything to forcing up crude output in the late 1970s and early 1980s. The Soviet daily press, technical journals and speeches by members of the ruling Politburo are filled with details of what has gone wrong. At the main oil fields "ever-increasing amounts of water are issuing from the wells along with petrolum," reports *Izvestia*. "The time when the oil spewed forth from the ground in gushes under its own tremendous pressure is largely behind us."

Gorbachev saw the consequence of past policies last week when he visited the vast oil fields of Samotlor, the largest in the country, if not the world. Production peaked at 155 million tonnes in 1980, but, say Soviet oil specialists, at the cost of tearing up its production plan so that "oil production has run almost four years ahead of the construction of oil field facilities." Almost 1.5 billion roubles' worth of infrastructure facilities originally considered essential to the running of Samotlor have not been built. As a result of such failures, reservoir pressures have dropped, oil pipelines often crack (sometimes causing fires and explosions) and other pipes are badly corroded, says Samotlor's chief engineer. Few Soviet oil specialists are passing up the present opportunity to point out that they predicted such an outcome years ago.

"Our proposals have not been carried out at Samotlor," said the director of the Petroleum Industry Research Institute recently. He claims that the Ministry of Chemical and Petroleum Machinery is ten years behind in equipment deliveries.

Not everything can be blamed on bad planning or overexploitation of existing reservoirs. Tyumen province, where oil and gas were first discovered in large quantities in the 1960s, is among the least hospitable places on earth. A vast swampy plain, it stretches east from the Ural Mountains across Siberia, frozen in winter and impassable in summer as the ice melts and the tracks dissolve into the marsh.

The Politburo has recently given priority to housing, electricity and roads, but even when these are built it will be difficult to get oil workers to live in an environment where oil wells are often isolated by floods or storms. Conditions are much worse than in the North Sea. Winter temperatures can drop to minus 45 degrees centigrade for long periods, and some of the oil fields are in permanent frost areas where the ground is frozen hundreds of metres deep. This makes construction difficult and costly.

Infrastructure will take time to build up, especially since Gorbachev made clear last week in Tyumen, as he had hinted before in Moscow, that the oil industry cannot expect a larger proportion of capital investment. Fuel and energy are already getting 40.8 billion roubles in 1985—an 11 per cent jump on last year—with oil the biggest single spender, absorbing 19 per cent of the capital investment going into Soviet industry as a whole. To invest more would disrupt Gorbachev's plan to double the money spent re-equipping industrial plant in the old industrial centres of Moscow, Leningrad, Urals and the Ukraine.

The emphasis in current Soviet criticism of the oil industry is not shortage of investment but the way in which it has been spent. The call is for a complete management reorganisation. "The lack of one person in charge of the Western Siberian oil complex and the corresponding lack of a balanced plan has created many substantial difficulties," says one senior central planner involved in Tyumen. He blames managers in the area for always looking to the different ministries in Moscow as their ultimate masters, making central control impossible.

Few of the former stars of the Soviet oil industry have escaped unscathed since the news from Tyumen turned sour. Nikolai Maltsev, the Oil Minister, lost his job at the beginning of the year, together with senior Communist Party officials involved in the oil industry in Tyumen. The ferocity of press attacks, which must have been sanctioned by the Central Committee secretariat, have increased as the news worsened over the last three years.

The criticism reaches to a high level. Gennadi Bogomyakov, the Communist Party leader in Tyumen since 1973, was strongly attacked this year by the daily *Sovietskaya Rossiya*, which said that "his sharp and tutorial attitude" expressed at a party meeting called to discuss the problems of Soviet oil stifled all debate on what has gone wrong. Speakers from the floor were waved aside. Communist Party leaders subjected to such public attack sometimes survive, but the casualty rate is high.

If new management is able to introduce advanced secondary recovery techniques into the oil fields, the gains in output could be substantial. According to Vitali Vorotnikov, a senior member of the Politburo, the existing oil fields are being exploited to only 40 to 45 per cent of their capacity—he quotes Soviet oil specialists as saying that this can be raised to 60 to 70 per cent. He accuses economic managers in the past of assuming that the natural wealth of Siberia is boundless and neglecting conservation of its resources.

The reduction of waste, rather than a leap in production, is at the centre of the energy strategy being pursued by the new leadership. Consumption is set to rise from 470 million tonnes this year to 484 million in 1990. The rest of the increase in demand, some 75-80 per cent of the total, is to be met by making economies, Gorbachev said earlier this year. As an example, 8 million tonnes of petrol were unnecessarily burned every year because the Soviet truck fleet had been slow to shift to diesel.

The very wastefulness of the Soviet economy's use of oil in the past means that there are now greater opportunities than in the West for conservation of resources. In 1983 the power stations were still using 2.5 million barrels of crude, of which 500,000 barrels a day have now been saved by substituting gas, and another 1.1 million barrels a day can be saved by 1990. The small boilers which heat homes and factories against the Russian winter are extremely inefficient in their use of fuel.

Gas output has consistently been the bright spot in the Soviet energy picture, so a substitute fuel is available where bulk new power stations are built or old ones modified. At current rates of extraction there is enough coal to last for 7,500 years, and only 18 per cent of Soviet hydroelectric power is utilised.

The scope for conservation is clearly considerable. If successful, it would also ensure that the Soviet Union has sufficient crude for the world market and to continue to supply Soviet allies in Eastern Europe with some 80 million tonnes of oil a year. A further drop in supply from Tyumen would reduce the amount Moscow has available for both markets, leading to a sharp reduction in foreign earnings and potential political difficulties with Comecon.

Overall, Gorbachev also wants a better return from investment in the oil industry because he needs an early success in his campaign for economic reform. His central problem is that the Soviet Union does not have the necessary capital resources to refurbish existing plant with high-technology equipment and at the same time continue to pour some 55 per cent of total capital investment into energy and agriculture.

Resources cannot be taken from other parts of the economy. Defence spending is apparently going up a little, and Gorbachev says he does not want to cut back on the supply of Soviet consumer goods. This explains the strength of the reaction in the Kremlin to the fall in oil output in Western Siberia. Given the narrow margins on which Gorbachev is operating, he cannot afford to see the most successful economic programme of the Brezhnev years go spectacularly wrong if he is to reform the rest of the economy. A serious failure in the energy programme now would dislocate Soviet planning for the rest of the century.

10 September 1985

Agriculture: The Ball and Chain

Yegor Ligachev chose the traditional meeting of the Soviet leadership on 6 November, the eve of the anniversary of the Bolshevik Revolution, to unveil the best piece of economic news Mikhail Gorbachev has had since he became leader. He announced that the Soviet grain harvest in 1986 was 210 million tonnes—30 million more than the average for the last five years. Gone are the days when, under Brezhnev, the size of the harvest was a state secret; this year's good news has been given wide publicity.

The larger harvest comes at a very convenient moment for the Soviet leadership: it reduces the need to import grain from the West at a time when Soviet hard currency earnings are down as a result of the fall in the price of crude oil; and it means that Moscow can, if it wishes, do without importing any grain from the USA, the only significant trade between the superpowers over the last decade. The timing could scarcely be worse for the world grain trade, however: it has relied heavily on the Soviets as its largest customer at a time when sales are severely depressed. Imports this year could fall from their peak of 55 million tonnes in 1984–85 to as little as 10–15 million tonnes, assuming that consumption is 220 million tonnes. Indeed, US market experts are forecasting that the Soviet Union may buy no maize at all from the USA this year—for the first time in sixteen years.

The size of the grain harvest has become a symbol of the economic health of the country as a whole and is a matter of great political significance. But while publication of the grain figures for 1986 reveals increased production, it does not analyse the causes. The harvest clearly benefited from good weather in the spring and autumn, enabling farms to overcome the effects of a midsummer drought. But did it also, as *Pravda* claimed earlier this month, increase because of the improvement in procurement prices, incentives, management and transport introduced since 1982?

The sensitivity felt by the Kremlin over the state of Soviet agriculture is understandable. It affects not only the country's overall economic performance but the daily lives of ordinary Soviet citizens, a third of whom—some 96 million out of a total population of 280 million—still live in the countryside. This is a much higher proportion than in Western Europe or the USA. The two-thirds of Soviet citizens who live in cities and towns can scarcely ignore the failings of the agricultural sector, any more than their rural neighbours—queues outside food shops and shortages within are a constant reminder.

Shortages continue despite enormous investment and 40 billion roubles in annual government subsidies for meat and milk production.

The problem, as in the rest of the Soviet economy, is not that production has failed to go up (since the last war Soviet agricultural output has gone up by 3.4 per cent a year compared with 2 per cent in the USA) but that demand, propelled by very low prices, has risen much faster.

The retail prices of all the main foodstuffs have not risen since 1962. Over the same period, money incomes have almost doubled. Meat in a state shop costs 1.75 roubles a kilogram, while production and distribution cost 4.70 roubles. At this price, output will never catch up with demand. The lack of balance between the retail price of food and rising real incomes has led to the highest food subsidies in history, and Soviet attempts to boost the politically sensitive supply of meat to the population has led Moscow to become the world's biggest importer of feed grains as the number of livestock shot up in the late 1960s and early 1970s.

Is this period now coming to an end? Will Soviet grain output achieve in the near future the level of 200 million tonnes in a bad year and 250 million tonnes in a good year, which Gorbachev says is perfectly attainable? Will Soviet agriculture cease to be a ball and chain for the rest of the economy?

Soviet agriculture remains primitive compared not only with Western Europe but with Eastern Europe. Grain yields per hectare are only half those of Bulgaria. This means that the basic development of the Soviet countryside will continue to absorb a third of all capital investment for the foreseeable future. On the bright side, however, there are signs that better procurement prices, incentives and infrastructure appear to be leading to increased output.

Nevertheless, even if grain production has increased slowly over the past quarter of a century, harvests are still very variable. The peak of the last decade was 237 million tonnes in 1978 and the trough 158 million in 1981. A really poor harvest does not cause famine, but it leaves the Kremlin no choice but to import grain unless it wants to take the delicate decision to slaughter some livestock.

The wide variation in the size of crops and the failure of output to respond quickly to high investment is largely explained by climate and history. The southern steppes, the vast prairies where much of the Soviet cereal harvest is grown, gets on average only two-thirds of the rainfall needed to grow wheat. These climatic disadvantages are exacerbated by the underdevelopment of the countryside. At the time of the 1917 Revolution, the peasantry were either self-sufficient or produced only a tiny marketable surplus using wooden ploughs and the medieval methods of agriculture they had employed for 500 years.

Stalin's forced collectivisation of agriculture in 1929 was basically a decision to confiscate food from the villages to feed the workforce in the cities. Soviet heavy industry was built at the expense of the countryside and repression was all the greater because of Stalin's exaggerated fear that the peasantry, still the majority of the population, constituted a potential political threat to the regime. The origin of the state and collective farms, into which Soviet agriculture is organised, as instruments of economic confiscation and political control, combined with very low prices for produce and very limited capital investment, meant that the countryside only really began to enter the modern world in the 1950s under Khrushchev.

Poverty in the countryside is well illustrated by a study of the collective farm peasantry in the rich grain-growing land of Stavropol, carried out by Raisa Gorbachev for her doctoral thesis. She discovered that in 1964 the average monthly pay for an unskilled labourer on a collective farm in this region was between 33 and 50 roubles. Since then, wages of collective farm workers have risen sharply as procurement prices have gone up. To stem migration to the cities, money has been put into supplying electricity and water, and building better roads to the villages. But there is still some way to go: a recent cartoon in a Soviet newspaper shows two peasants staring gloomily at a heap of fertiliser in a field. "What will the inspector say when he sees the fertiliser lying unprotected in the open?" asks one peasant. "Don't worry," says the other comfortingly, pointing to a rutted track beside the field, "What inspector could reach us over a road like that?"

Conscious of these failings, successive Soviet leaders have allocated between a quarter and a third of total Soviet capital investment to agriculture. Conditions have improved, but the return on investment has never been anywhere near as good as the Kremlin hoped. Large sums were spent. Farmers' incomes rose and there was heavy investment in buildings and agricultural equipment, but little clarity about which of the numerous schemes to improve agricultural output would show the best return. The most important initiative was the 1982 Food Programme. Meat and milk output was to be increased by a spectacular jump of 15 billion roubles in procurement prices for 1983, none of the increase being passed on to retail prices.

Gorbachev was the Communist Party official in charge of Soviet agriculture from 1978, but his real authority was limited. Only now are the differences and similarities between his agricultural policies and those of his predecessors becoming clear. He has retained the food programme's emphasis on rapidly increasing the supplies of meat, milk and eggs to the population and is keeping the proportion of capital investment devoted to agriculture at one-third of the total, but big new irrigation projects have been displaced by more cost-effective schemes to improve existing land. Plans to divert water from the rivers of Northern Russia and

Siberia southward to the Volga and the plains of Central Asia have been dropped.

More significant, however, are reforms in two other areas: to reduce the fragmentation of authority and investment, Gorbachev set up the state agro-industrial committee, or Gosagroprom, under Vsevolod Murakhovsky in 1985. It unites six agricultural ministries and other agricultural organisations. Gorbachev himself keeps close personal control of the agricultural sector.

The second reform came in the form of a 7,000-word decree on agriculture published at the end of March. It introduces a number of important changes:

- A 50 per cent price bonus on the production of major commodities above the average level actually achieved in 1981–85. These rewards apply to grain, meat, milk, cotton, soya, sugar beet, tea and wool. Previously, bonuses were tied to surpassing plan targets which were too high. The government has also promised that a state or collective farm which achieves a bonus this year will not immediately find its planned production target raised next year.

- State and collective farms will be able to sell 30 per cent of their fruit and vegetables profitably at prices above those of the state but below those of the free market. Previously only collective farms could do this, and they had to meet the plan target first. The effect of this is already apparent in Moscow: trucks from the south have been selling watermelons for one rouble. Last year the only watermelons on sale cost 8 roubles in the free markets.

- Local authorities in charge of "oblasts"—districts about half the size of an average English county—will have the power to fix prices in the local state shops. Prices will vary according to demand, an important change in a country where all prices have hitherto been determined centrally. This is in line with the tendency under Gorbachev for goods to be increasingly sold through co-operative shops at prices set midway between the rock-bottom state shop prices and the extortionate prices, three or four times higher, charged in the peasant markets.

The grain harvest this year appears to have benefited from these incentives combined with better distribution of fertiliser, feedstuffs and pesticides. Even where the harvest was not very good, state procurement increased, presumably because of a greater desire by farm workers to send what they grow to the silos.

It is still too early to say that Gorbachev has definitely managed to set the Soviet Union on the road to producing enough grain to feed its vast livestock herds, but the signs are that the country is moving closer to being able to produce the 220 million tonnes it needs for self-sufficiency in grain. This still leaves Soviet agriculture well behind the rest of Europe and North America, but it is the sort of boost Gorbachev needs. More and better sausage in the shops of Moscow does far more for the credibility of his economic reform programme than any amount of statistics published in the pages of *Pravda.*

24 November 1986

The Prices Test

"I am a conservative by nature," said Nikolai Glushkov, chairman of the State Committee for Prices, when asked about reform of the Soviet price system earlier this year. He ruled out any change before 1990. As the man who set all prices in the Soviet Union for eleven years, Glushkov was among the most powerful figures in the country and his dismissal last month is one of the most important changes in the Soviet economic leadership to be carried out by Mikhail Gorbachev.

The issue of prices crystallises the political differences between those Soviet leaders who want to see the present economic system, established in the late 1920s and early 1930s, run more competently, and those who want to transform it. Glushkov's vociferous defence in the press of his conservative views—despite criticism from Gorbachev—indicated that he had the support of some Politburo members. By the same token, his departure opens the door to a change of policy which was ruled out for as long as he held his job.

At stake is the way the Soviet economy is run. Soviet wholesale and retail prices are established by administrative fiat from above, based theoretically on the cost of production, not on demand. They are a system of rationing developed in conditions of scarcity of almost all goods in the fifty years before 1970.

But Gorbachev's demands for self-financing, managerial independence of enterprises, profitability, an adequate return on assets and accounting will all remain meaningless if the Soviet manager or head of an enterprise has no control over the costs of his inputs and outputs, which are determined in Moscow under the five-year plan. Soviet economists complain in particular that this leaves enterprises with no incentive to introduce better technology.

This makes price reform and an alteration of the way Soviet prices are decided the key to change in the Soviet economy over the next fifteen years. The problem is that while economic reformers can see the anomalies in the present system, they do not seem clear in their own minds that the implication of radical price reform is a change in the supply system as a whole.

At the moment, prices are determined by the all-powerful State Committee for Prices. The key relationship for any enterprise is not with its customers or other enterprises but vertically with the top, with Moscow. Suppliers and clients are not free to choose each other. They must make requests to the State Supply Committee (Gosnab), which then allocates supplies. "Obtaining the raw materials and equipment needed to fulfil the plan on time is far more important than loans or profits, for without an allocation voucher money is valueless," writes Dr Basile Kerblay in his authoritative book *Modern Soviet Society*.

Today, there is no trade in industrial products between enterprises, but a system of rationing administered from the top. Current wholesale prices were set in 1982, modified last year, and were not due to be changed again until 1991. Reformers such as the economist Dr Abel Agenbegyan and other radicals want a change earlier, in 1988, but it is not known where Valentin Pavlov, the new head of the State Committee for Prices, stands on this issue.

Retail prices are also determined centrally, and change in these is politically sensitive. Essentials such as bread and meat are very cheap; shop prices of bakery products, sugar and vegetable oil were last changed in 1955. The prices of meat and milk products were last raised in 1962 and have been static ever since. To travel any distance by Metro, bus or trolleybus in Moscow costs only 5 kopecks. Housing rent normally costs only 3 per cent of income. These prices have been kept stable despite increases in the procurement prices to state and collective farms; this means that meat which sells for 2 roubles a kilogram is officially acknowledged to cost the state 5 roubles to produce. The meat subsidy alone is 20 billion roubles a year.

Such low prices make it possible even for Soviets who get much less than the average monthly wage of 195 roubles to survive at a basic level. Anything more than the essentials of life, such as furniture and many articles of clothing, are very expensive and often in short supply. Good-quality women's winter boots can cost up to 140 roubles a pair. Goods not considered necessary, such as cars, are sold at a price fixed by the government's view of what the market will bear. The 12 million Soviet private car owners have each paid 7,000–8,000 roubles for their cars and on average saved for eight years.

This system of pricing and procuring goods, rough and ready at the best of times, was devised after the 1917 Revolution and systematised during industrialisation in the 1930s as a form of egalitarian rationing. As the economy developed, the price system has remained unchanged, despite growing disadvantages. The result today is that manufactured goods are generally too expensive, and food prices—indeed raw material prices as a whole—are too low. The most serious problems in the retail sector are:

- The great increase in purchasing power, much greater than the growth in supplies of basics. Real incomes increased by 43 per cent between 1970 and 1983. At the same time people have moved from the countryside into the towns and cities, which means the number of people buying in town shops rather than village markets has gone up by 57 million in the last twenty years.

- Low prices mean long queues and often poor-quality goods. This leads to large secondary and black markets. In the legal peasant markets, a kilo of meat costs 8 roubles and there are no queues. It also means that many quality goods miss out on legal retail trade entirely. People in Moscow and Leningrad are increasingly well dressed, but the cloth for their garments is often imported. Many of their clothes are bought at great expense from private tailors and dressmakers who operate illegally.

- Emphasis on quantity rather than quality means overproduction of some items. For instance, in 1984 the Soviet Union, with a population of 280 million, produced 740 million shoes—more than the USA, Britain, France and West Germany combined. Yet many of these are unsaleable and people's preference for sports shoes or sandals is evident in the streets of Moscow.

The wholesale pricing system determined by Glushkov's committee has prevented any form of industrial trading or contracts between different enterprises. Soviet industry thinks in terms of the acquisition of material supplies by administrative means rather than the purchase of goods needed.

The state committee has devised a cumbersome method of rewarding quality and punishing production of poor quality goods, but this is almost a caricature of Soviet bureaucracy at its worst. Glushkov explained the wonders of his method of distinguishing between good- and poor-quality goods by a system of fines on producers in an interview earlier this year. In the first year of producing inferior-quality goods, he said, "we lower the wholesale price by 5 per cent, in the second year by 10 per cent and in the third year by 15 per cent. After that, if the goods continue to sell, we cut the price by another 30 per cent. Then we abolish paying any price at all for those goods, which means their output is stopped."

It is easy for reforming Soviet economists to make fun of a scheme which allows five years before inferior-quality goods stop being sold, but the ability of state-owned enterprises to negotiate prices would not necessarily lead to much competition in Soviet heavy industry. Soviet enterprises are often not only very large but have a monopoly in what they produce. Reasonably enough, the men who planned the rapid industrialisation of the country saw no reason to waste scarce capital investment on creating more than one supplier for each product.

An increase in Soviet manufactured exports is one method of increasing quality production. From the beginning of next year the monopoly of the Ministry of Foreign Trade over hard currency exports and imports worth $60 billion last year will be broken up. Individual ministries and some enterprises with export potential will be able to trade directly with foreign companies.

A complete change in the price system, however, is neither feasible nor expected. But retail prices could be shifted, as in parts of Eastern Europe, to a three-tier system of fixed prices for basic foodstuffs, free prices for luxuries and maximum prices for goods in between. If, for instance, Gorbachev's plans for enterprises to have financial autonomy were to lead to better-quality clothes at higher prices, popular enthusiasm for a new price system would increase.

Low and heavily subsidised basic food prices are too much an accepted part of the Soviet political system to be easily raised. Even if real incomes have risen, there are still plenty of people who would be badly hit by an increase in the cost of living. When the price of hard sausage meat was raised from 4.5 roubles to 9 roubles a kilogram in August, there were fears of other food prices going up. Better-quality food supplies should not be difficult to achieve at prices in between those in state shops and the free market. In industry, the organisational problem of transferring much of the decision-making on prices to individual enterprises responsive to demand and away from the administrative tutelage of the centre is far more complicated. It will fundamentally change the way the Soviet economy has been organised over the past fifty years, and also entails an important devolution of political power away from Moscow.

It is not surprising that many Soviet leaders found Glushkov's conservatism a comforting barrier against any real measure of economic reform. His departure means that the chance of a significant price change is much greater, though its implementation is by no means assured. It is becoming clear, however, that over the rest of the decade the Politburo's decisions over prices will be the best barometer of the balance of forces in the struggle between the economic radicals and conservatives within the Soviet leadership.

17 September 1986

Opening to Moonlighters

By the end of next year, two or three million people should have started to take advantage of a Soviet law allowing them to hold a second job in the private sector, Ivan Gladky, Chairman of the State Committee for Labour and Social Issues, said this week, after the legislation had been passed by the Supreme Soviet. Eventually, the number may be far larger. Soviet social scientists estimate that between 17 and 20 million people out of a total labour force of 151 million participate in the secondary economy in the Soviet Union, though this is invariably in addition to another full-time job.

The new law names twenty-nine different types of individual labour which will be legal, including everything from private taxis to house repair and mending fishing rods, but the list is not exhaustive and may be added to by local authorities.

Those who currently supplement their earnings by part-time jobs and individual labour are usually in food production or services; demand for both has risen sharply over the past twenty-five years. The concentration of state investment on industrial development, neglect of the consumer sector, and the imbalance between prices and rising incomes have all encouraged the growth of a massive secondary economy. Soviet specialists estimate that in cities private handymen repair 50 per cent of all shoes, 45 per cent of all apartments, 40 per cent of cars and 30 per cent of all large household appliances. In the countryside, where services are worse, the figure rises to 90 per cent.

Given that there are 80 million apartments in the Soviet Union, this is big business. The size of the secondary economy is also underlined by surveys of family expenditure showing that a third of all spending is in the secondary economy, not including the high-priced peasant food market.

The aim of the new law, which comes into effect from 1 May next year, is to distinguish between individuals who work and businessmen who employ others. The latter remains strictly forbidden and is never likely to be countenanced by the Communist Party on the grounds that this really would allow capitalism to get a foot in the door.

What will the impact of the new law be? The full text has not yet been published, but it will have three big effects:

- It will legalise a large part of the secondary economy—primarily, but not wholly, in the service sector. It will enable the high incomes sometimes earned by individual craftsmen to be taxed.

    In the Baltic Republic of Latvia, for instance, half the money on deposit in the banks is held by 3 per cent of depositors, the average account of this top layer being 20,000 roubles.

- The private sector will expand and become better organised. Gladky says there is nothing in the legislation to stop somebody opening a café. Local Soviets or councils have been granted the power to decide who will be able to hold an individual job, but this will vary in different Soviet republics.

    There is a vast difference, depending largely on tradition, on the extent of the service sector, which is larger in the Baltic or Black Sea areas than in the central Russian cities, where it is limited.

- The legalisation of a large part of the secondary economy is being accompanied by a crackdown on the black market and on corruption. In certain sectors of the economy, such as food retailing, corruption had become all-pervasive by 1982, when the present clampdown started.

The law immediately raises the question of whether the general pattern of state control of the Soviet economy is changing. While this measure is likely to be important in raising the Soviet standard of living and the availability of consumer services, there is no evidence that it will alter the economic and social balance of power in the country.

Even a much wider release of free enterprise would not achieve the impact that such reforms have had in China because two-thirds of Soviet citizens live and work in cities, whereas in China most of the population are peasants relying on individual or family labour.

21 November 1986

Why Soviets Buy Cars

In the winter snows, the 11 million car owners in the Soviet Union often protect their vehicles by leaving them in garages for three or four months. On average, a Soviet private car runs for only nine months of the year, and where garage space is not available it is covered with a tarpaulin to protect it until spring.

There is good reason why Soviet citizens devote such care and attention to their cars. The difficulty of buying a car has gone down in recent years but the price is still high: between 8,000 and 9,000 roubles for the most popular makes such as the Zhiguli (sold in the West as Lada). Despite this, private car ownership is increasingly common in the Soviet Union, even if the phenomenon is comparatively new. In 1980 there were only 6.3 million private cars in the country, giving an average of 24 cars per 1,000 people, compared to 256 in Britain and 526 in the USA. Last year, Soviet citizens bought 1.1 million cars.

In the shopping rush before the New Year holiday, the streets of Moscow have been crowded in the evening with medium-size Zhighulis and Moskvitchs (80 per cent of private cars), tiny Zaporozhets (17 per cent) and the good-sized Volgas (3 per cent).

Nevertheless, the backbone of the Soviet transport system for individuals remains buses, trams, trains and aircraft. Every city with a population of more than a million has a right to have its own Metro system. Fares are low. "It costs me five kopecks for a forty-five minute Metro journey to work and the same to go home," said one Muscovite with a car, explaining why he does not drive to work.

Yet the demand for cars is great, despite the high price of purchase and maintenance. Soviet drivers advance two reasons for this. In the cities, where two-thirds of car owners live, new housing projects are often a long way from work. However, leisure trips outside the city on days off, not access to work, are the main reason advanced by 56 per cent of Soviet citizens who were asked why they bought a car. Only 10 per cent of those questioned said shorter travelling time to work was their prime motive.

Moscow and Leningrad are both surrounded by dachas, to which people from the city flood for summer weekends and holidays. Given that city flats are often very small and prefabricated and that dachas can be bought for as little as 2,000–3,000 roubles, ownership of a place in the country is often regarded as essential rather than a luxury. "The problem is that it takes me and my family half a day to reach our dacha by public transport," said a Muscovite who had just bought a car.

In the countryside itself, the private car has been slower to make an impact. This is in part because of lower incomes, greater difficulty in maintaining a vehicle and lack of petrol pumps. However, motorcycles, of which there are 12 million in the Soviet Union, are common in the villages and small towns. At about 1,000 roubles they cost one-seventh the price of the cheapest car and are therefore much more accessible to the less well off and the young.

Buying a car in the Soviet Union is more than a question of raising the cash. Every factory, ministry, state organisation, republic and public institution in Soviet life has its allocation of cars. Where the allocation is sizeable, such as in a factory which needs to attract skilled workers, waiting time is often a matter of months. In professions with a small allocation, the aspirant car owner may have to wait much longer. He may then try to take a short cut and buy on the second-hand market, but to do so he will pay a price. If, for instance, pointed out a Soviet citizen with an interest in cars, "a new Zhiguli cost 9,000 roubles if bought from the factory through the allocation system, it will cost some 12,000 roubles if bought five days old on the second-hand market."

A five-year-old second-hand car in good repair costs the same as a new car bought through the state system. It is therefore difficult for people in their twenties and thirties to buy a car. They lack seniority at their workplace, or accumulated savings. The typical Soviet car owner is a man between forty and fifty-nine who has saved for eight years, and six out of ten motorists are white-collar workers.

Nor does expense end with the purchase of a car. There is a chronic shortage of some spare parts and official mechanics to instal them, partly because the bureaucracy assumed that the life span of a Soviet car would be seven years. In fact, the true figure is turning out to be an average of fifteen years because cars in the Soviet Union are too valuable to dump.

The result of these shortages is that car owners turn to the black market for repairs and spares. Both cost money: a piston ring up to 40 roubles, a battery up to 180 roubles. An estimated 60 per cent of all serious repairs are done privately.

A shortage of petrol stations, and in some areas their complete absence, also means that much petrol is bought illegally. One survey showed that 38 per cent of all petrol used by private car owners was bought on the black market below state prices, now 4 roubles for 10 litres.

The overall losses to the state are enormous. The Interior Minister pointed out that in the last seven years the number of private vehicles on the roads had risen by 180 per cent, but the official sale of petrol by only 20 per cent. The difference was made up by the black-marketeers whose access to supplies is all the greater because a large part of the Soviet truck fleet runs on petrol, not diesel fuel.

Widespread theft of petrol is inevitable until the number of petrol stations is increased. It is not clear, however, why state fuel depots should not sell petrol direct to the customer at the official price. It is in this area, in services, rather than in the structure of the Soviet car market as a whole, that change can be expected over the next fifteen years. A cheap car costing 3,000–4,000 roubles is likely to remain a consumers' pipe dream.

4 January 1986

At Togliatti Car Plant

The vast Togliatti car plant on the bank of the Volga River, 1,000 kilometres east of Moscow, is the Kremlin's main concession to private car ownership. Every minute the three assembly lines, each 2 kilometres long, produce three cars—or about half the total car production for the whole country. The plant is also important because last year it became the testing ground for a new system of management autonomy and incentives which Gorbachev wants to see spread to the whole country.

The Soviet Union has always been ambivalent about private cars. In 1950 there were only 64,000 in the country, and under the leadership of Nikita Khrushchev officials complained of having to travel around by truck to conduct official business. Only in the mid 1960s was the decision taken that more private cars were needed as an adjunct to public transport.

The Volga automobile plant—known to Soviets as Vaz—where car production started in 1970, is the centrepiece of this policy. Over the past sixteen years it has produced 10 million cars, mostly based on the Fiat 124, of which 3 million have been exported as the Lada. The Zhiguli, the Soviet trade name for Togliatti's products, remains by far the most common car on Soviet roads, and 720,000 are produced annually.

Togliatti, named after the wartime Italian Communist leader, has become the fastest-growing city in the Soviet Union, with a population of 640,000. Its appearance, like that of many new Soviet cities, is aseptic, though alleviated by the planners' decision to divide it into three, leaving a large triangle of forest in the centre.

Demand for cars in the Soviet Union is always higher than supply. The Samara, the new front-wheel-drive car from Vaz, is being produced at a rate of 300 a day, climbing to a third of total output by 1988 at a cost of 8,300 roubles a car. The management at the Togliatti plant make it clear that although they are investing in improving their product, they do not plan to raise output. Total Soviet car production will stick at about 1.4 million a year, 1.1 million for the domestic market, up to the end of the century, say Vaz managers. "We don't regard cars as a prime necessity," Nikolai Glushkov said last month.

But the very fact that some 35 per cent of the Togliatti plant's production is exported makes it different from other Soviet enterprises. The Lada is almost the only Soviet-manufactured export which competes directly in Western markets. The Soviet Union's exports are mainly oil, gas and other raw materials.

The factory differs from others in the Soviet Union in three other important respects:

- The plant is bigger than most. Almost all components for the car are manufactured at the plant itself. The total workforce is 125,000, of whom 97,000 work in three shifts.

- The cost of manufacturing a Zhiguli is put at between 1,800 and 2,200 roubles by Boris Krupyenkov, director for economics and planning at the plant. The retail price is 6,000 to 7,000 in the Soviet Union and more for the new Samara. The profit is split 47.5 per cent each for the plant and the state, with the remaining 5 per cent going to the Ministry of Automobile Manufacture.

- Much of the heavy capital equipment is concentrated on foreign manufacture. Togliatti does not seem to have suffered from the dearth of modern machinery seen in so many Soviet plants. This is probably because it was started based directly on the Fiat 124 and has always produced significant foreign exchange through exports.

The forge, the pressing plant and the assembly lines all have large quantities of foreign-made equipment. This includes some robots for contact welding and plans to introduce more. Under the economic experiment introduced in the plant at the beginning of last year, management obtained control of 40 per cent of foreign exchange earning, though still acting through the Foreign Trade Ministry.

How far is this independence real? Alexei Nikolaev, the first deputy managing director at Vaz, says that "our role is decisive; the Foreign Trade Ministry only does the paperwork". According to *Izvestia*, however, Vaz still has to obtain a document from the Machine Tool Ministry stating that an item is not produced in the USSR before it can import it. "Naturally nobody wants to acknowledge their own impotence," the newspaper quoted a Vaz manager complaining. "They say it will be done, but not tomorrow."

Gorbachev made it clear, when he visited Togliatti in April, that he saw it as a potential model of the way other Soviet enterprises should develop. He said the experiment at the plant "has shown once again that the system of self-financing is an effective method of combating the notorious method of gross output. It acts as a cost-cutting mechanism."

The experiment has certainly had some effect on quality of work. The head of quality control at the end of the assembly lines says that he used to reject between 15 and 17 per cent of the cars delivered. The new system of incentives, where up to 30 per cent of wages is tied to performance and productivity, has cut the rejection rate to 2 per cent. This claim of better-quality work is confirmed by foreign companies selling the Lada overseas, who say that defects on cars delivered to them have dropped very significantly over the past six months.

An increase in quality also seems to be reflected in the new Samara—70 per cent of whose components differ from the old Zhiguli—which looks a more impressive car than its predecessor. "The Samara 2108 was wholly developed by our design engineers in this plant," says Vladimir Akoyev, the first deputy technical director, nettled by the suggestion that Porsche had any input into the design.

In many respects the Vaz plant at Togliatti is indeed the exemplar of the kind of factory Gorbachev would like to see across the Soviet Union. Its management sounds more energetic and flexible than the directors of other Soviet plants. The experiment, while still in early stages, has succeeded in raising quality. But Togliatti has many advantages over other Soviet plants. It competes in export markets, has modern capital equipment and sells a single and very profitable product. A real test of the effectiveness of the new experiment would be if the plant was able to raise its output to cope with any increase in foreign demand for its products following the launch of its new model.

20 June 1986

Wages and Prices

Soon after he was elected Soviet leader in 1985, Mikhail Gorbachev went to visit Hospital Number 53 in Moscow. The chief surgeon pointed out that he was the only surgeon in the hospital capable of performing complicated operations. For this he was paid 5 roubles for each operation, less than his taxi fare home if he missed the bus or Metro. Nursing sisters in the same hospital complained that they earned only between 60 and 80 roubles a month. The Politburo did raise medical salaries shortly afterwards: from 130 roubles to 200 roubles a month for surgeons and those working in intensive care units. This is still less than most factory workers earn and only just above the average wage.

Lack of wage differentials rewarding skilled or professional workers is increasingly blamed by Soviet economists for the country's low productivity, running at only 55 per cent of US levels in industry and 25 per cent in agriculture.

Gorbachev's government is now seeking to reverse the trend towards narrowing differentials by boosting professional salaries and the wages of specialist and skilled workers. Last month it announced an increase of between 30 and 35 per cent in skilled workers' wages. This should also improve the quality of public services such as health and education, which have suffered because of the pay gap with production workers. In

1940 the difference was only 4.5 per cent, but by 1984 production workers were earning 30 per cent more.

Lack of incentive payments for high productivity also helps to explain why two-thirds of Soviet workers say they do not work to full capacity, according to a survey cited by Tamara Zaslavskaya, one of the economic reformers who have come to the fore under Gorbachev. Another survey shows the impact of poor pay and lack of authority on Soviet management, revealing that only 9 per cent of managers and 13 per cent of middle management in state and collective farms in Siberia wanted promotion, while 30 per cent of the former and an astonishing 72 per cent of the latter actually wanted demotion because of the lack of rewards.

Writing in the monthly party journal *Kommunist*, Zaslavskaya argues that a combination of greater managerial control over hiring and firing, and increased rewards for managers and skilled workers, would solve the labour shortage which impedes progress in the Soviet economy. A decline in the birth rate in the 1960s has meant that the Soviet labour force is no longer growing fast enough to meet the needs of industry. The article points out that of the 151-million-strong Soviet labour force, "more than 30 per cent of those engaged in industry and 70 per cent of those engaged in agriculture are performing simple manual work". Soviet enterprises hoard physical assets such as labour and raw materials in the same way as a Western company builds up financial reserves. Looking at the consequences of a more fluid Soviet labour market, Zaslavskaya says that as better technology is introduced "millions of poorly qualified workers will be discharged from the production branches".

Another Soviet economist estimates that between 15 and 19 million might be affected over the next fifteen years, some of whom could be immediately re-employed by factories which want to increase their number of shifts. The Soviet government often berates ministries for building new plant when existing factories are working only one shift. Greater labour mobility within the country would also allow re-employment.

The increase in differentials and managerial independence is to be accompanied by greater emphasis on labour discipline: Zaslavskaya acknowledges that high productivity and high rewards are to be found in the private sector and the black market. Both developed strongly under Brezhnev's leadership as output of goods and services by the state failed to keep up with the rise in real incomes.

Some individuals have made fortunes. The article suggests that some of these profitable private activities be legalised and made subject to a progressive income tax. The top rate of Soviet income tax at the moment is 13 per cent, but it is not really used as an instrument of policy.

More controversial than changes in the wage structure are Zaslavskaya's arguments that these must be accompanied by a new price structure. The price and availability of goods differs greatly across the Soviet Union and has enormous impact on the mobility and distribution of labour. The timing and form of an overall price change is still being debated, but food prices are already going up as more produce is channelled through co-operative shops.

Much of what Zaslavskaya writes remains theory for the moment, but greater control of individual enterprises over hiring and firing as well as pay differentials, are clearly crucial to making Soviet enterprises self-supporting and autonomous, as the government has promised.

29 October 1986

Economic Change Promises Quick Improvement to Soviet Lifestyle

Mikhail Gorbachev became Soviet leader largely because of his reputation as an economic reformer. Only over the last two months, however, has the extent of the economic changes he plans to introduce become clear.

The most radical change planned is the legalisation of manufacturing and producing enterprises organised on a co-operative basis. This is likely to become law next year according to Dr Leonid Abalkin, who became head of the influential Institute of Economics in Moscow last June and is a member of Gorbachev's advisory team during the Soviet leader's trip to India. Dr Abalkin says that individuals will be free to establish manufacturing and producing co-operatives, which will be largely free to market and price their products without state control. This will add an entire new sector to the Soviet economy and could contribute between 10 and 12 per cent of the country's national income (roughly equivalent to gross national product) within ten years.

These enterprises, producing mainly quality goods for the consumer market, will have a greater impact on the Soviet economy than the individual labour law passed by the Supreme Soviet last week. This law will affect between two and three million people, out of a total Soviet labour force of 151 million within a year, say senior Soviet officials. It should double the estimated contribution to the economy of legal and illegal labour of between 10 billion and 12 billion roubles.

Other changes in Soviet economic management to be introduced from the beginning of 1987 include:

- Freeing light industry from central planning direction over quantity and quality of output, all of which must be sold under contract to other enterprises.

- An end to the monopoly enjoyed by the Foreign Trade Ministry over foreign commerce since the 1930s under which twenty-one ministries and seventy enterprises will get foreign trading rights.

- Changes making five important ministries self-financing so that they must fund themselves out of their profits.

The most radical changes are concentrated on the neglected service sector, the production of consumer goods and agriculture. Here, economic management should look completely different from that under Leonid Brezhnev and his predecessors. Brezhnev was also eager to increase the supply of food, consumer goods and services to the population but despite food subsidies, which will total 58 billion roubles in 1987, he failed to do so.

Gorbachev has decided to take a different and more radical approach. He needs to, because Soviet capital resources are already tightly stretched. Capital investment in re-equipping Soviet industry has gone up and agriculture, energy and defence all require large resources.

Only by introducing a degree of private or co-operative initiative in small-scale manufacture of consumer items, allowing craftsmen to work privately and legalising second jobs, can the supply to the consumer be increased to anywhere near the amount needed to satisfy demand.

The commanding heights of the economy, and most of the foothills, remain firmly in the hands of the state, for the restructuring of ownership is put in the service and consumer sector. Heavy industry, transport and raw materials remain in the hands of the government. The reforms will nevertheless change the style and standard of living for many, perhaps most, Soviets. The impact will vary across the country. Dr Abalkin said he is concerned that in central Russia, where there is little tradition of small businesses and craftsmen, the impact of the new laws may be much less than in the Baltic republics. In cities like Moscow he expects tailoring, car repairs, household repairs and cafés to attract individual workers.

The state banks will provide credit for individual workers and co-operatives. Small-scale manufacturing of basic items in short supply should find a ready market in the smaller towns and villages.

Soviet planners have looked at the experiments in East Germany,

Hungary and China when deciding on their changes. East Germany is the model most often cited: it has a well-developed private sector of 82,000 craftsmen and 3,000 co-operative outside state planning, providing two-thirds of services.

Hungary is less often mentioned by Soviet economists as a useful example, although they say they have looked at the Hungarian experience of second jobs and individual labour. They see China as a largely rural country, well behind the Soviet Union in development. Allowing Chinese small farmers to market a proportion of their produce at free market prices has a much greater impact on the Chinese economy than it would in the Soviet Union, where two-thirds of the 280 million population work in the cities.

The changes are unlikely to spur the Soviet Communist Party into diluting its control over the country, but the decentralisation of economic decision-making in agriculture and the service sector will inevitably give more authority to the regions. Moscow will retain its control over the allocation of investment, however, and the price of basic commodities will still be determined centrally, although links between increased quality and higher prices will be closer.

Dr Abalkin says a general price rise, combined with an increase in wages to help low-income families, was considered but rejected in favour of higher prices for better-quality goods.

28 November 1986

Dawn of the Enterprise Culture

Journalists to the back of the queue—so says Andrei Fyodorov, manager of the new co-operative café at 16 Kropotkinsky Street in central Moscow. His aim: to limit the number of Soviet and foreign correspondents pursuing stories other than food.

So far Fyodorov runs Moscow's only co-operatively owned café, although other aspirant restaurant managers are searching for premises, planning to take advantage of a new law on individual labour which takes effect today. They face many of the same problems already confronted by 150 other new co-operatives established over the last six months, as they try to find their niche in the state-controlled economy.

Most of the new ventures offer repair services for houses, clothing or furniture. Typical is a co-operative with a hundred members in Dmitrov district on the edge of Moscow which offers to build and repair dachas. Some more esoteric services have also appeared, such as a hairdressing salon for dogs in Vilnius, Lithuania, and another for ballet shoes in the capital.

By the end of this year about 1,500 service co-operatives are expected to be in existence—and this excludes other forms of co-operative. Their popularity reflects a desire on the part of ordinary Soviets to earn extra money through a second job: a recent poll carried out by the Institute of Sociological Research in Moscow showed that 27 per cent of those questioned wanted to earn more in this way.

These changes could mean a major boost for the economic reform programme of Mikhail Gorbachev. They will help increase the supply of services and goods to consumers beset by shortages, and can be expected to take effect quickly. This last point is important because Gorbachev's other economic reforms are not expected to produce benefits until the end of the decade. Greater reliance on individual and co-operative labour will also have the advantage of providing services at no extra cost to the state.

But the scope to be allowed for co-operative and private labour has not yet been decided, largely because the Communist Party is still debating the future shape of the economy, which is run very much as it was during Brezhnev's years in office.

Only this year is the government starting to make structural economic reforms—notably the draft law shifting the emphasis from administrative fiat to assessment by profit and loss. The radicalism of the changes will become clear only at a key meeting in June of the 307-member Central Committee.

Party conservatives are resisting plans to give the private sector more scope, though Gorbachev has firmly backed the reform. He argues that the Communist Party, even under the most radical interpretation of the new laws, will retain control of all the commanding heights and most of the foothills of the economy. Nor will the individual labour law introduce entirely new forms of activity. In many cases it will simply allow people to do legally what they have previously done on the side. Soviet surveys show that between seventeen and twenty million people out of a total labour force of 151 million make money through second jobs.

The incomes of Soviet wage-earners have increased faster than the supply of consumer goods and services over the past thirty years. The result is that private handymen working on their own account satisfy a high proportion of consumer needs. In the republic of Russia, the Transport Ministry says it meets only 42 per cent of the public demand for taxis, the rest being met, if at all, by drivers of the 12 million privately owned cars.

Failure to meet demand, surveys show, means that the average Soviet citizen spends 10 per cent of income on services, but would like to spend twice as much. Instead bank savings have risen steeply, so even high-priced goods such as new cars or expensive furniture find immediate buyers.

Dr Lev Nikiforov, responsible for research into co-operative and individual labour at the influential Economics Institute in Moscow, says that if individual and co-operative labour only provides legally what is currently illegal it will be supplying a third of all services.

But the aim of the individual labour law is more ambitious than just to legalise a piece of the black or grey market. The government's main desire is to draw a line between serious corruption and individualistic labour activities—although an added benefit will be that the reforms will boost tax revenues.

Dr Leonid Abalkin, one of the Soviet Union's most influential proponents of economic reform, says he expects that the right to hold second jobs legally will double the contribution of private labour to the national income over the next five years, from 2 per cent to 4 per cent. But he sees the development of co-operatives as being of far greater significance for the economy as a whole. In theory, they already exist in the co-operative farms (kolkhoz) set up after the collectivisation of agriculture in 1929. However, the peasants were coerced into joining kolkhoz and the appointment of chairmen is always from above.

The new co-operatives are different. In theory, individuals can set them up by registering with local financial authorities and paying a small fee. There is plenty of demand for jobs. When a co-operative providing some thirty different services in Ulyanovsk advertised for up to fifty people wanting a second job, it had 800 applicants. Start-up credit at low interest from the bank is also easy to arrange.

In practice, however, Dr Nikiforov says the co-operatives face three serious difficulties: supplies of raw materials and machinery, provision of full-time skilled labour, and relations with local government and ministries. The greatest difficulty is supplies. The wholesale customer in the Soviet Union cannot just arrive at the appropriate state organisation with a cheque and sign an order for raw materials or equipment. Allocation of resources is decided centrally by the State Supplies Committee, which is not geared to supplying the new co-operatives with small batches of material or a few machines.

"If we are serious about co-operatives they should have the same rights as state organisations in the allocation of resources," says Dr Nikiforov. He cites a co-operative making footwear in Armenia which gets most of its raw materials from a local factory but cannot buy specialised machines. In theory all Soviet industry is meant to be shifting towards contracts (where prices are determined by supply and demand) but at present the lack of trade in industrial products severely hampers new co-operatives.

The supply of labour for second jobs is no problem and the co-operatives will also use pensioners, housewives and students. A difficulty is that the co-operatives will also need full-time skilled workers and technicians whom state enterprises want to keep. In some cases part-time workers, such as would-be taxi drivers in Tallinn, Estonia, have been unable to get documents from their main place of work to allow them to take on secondary employment. The attitude of local authorities and ministries is also critical if individual and co-operative labour is to produce the surge in growth which Dr Abalkin believes to be possible. This means provision of premises, electricity and gas at reasonable speed.

It is also vital that the government should not try to control the new co-operative or individual ventures to the point where they are stifled. For instance, the Transport Ministry wanted to decide the prices charged by private taxis, and exactly when and how they should operate. Other ministries have tried to keep a grip on costs, salaries and management because this is their traditional behaviour and because they want to prevent competition with state services.

The degree of official discouragement or support varies across the country. In Moldavia, the government is willing to turn over loss-making catering enterprises to co-operatives. In Khabarovsk, a large city in the Soviet Far East which is notably short of consumer goods and services, the party leader was dismissive of the whole idea. He knew nobody who wanted to be a pastrycook.

Tax rates demonstrate the government's determination to stop entrepreneurs becoming millionaires. For the first time it has introduced a progressive tax. On an individual's net profit up to 3,000 roubles per annum tax is levied on only 11 per cent of income, but then jumps to 60 per cent on profits between 3,000 and 5,000 roubles. Co-operatives pay 5 per cent for three or four years and then 10 per cent.

The Kremlin is clearly conscious that more private initiative will be seen as a sign that capitalism has a toe in the door. To give present moves ideological respectability, protagonists of change point to Lenin's New Economic Policy in the early 1920s, which allowed private trade. But the Kremlin's economic policy has far from gelled and will start to clarify only after the June meeting of the Central Committee. Gorbachev's reputation as an economic reformer long preceded actual achievement. The first test of how much radicalism he wants or can force through will be the scope given to private and co-operative labour.

1 May 1987

Joint Ventures with Western Companies

A central aim of the Soviet decision to end the Foreign Trade Ministry's monopoly control over exports and imports announced this week is to make it easier to set up joint ventures with Western companies.

In the biggest shake-up in the organisation of Soviet commerce since the 1920s, the new decree gives some twenty-one ministries and sixty-seven state enterprises the right, from the beginning of 1987, to import and export on their own account outside the control of the Ministry. Soviet foreign trade, worth a total of $60 billion last year, consists largely of the export of raw materials such as oil, oil products and gas, and the import of machinery and grain. Soviet-manufactured exports, apart from arms, are very limited.

The weakness of the Soviet trading position has been underlined by the fall in the price of oil and a steep decline in the Soviet terms of trade. Its exports are largely denominated in dollars and imports in Western European currencies. It now takes five times the amount of Soviet crude to buy one West German machine tool as it did when the price of oil was at its peak.

Under the new decree it is hoped that manufactured exports by those industrial ministries considered to have export potential will be increased. These ministries will be given priority in allocation of foreign exchange if the equipment purchased can be used to increase exports or substitute for imports. The reorganisation will initially affect only some 6 per cent of Soviet foreign trade because the Foreign Trade Ministry's control of raw materials exports and imports will not be affected. The Ministry will also continue to handle the import of new plant requiring major foreign investment and the imports of Soviet ministries which only occasionally need to buy goods from abroad.

Under a new organisation, called the State Foreign Economic Commission of the Council of Ministers (SFECCM), the twenty-one ministries will be able to establish direct links with foreign suppliers for imports of equipment. They will be able to arrange compensation deals and use 90 per cent of their hard currency export earnings to import equipment to increase production capacity for home or foreign markets. The government will take 10 per cent of their hard currency earnings in tax.

In the past Soviet enterprises, even where they produce a product with export potential, have seen little benefit in exporting since they received no benefits themselves and had to produce better-quality goods. The Vaz car plant at Togliatti is one of the few Soviet enterprises to sell manufactured exports requiring major capital investment directly in foreign markets.

Soviet Foreign Trade Performance
(Roubles bn)

	1985 (1st half)	1986* (1st half)
Trade turnover		
All countries	70.5	66.8–68.3
Socialist	43.2	45.2–45.7
Non-socialist	27.3	21.6–22.6
Exports		
All countries	34.2	33.2–34.8
Socialist	21.5	22.8–23.1
Non-socialist	12.7	10.4–11.7
Imports		
All countries	36.2	32.6–34
Socialist	21.6	22.4–22.6
Non-socialist	14.6	10.2–11.4

*Estimate based on officially reported 4 per cent drop in total trade turnover to R67bn, a level of exports of R34bn as reported in the Soviet press, and official foreign trade performance during the first quarter of 1986, as reported in "Foreign Trade".

Note: Figures may not add due to rounding.

The enterprises will still have to receive authorisation from the Foreign Trade Bank (FTB), where hard currency deposits must be made, but the bank will open branches all over the Soviet Union. Final say by the bank allows the state still to have final control over spending and imports. The FTB is a powerful institution which should allow Moscow to avoid a flood of imports, as happened in Poland in the 1970s and China in the 1980s. Enterprises will have access to foreign currency which they have earned themselves or which will be advanced in the form of a four-year hard currency loan by the bank, to be repaid out of export earnings.

At the moment, the Foreign Trade Ministry exercises its monopoly over commerce through a large number of foreign trade organisations, some of which will now be split up and their different departments hived off to the appropriate ministry. Some ministries already have import and export departments, but in the past the final say was always with the organisations. The Soviet Union also intends to decentralise its external commerce to make it easier to set up joint ventures with Western companies, say Western diplomats in Moscow. This idea emerged earlier this year but was never spelled out.

It now appears that the Soviet Union wants to promote joint investment on a 51 per cent Soviet/49 per cent Western basis. These companies will be able to repatriate profits, control the prices of their own products and not be subject to any control by the State Planning Organisation, Gosplan. Joint venture companies will also allow the foreign partner to have a say in management and quality control. In the past the Soviet side refused Japanese companies the right to appoint their own quality control manager in joint venture projects, which as a result did not get off the ground.

Soviet officials, aware of their lack of marketing organisations, are clearly conscious that they need Western marketing networks. The new state committee will also try to promote Soviet and Western supply of plant to third countries. This may prove attractive to companies wanting to do business in countries such as Libya or Iraq, which have close links to the Soviet Union.

Foreign companies have so far proved cautious about the idea of joint ventures. But the decentralisation of the powers of the Ministry of Foreign Trade, combined with a campaign against corruption within the foreign trade organisations, is disrupting traditional links between suppliers and clients. This will probably lead to ministries looking for alternative suppliers.

25 September 1986

The Shift to Radical Economic Reform

In the battle to reform the Soviet economy, Mikhail Gorbachev is facing a critical moment. The balance of power between radicals and conservatives is so even that economists will predict only that the struggle will be prolonged and intense. At stake is the shape of the Soviet economic system, largely created between 1929 and 1932, under which the central authorities in Moscow allocate resources of goods and labour and determine the value at which they are sold.

Soviet reformers have realised that piecemeal economic reforms introduced since Gorbachev came to power have been thwarted by the unaltered control of the commanding heights of the economy by organisations such as Gosplan and Gosnab—which together control the Soviet supply system—and by the ministries in Moscow.

The key issue at tomorrow's planned meeting on the economy of the Communist Party's Central Committee will be the production of a coherent plan to reduce the power of these central bodies so as to allow enterprises to allocate resources by negotiating contracts at prices which reflect supply and demand. The proposed reforms would change more than the method of economic management. In a centrally run economy political and economic leadership are the same, so the reforms would curtail or end the authority of some of the most politically powerful men and organisations in the Soviet Union.

Not surprisingly there is strong, if covert, resistance in every party and government institution, from the Politburo down, as the implications sink in. Conservatives "are afraid that with the abolition of directional planning there will be anarchy of production," says Dr Boris Kurashvili, a specialist on the reform of the Soviet state and economy at the Institute of State and Law in Moscow.

The Central Committee will discuss a new law on state enterprises, already published in draft form, which aims to increase the independence and rights of individual enterprises, but economic reformers say the extreme ambiguity of its language reflects rather than resolves key questions. A senior manager at the Sumy engineering plant in the Ukraine, which has conducted an experiment in financial autonomy over the past three years on whose results the new law is partly based, said earlier this month that the Moscow ministries were still very much in control. "In practice, the quantity of goods produced remains the index by which we are judged," he said.

Gorbachev told a recent conference that it was the power of the central economic bodies which frustrated the more limited reforms attempted in the 1960s and 1970s, ensuring that they were applied "in a very truncated form".

The fate of the modest reforms introduced during Gorbachev's own two years in the Kremlin suggests that in any contest for authority between central bodies and newly enfranchised enterprises, the former tend to triumph. Enterprises may have received more rights, but in practice they have neither the incentive nor the strength to use them. For example, the ministries and enterprises which received the right to trade abroad from the beginning of this year have shown little interest in competing for foreign markets. A principal cause of this is lack of experience, since these organisations do not compete on the domestic market, where their inputs and outputs continue to be planned in the traditional centralised way.

The fact that the Soviet economy is managed through the central allocation of goods and labour, and not through direct negotiations between producer and consumer, is also neutralising the effect of regulations introduced over the last year to allow people to set up co-operatives or engage in jobs.

As an illustration of problems facing new ventures trying to trade legally within the present system, Dr Alexander Levikov, head of economics at *Literaturnaya Gazeta* and an advocate of reform, cites a co-operative recently established to build wheelchairs in Estonia. The co-operative needed steel pipe, and the engineer who set it up knew some was being discarded as scrap by a nearby plant. The plant was willing to sell it to the co-operative, but could not because its plan for scrap had been devised in Moscow. If the pipe were sold at a higher price to be made into wheelchairs, there would not be enough metal left to fulfil the plan for scrap.

Every commentary, from anecdote to scientific survey, indicates that economic reform is failing to make headway. A professor conducted an experiment to try to make a collective farm, in the Altai region of Siberia, self-financing and economically independent, but he found it could not cut free from central direction. "If the farmers do not follow instructions they are denied equipment and other needs," he said.

Dr Otto Latsis, an economist on the party's theoretical journal *Kommunist*, says the new laws—on individual labour, co-operatives, joint ventures, foreign trade and the right of collective farms to sell part of their produce on the free market—will have only limited effect unless there is fundamental change in relations between buyer and supplier, in favour of the former.

Frustration at the failure of the earlier Gorbachev reforms has led to much sharper criticism of central government organs, such as Gosplan and Gosnab, the Finance Ministry and the fifty or so industrial ministries. "If you want to kill an idea, just turn to Gosplan. They will arrange a funeral at the highest level," two economists wrote recently.

Bitter jokes like this were often told in the past, but never published in the press. Last month Dr Nikolai Shmelev, an economist, went further and denounced the whole way the Soviet economy had been run for the past fifty years. "Today we have an economy of shortages, totally unbalanced and unmanageable, and to be perfectly honest, virtually unplannable, and which still does not accept scientific progress," he wrote in *Novi Mir*. He even denied that socialist ideology required central administration of the economy, an important charge since it undermines one of the chief defences of the central economic bodies—that any shift from plan to market is a betrayal of the central core of belief on which the Soviet state was founded.

More temperate criticism holds that allocation of scarce resources from above may have been necessary in the 1930s and 1940s, to industrialise the country and win the war, but that these methods are obsolete. The economy is beset by chronic imbalances between supply and demand, which are choking growth. "Supply deficiencies, like long-range guns, hit their targets a long way ahead," said one writer in *Socialist Industry*.

The fact that almost all Soviet citizens have suffered from this long-range bombardment is the strongest card in Gorbachev's hand. The problem is that his remedies require a revolution from above and a degree of upheaval which frightens many party and state officials. It is significant that the reform which works best is the establishment, early this year, of a centralised organisation for quality control with inspectors in most big factories. Adopted from the military industries, it has improved the quality of output.

It is clear, says Dr Levikov, that the system of price formation must be changed and "if it doesn't happen, then all the other reforms are useless." At present prices are determined in Moscow, but if the financial independence of enterprises is to have any meaning, they must be free to negotiate contracts with other enterprises.

The cost of basic food and services presents a different problem. Reform economists advocate state-fixed prices, but at a level which better reflects the balance between supply and demand and relieves the state of paying heavy subsidies. Going by the experience of Communist governments in Eastern Europe, it is the success or failure of price reform which is the key to the success of economic reform. In Hungary, a change in the price system was successfully introduced, but in Poland it provoked riots in 1970, 1976 and 1980. The issue of prices also provides an opportunity for conservatives within the party to look for popular support against a rise in the cost of living.

How quickly can the reform of the Soviet economic system be carried through? Gorbachev has spoken of the state enterprise law coming into effect by the beginning of 1988, together with changes in the powers of the central bodies. Complete change in the economic mechanism would come from the start of the next five-year plan in 1991.

Working groups will consider the future of the central economic bodies, and there is a scheme to cut the staff of Gosplan by 50 per cent. But the determining factor in the tempo of reform is the political struggle within the party and state. It all depends, says Dr Kurashvili, on "how long it will take to break the resistance of the apparat". This is still strong at all levels. Many members of the Politburo and the Central Committee have risen through managing the present system. If anybody benefits from the unreformed Soviet economy, it is they.

The radical supporters of Gorbachev in the Politburo and party secretariat, such as Eduard Shevardnadze and Alexander Yakovlev, the party secretary for propaganda, are generally in political rather than economic jobs. Nikolai Ryzhkov, the Prime Minister, and Nikolai Talyzin, the head of Gosplan, have backgrounds as competent administrators rather than reformers.

At tomorrow's Central Committee meeting it will be important, therefore, for Gorbachev to demonstrate his overall political strength by promoting some of his supporters. Diplomats say he wants to give either Yakovlev or Boris Yeltsin, the status of full Politburo members.

Gorbachev's commitment to radical economic reform rather than the incremental change of the last two years cannot be in doubt, but tomorrow he needs to persuade the Central Committee that the transformation of the system which they manage is feasible and necessary—and that it can be carried through without reducing the economy to chaos.

24 June 1987

Soviet Economic Motor Changes up a Gear

The final decision of the Soviet Communist Party to break with the system of a centrally administered economy devised by Stalin in the 1930s came with surprising ease after two years of debate and growing criticism of present economic management. The party's Central Committee also heard, on 25 and 26 June, that the piecemeal reforms introduced over the past twelve months were having very limited impact on the economy.

Instead, Mikhail Gorbachev put forward a coherent framework for economic change to be introduced over the next three years, in time for the start of the 1991 five-year plan. In his three-hour speech he argued that complete direction of the economy from the centre might have been necessary to build heavy industry in a peasant country fifty years ago, but today ministries in Moscow are manifestly incapable of directing the day-to-day activities of every Soviet enterprise.

Describing the Soviet economy as having reached a pre-crisis situation, Gorbachev said the most alarming consequence of this was that the Soviet Union had dropped behind the West in technology and the efficient use of resources. The system had been kept going only by massive exports of oil and other raw materials to make up for the basic inefficiency of the economy. Gorbachev also left no doubt about what the Soviet Union should do about this. Democratic centralism, the core of Lenin's concept of Soviet government, needed to become much less centralised and more democratic, he said. The main question was "how to create even more powerful stimuli than under capitalism for economic, scientific, technological and social progress".

It is the patent failure to compete successfully with the West in any of these areas over the past fifteen years which played a key role in making Gorbachev General Secretary of the Communist Party in 1985, though many party leaders who supported him then expected reforms of a far less radical nature.

In many respects Gorbachev's attitude to Soviet socialism today has a parallel with President Roosevelt's towards American capitalism in the 1930s. The Soviet leader, like President Roosevelt, is saying to his political establishment that if its members want their method of running society to stay in business at all, they must accept a new deal. Again like the USA in the 1930s, many conservative members of the Central Committee go along with Gorbachev because they cannot think what else to do and they know that doing nothing could be very risky indeed.

The new deal proposed by Gorbachev is very radical. At present, if the manager of one Soviet enterprise wants to obtain a product from another, he must obtain a piece of paper from the appropriate ministry or central government organ in Moscow to do so. By 1991 this will all have changed. Authority will be devolved downwards. Enterprises will decide independently most of their inputs and outputs through whole-sale trade at prices reflecting supply and demand. At the same time, the role of Gosplan and Gosnab will be sharply reduced.

Nor are the changes purely economic. Political and economic leadership are welded more closely together in the Soviet Union than they are in the West, so economic decentralisation should automatically reduce the ability of the top ranks of the party to monopolise political power.

Advocates of reform in Moscow seem surprised by the extent of their victory. The Central Committee's final decision reads like a compendium of the ideas of radical Soviet economists. A symbol of this is that the press conference at the end of the meeting was given by Dr Abel Agenbegyan, not a Central Committee member but for twenty-years the most prominent and cogent of academic reformers.

Such changes could not have occurred a year ago. Although Gorbachev became leader partly on the strength of his vague reputation as a supporter of economic reform, it was never clear what this really amounted to. In his past as a provincial administrator in the grain lands of southern Russia, and then as the party expert on agriculture, there was little to suggest that he would seek to change the system as a whole. As recently as summer 1986 it was easy to find senior officials such as Vladimir Glushkov, the head of the State Committee for Prices, saying that they saw no reason for more than a little tinkering with the price system. Given that the key element of reform is to allow the enterprise to set its own prices at a level reflecting supply and demand—a right essential to financial independence—the policies of men like Gluskhov blocked all real managerial change.

There was a committee on reform set up under Nikolai Talyzin, the head of Gosplan, which co-ordinated the activities of twenty-six working groups of academics and senior managers producing plans for change in different areas of the economy. These reported last summer, but Soviet economists say that it was only after Nikolai Slyunkov became head of economic administration in the party secretariat at the beginning of 1987 and told the groups to prepare radical proposals that these reports began to turn into policies.

Day-to-day management will be in the hands of the enterprise. By 1991 it will engage in wholesale and retail trade to meet its needs and sell its products. It will be able to go bankrupt— a fate deserved by several thousand companies, according to Dr Agenbegyan—and the government will in general stop keeping unprofitable enterprises going with the profits of profitable enterprises.

But this will be true of only part of the economy. For if the June Central Committee meeting saw a victory of the reformers, it also saw a historic compromise on the part of the central organs of government. At the centre of this compromise are state orders. In the transition to wholesale trade the state will order goods, in theory through competitive bidding, from enterprises. At first this will account for some 60 per cent of business, though this should drop to 25–30 per cent, Dr Agenbegyan estimates.

This part of the economy will continue to be run by Gosplan and Gosnab. State orders will become the main source of supply for the armed forces, always fearful they would lose their priority position in a Soviet economy in which allocation of resources by decree plays a reduced role.

The other key area during the transition period over the next three years will be prices. Here, the documents outlining the main guidelines for reforms produced by the Central Committee meeting are at their vaguest. Not only do price changes have a politically explosive potential, but the situation is complicated because a number of problems need to be solved simultaneously.

Unfortunately for the Kremlin, Glushkov and his predecessors ran the Soviet price system very badly. A commitment to keep the basic cost of living low became an obsession. Gorbachev also pointed out in his speech to the Central Committee that the price of energy and raw materials was too low to encourage efficiency in the use of either.

In both cases it makes sense to raise prices. The difficulty is that this would require a whole new system of state prices, to be worked out at the very moment when many enterprises should be planning to shift to wholesale prices. The latter change will start only after three years and could take ten years to complete. In theory, the state enterprise law comes into effect from the start of 1988, as will the reduction in the authority of central organs, but real financial independence must wait upon the switch to supply by trade rather than injunction in 1990–91.

For quick returns during the transition period, the best chance for Gorbachev is likely to be the introduction of limited private and co-operative enterprise on the margins of the economy in agriculture and services. This could produce a quick boost to output, while the heavy industry core of the economy will take longer to respond to change.

All these are difficulties Gorbachev will have to face over the next few years. "Economists are terrible on transitions—they tell you to go from A to B, but they can't tell you if you'll fall off a cliff on the way," remarked a specialist on the Soviet economy last week. But whatever the nature of the cliffs, the Soviet Union is now committed to an agenda and time-scale for the transformation of the way its economy has been managed for more than half a century.

7 July 1987

PART VI
Foreign Policy and the Military

After summer 1985 Third World ambassadors in Moscow all asked the same question: how far would the Soviet Union under Gorbachev sacrifice its former allies in order to cultivate better relations with the USA and end the Cold War? The question was difficult to answer because the instinct of Gorbachev and Eduard Shevardnadze, in contrast to Brezhnev, was to increase the political input into security policy at the expense of the military. In 1985–86 there was no open attack on the army itself. This came in May 1987, when the Defence Minister and Air Defence Chief were sacked after Mathias Rust, a young West German pilot, landed his plane in Red Square.

Memories of War

Less than two months before the Soviet Union celebrates the fortieth anniversary of victory over Nazi Germany, the murder of an old man in a village in the south of the country illustrates the depth of popular feeling about the events of the last war.

The man who died was Ivan Dergachov, an old man who lived alone and made a living collecting empty bottles in the village of Orlovka in Donetsk province. He was also one of the few men to survive the war in Orlovka. Some 207 people, almost the entire male population of the village, were killed by the Germans between 1941 and 1945. After the war, a rumour spread through the village that the bottle collector lived when the others died because he had collaborated with the Gestapo, but nothing happened for almost forty years.

One day recently, Dergachov, by now an old man, tried to collect empty bottles from two young men called Kolya and Tolya who were drinking behind the village hall. They refused to hand them over, a fight started and the old man was beaten up and eventually throttled with a belt. Two days later he died, and Kolya and Tolya were sentenced to seven years in prison for his murder.

Almost immediately, 300 people in Orlovka wrote to *Komsomolskaya Pravda*, the daily newspaper of the Communist youth organisation Komsomol, to which Kolya and Tolya belonged, demanding their release. When the newspaper sent a reporter to interview people in the village, he was told by a local teacher: "I have no pity for a man like Dergachov. Hatred gives them the right to raise their hands against him."

The reporter denounces the murderers as drunken louts who deserved all they got and is shocked that the people of Orlovka justify the crime. But murder, justified by the suspicion of collaboration long before the killers were born, illustrates the extent to which popular feeling in the Soviet Union is still conditioned by the trauma of the last war.

3 April 1985

Before the Geneva Summit

Mikhail Gorbachev will lead the Soviet Politburo on to the top of Lenin's tomb today to review the annual march-past of the Soviet army in celebration of the anniversary of the 1917 Revolution which brought the Communist Party to power.

For thirty minutes the new Kremlin leadership will watch the Kanti-mir and Taman Guards division, Moscow's elite garrison troops, march through the square followed by squadrons of tanks, rockets and military hardware. This display of Soviet military strength comes at a time when there is decreasing belief in Moscow that the summit meeting between Reagan and Gorbachev in Geneva in two weeks' time will produce much in the way of arms limitation, though it may stabilise relations between the superpowers.

Soviet pessimism has grown since President Reagan's speech to the UN in which he emphasised the Soviet role in regional conflicts around the world, not arms control, as the prime topic for Geneva. Last week the President further underlined his commitment to Star Wars, the Strategic Defence Initiative programme which, the Soviets insist, precludes agreement on limiting offensive nuclear weapons.

Shultz's visit to Moscow this week produced no sudden zigzag in US or Soviet policy, and on substantive issues the two sides are very far apart. "It is difficult to imagine any broad agreement in Geneva," writes Alexander Bovin, an authoritative Soviet commentator. This does not mean that the summit will end in disaster. The degree of animosity between the superpowers today is less than during the first three years of President Reagan's administration. Both Gorbachev and Reagan have good reasons for appearing—and to some degree for being—conciliatory when they meet.

The Kremlin feels that the Soviet diplomatic offensive of the last three months has markedly improved its image in the eyes of foreign governments and world opinion. "Moscow has taken over the initiative in the political and psychological preparation" (for Geneva), claimed four Soviet journalists who interviewed President Reagan last week.

There are other Soviet gains. Dr Georgi Arbatov, the head of the USA and Canada Institute in Moscow and an important adviser to Gorbachev, told Soviet television viewers last weekend that the US administration is divided on relations with the Soviet Union, and tension between the USA and its allies has "reached a scale without precedent in postwar history". But the significance of Gorbachev's public-relations triumphs in Paris and elsewhere can be exaggerated. He gained the political initiative by publicly producing, for the first time, a Soviet plan for a 50 per cent cut in nuclear arsenals, but there is little sign yet that the USA will seriously modify its defence plans.

Although public comment concentrates on Star Wars and cruise and Pershing II missiles, Moscow is worried by the level of US defence spending as a whole. Last week *Pravda* pointed to the US defence budget of $302.6 billion for fiscal year 1986 as the real measure of US policy in Soviet eyes.

This is very serious for Moscow. Better relations with Washington after the Geneva summit may reduce the degree to which Soviet leaders feel threatened by President Reagan, but at the end of the day they have always seen détente as being based not on perceptions but on parity in nuclear weapons and the means to deliver them. This, they believe, they achieved in the late 1960s when they deployed Intercontinental Ballistic Missiles able to hit the USA. They reinforced strategic equality when they were able to match the USA in placing Multiple Independently Targetable nuclear weapons (MIRVS) on each missile in the late 1970s, and today they have parity in warheads.

The Soviets see high US defence budgets as an attempt to erode this parity—based on unavoidable mutual destruction—in the event of nuclear war and to reassert the superiority enjoyed by the USA in the twenty-five years after 1945. They are also worried that in seeking to compete with the USA in defence spending, their economy will be seriously overstrained. Senior Communist party Central Committee officials have quoted Caspar Weinberger, the US Defence Secretary, as saying in 1980 that in trying to keep up, the Kremlin might break the back of the Soviet economy.

This is a little overstated but Gorbachev, and most of the men around him, rose to power as proponents of economic reform. A more hostile international environment means higher defence allocations, less investment in the civilian economy, and a more limited chance of success in changing the way the Soviet economy is run.

The Soviet defence budget is already estimated to take up to 13–14 per cent of the Soviet gross national product and is a serious burden on the economy. To accelerate growth in defence spending would mean a reallocation of resources from the civilian to the military sector. Gorbachev has already said that he needs a growth rate of at least 4 per cent a year if he is to meet the competing needs of investment, consumption and defence. This is almost twice recent performance.

An escalation in the Soviet defence budget now would be all the greater shock to the economy because it has not been rising fast in recent years. A CIA report to Congress on the topic last year concluded: "There have been two distinct periods in Soviet defence spending since 1965: before 1976, growth in defence spending averaged 4 to 5 per cent per year; after 1976, the rate of increase in spending dropped appreciably to about 2 per cent a year." The fall-off was probably motivated in part by the problems of the economy and the low rate of growth as a whole during the last years of President Brezhnev. But détente, at its peak after the Vladivostok accords in 1974, and the belief that a strategic balance with the US had been attained, also played a part.

Despite the increase in US defence spending since the last years of

President Carter, there has been no parallel jump in Soviet defence allocations, although there have been muffled cries of anguish from senior Soviet military officers. Marshal Nikolai Ogarkov, until late last year Soviet Chief of Staff, was the most eloquent advocate of the Soviet armed forces competing with the USA in introducing expensive high-technology conventional weapons. He argued that "given the quantity and diversity that has been achieved in nuclear missiles", a first strike without retaliation is impossible. The real change in warfare, said Marshal Ogarkov, was in high technology, which was "making it possible to increase sharply, by at least ten times, the strike potential of conventional weapons." Implicit in this analysis of Soviet military needs is higher spending.

Marshal Ogarkov's dismissal at the end of last year, never fully explained, was almost certainly a consequence of this demand for more allocations to match the US military build-up. On the day before his removal, *Pravda* ran an editorial implying that the Soviet leadership had turned down a proposal to cut consumer programmes to strengthen defence: "Despite the current tense international situation, which requires diverting considerable resources to strengthening the security of the country, even thinking about cutting the social programme is inadmissible." On the day of Ogarkov's dismissal, the military newspaper *Red Star* ran the same editorial.

The removal of the Soviet Union's senior professional soldier is the most dramatic outcome of the debate within the leadership on how they should react to US defence expenditure. Overall, however, they seem to have concluded that the USA will find it very difficult to change the present military balance, though it might obtain an edge in some areas such as Star Wars.

The US defence build-up is all the more significant for US–Soviet relations because in other areas President Reagan's confrontational attitudes have not been translated into confrontational policies. In the Third World, China and Western Europe, US competition has not proved noticeably more intense over the past four years than under President Carter or his immediate predecessors. In the regional conflicts in Afghanistan, Angola, Cambodia, Ethiopia and Nicaragua, where President Reagan has accused the Soviets of being the hidden hand behind local wars, there is, apart from Afghanistan, only limited superpower involvement. The most serious defeats for US foreign policy in Iran and Lebanon were not inflicted by the Kremlin. There is nothing today, diplomats point out, on the scale of superpower confrontation in Vietnam and the Middle East in the early 1970s, when détente was supposedly at its height.

Both the extent of US defence spending and the lack of sustained geopolitical confrontation in the Third World and elsewhere in the first half of the 1980s have come as a surprise to the Kremlin. When President Reagan was elected in 1980, the Communist Party Central Committee had a study made, not on whether he would increase defence spending, but by how much the USA could afford to do so.

The Soviet view is somewhat more confident today. Diplomatic dialogue, such as Shultz's mission to Moscow and the impending summit in Geneva, has partly displaced the hardline rhetoric of 1980–83. This is an improvement, but it is doubtful if relations have improved to the point where substantive negotiations will produce significant restraint on the military arsenals of the two sides.

7 November 1985

After the Geneva Summit

Mikhail Gorbachev returns to Moscow this weekend announcing that a sustained political dialogue with the USA has started, but admitting that he has achieved very little narrowing of views, still less agreement, on arms control. Dialogue with the USA is significant, Gorbachev said, "if followed by practical steps". It is the extent of these steps over the next six months which will decide the Soviet attitude to Geneva.

The failure to achieve movement towards banning the US Star Wars programme may have disappointed but will scarcely have surprised Gorbachev and Eduard Shevardnadze. Ever since George Shultz visited Moscow at the beginning of the month, in an abortive bid to narrow differences, it has been evident that the Geneva meeting would contribute little to the control of nuclear arms. None the less, the Soviets are clearly pleased that dialogue with the other superpower has restarted after seven years. The level of rhetoric in the first three years of Reagan's presidency seriously worried the Kremlin to a degree not wholly appreciated outside the Soviet Union.

President Reagan's speech denouncing the Soviet Union as "an evil empire" and an ideological offensive placing Moscow at the centre of American demonology has concerned the Soviet leadership almost as much as the acceleration in the US defence budget. "For us words are deeds," declared Anatoly Dobrynin, Soviet ambassador to Washington at the end of 1983, explaining the strength of Soviet reaction to this verbal assault, even though Washington did little to translate this new militancy into action against the Soviet Union.

Nor do the Soviets see the summit simply as a way of influencing the

view President Reagan and the USA as a whole take of the Soviet
Union. By going to Geneva and giving his lengthy press conference
yesterday, Gorbachev was able to put over the Soviet position on a
range of issues to a world audience—as his predecessors in the Kremlin
have failed to do for twenty years. This exposition of Soviet views leaves
him well placed to heap all the blame on the USA if the present dialogue
goes sour because it is not sustained by active measures of arms control.

Soviet commentary in the weeks before the summit indicates that the
Kremlin suspects that this is quite likely to happen. In recent days
Leonid Zamyatin, chief Soviet spokesman at the conference, has
expounded the virtues of a better atmosphere between the superpowers,
the significance of dialogue, and downplayed the failure to agree on Star
Wars or arms control. But Gorbachev was quick to say yesterday that
the Soviet Union would not fail to keep up with the USA in developing
the technology of nuclear war if compelled to do so. Throughout the
summit Moscow stuck to its position that Star Wars, and President
Reagan's entire defence programme, is aimed at ending military parity
and the political equality based upon it. The fireside chats with President
Reagan seem to have done little to modify the Soviet view that this is the
ultimate American intent.

Nevertheless, some Soviet specialists on relations with the USA argue
that a more amicable relationship between Washington and Moscow will
make Congress less sympathetic than in the past to funding weapons
programmes. In their estimation, Congressional action may be a better
bet for getting Reagan's defence plans cut back than the negotiations on
arms limitation in Geneva which this week's summit is meant to boost.

Gorbachev also feels that an explanation of Soviet policy in the Third
World and on other topics of dispute may diminish popular American
hostility to the Soviet Union. Yesterday, however, he restated the traditional Soviet view that the USA is wrong to accuse the Soviet Union of
fomenting revolutions that would have occurred anyway. If, asked
Gorbachev yesterday, there is a revolution in Mexico or Brazil, "are
people going to say this is the hand of Moscow?"

In Moscow Gorbachev's mission to Geneva is likely to be seen as a
qualified success. His failure to get anywhere on arms control will be
blamed on President Reagan. The demonstration of Gorbachev's ability
to conduct foreign policy will also strengthen his position in carrying out
extensive changes in the leadership in the lead-up to the next Communist Party Congress on 25 February. But Gorbachev will probably tell the
Congress, going by the outline of the five-year plan published just before
the summit, that the Soviet Union will maintain its defence allocation.
He will tell Central Committee that competition with the USA will
perhaps be more regulated in future. None the less, for Moscow the

arms race remains at the centre of this rivalry and is likely to continue unabated.

22 November 1985

Reykjavik Summit

Mikhail Gorbachev flew from Reykjavik to Moscow yesterday, disappointed at the outcome of the Iceland talks but having won clear political advantages over President Reagan. He is unlikely to face much dissension or criticism from Soviet leaders who stayed at home. He can say that the Soviet Union has done everything possible to achieve an agreement on the reduction of nuclear arsenals—indeed, by early Sunday morning had largely done so—but was frustrated by President Reagan's insistence on developing and testing the Strategic Defence Initiative. Gorbachev therefore holds the political high ground at home and abroad, but this will not be seen in Moscow as sufficient compensation for the failure at Reykjavik.

The Soviet Union has long wanted to find out if, at the end of the day, a right-wing US administration like that of President Reagan would make long-term agreements with it. In spite of all the negotiations since Reagan came to office in 1981 the answer to this question had remained unclear up to the two-day meeting in Iceland. Moscow may now feel that it knows the answer.

Gorbachev spelled this out at his press conference immediately after leaving President Reagan. He said he was not worried by Star Wars because he thought the USA could never create an effective anti-ballistic missile system to defend America against Soviet warheads. "I said to the President we are not concerned with the military threat of SDI," he said. On the contrary, the Soviet leader stressed that the true "danger of SDI is political" because it creates "an atmosphere of suspicion and distrust".

Serious questions immediately arise:

• *How far does the failure to achieve a more stable and controlled relationship with the USA damage the Soviet Union?*

The immediate economic benefits of even a high degree of nuclear disarmament can be exaggerated. Nuclear weapons are cheap compared with tank armies and conventional weapons. An end to the nuclear arms race would take time to translate into reduced Soviet military spending, and a major transfer of resources from the military to the civilian sectors of the economy.

In broader terms, however, there is a very real, though more subtle, connection between Gorbachev's desire to restructure Soviet politics and the management of the economy. To dismantle what is in effect a siege economy and the semi-military command structure and total authority of the Communist Party would be easier if the Soviet Union's relations with the outside world in general, but the USA in particular, were to improve.

• *Is there a danger for Gorbachev that other Soviet leaders and officials will see the concessions he offered in Reykjavik as a sign of weakness?*

No doubt that accusation will be made privately, but it is unlikely to carry much weight. Gorbachev is good at explaining his policies on television at home and abroad, and he is likely to carry conviction. Most Russians will believe he tried and failed, but blame the USA. Marshal Sergei Akhromeyev, the Soviet Chief of Staff, actually headed the arms control working group which agreed on the radical weapons cuts in the early hours of last Sunday morning. The Soviet military cannot complain that they were stabbed in the back.

Most ominously, the failure at Reykjavik appears to have left open the issue of the size of the Soviet delegation at the UN. If the USA goes ahead and expels twenty-five Soviet diplomats from the USA as it has said it will, then Moscow is probably in the mood to retaliate harshly to show that conciliation in Iceland does not mean it has become soft.

Yet Gorbachev has clearly gained advantages at Reykjavik which put him in a much stronger position tactically than Reagan. As a gloomy-looking George Shultz announced the talks' failure on Sunday night, the Soviet gains were immediately obvious. Enormous international attention will be focused on SDI which, Gorbachev says, was the cause of failure. Previously the Soviet Union could claim only that Star Wars frustrated its offer of weapons cuts. After Reykjavik it can point to actual agreements frustrated by SDI.

• *How will Soviet propaganda after Reykjavik seek to sustain and enhance these advantages?*

Gorbachev is too clever to beat the drum too hard when it comes to trying to influence US public and Congressional opinion against President Reagan's position at Reykjavik. He is likely to let the near-agreements at Reykjavik speak for him and wait upon events. It is unlikely that all the Soviet propaganda machine will behave with the same subtlety. "Repetition is the mother of learning," is a Russian saying which has been the rule for many Soviet writers on foreign affairs.

Although Gorbachev concluded his speech on Sunday with a few upbeat notes on US–Soviet relations, there is a serious danger that they will now deteriorate. The gloom of the senior Soviet officials on Sunday night as they heard the news of failure is not difficult to understand. They appeared to have decided—to reverse Mrs Thatcher's phrase—that Washington under President Reagan is not prepared to do business with Moscow.

14 October 1986

Stability between the Superpowers

The best reason for optimism over a US–Soviet agreement on the abolition of medium- and short-range nuclear missiles in Europe, followed by a second period of détente, is the extraordinary stability of the balance of power between Moscow and Washington in the 1980s. In the four main areas of superpower competition—the Third World, China, Western Europe and strategic arms—the relative strength of the two sides has shown no significant change over the past six years.

Compare the situation now with 1972, when President Nixon began the first period of détente by agreeing the first Strategic Arms Limitation Treaty (SALT 1) in Moscow. He did so at a time when the USA and USSR backed different sides in a major war in Vietnam and Cambodia and an intermittent war between Israel and the Arabs. In contrast, interruptions to US–Soviet dialogue over the last three years have come not from wars, or even Afghanistan, but from comic opera spy scandals.

President Reagan's contention is that the balance with the Soviet Union is so steady because of his administration's untiring vigilance and high defence budgets—the new dialogue is never to be confused with the old détente, which served as a smokescreen for the betrayal of US interests. In fact the Reagan administration has drifted into dialogue with Moscow since 1983 in unwilling recognition that a confrontational attitude towards the Soviet Union was extremely difficult to translate into an effectively confrontational policy. The only exception to this is Afghanistan.

The White House discovered that international relations had gelled. The first period of US–Soviet détente was based on two major developments: by the late 1960s the USSR had built enough intercontinental missiles capable of hitting America to achieve nuclear parity with the USA; at the same time détente in Europe was ushered in by settlement of Soviet and Polish territorial disputes with West Germany. But détente in the 1970s scarcely touched the two other key areas of superpower competition: the Third World and China. Washington feared and Moscow hoped that a series of successful revolutions in Africa and the Far East was the wave of the future. After the Chinese invasion of Vietnam in 1979 the Kremlin was always nervous that good relations between China and the USA would turn into a military alliance aimed at the USSR.

The present lack of friction between the two superpowers shows that the original basis for détente was sound: increased US defence spending since 1977 has not changed the military balance, and détente in Central Europe never really ended. In addition China has, for the moment, chosen the political distance it wants to keep from Washington and Moscow and has never become as close an ally of the USA as the Soviet Union feared. Revolutions supported by the Soviet Union in the Third World look in retrospect more like the final consequences of the collapse of the European colonial empires than of a new revolutionary upsurge.

The build-up of US conventional forces under Carter and Reagan has not significantly increased American capability for intervention in the Third World. The Iraqi missile attack on a US frigate in the Gulf, like the massacre of the US marines in Beirut in 1983, shows that in a world in which quite small states deploy strong and heavily equipped armies, superpower intervention is a costly and often fruitless business.

All this became evident in the first three years of the Reagan administration. The absurdities of Irangate are a measure of the frustration in the White House that America's inability to rescue hostages in the hands of Iran or its allies was as great in 1985–86 as it had been under President Carter in 1979–80. At that time President Reagan and his supporters had blamed poor leadership and enfeebled armies.

Relations between Washington and Moscow will always be a mixture of competition and dialogue, but the distance President Reagan has travelled towards the latter since 1980 is largely an accommodation to a world in which both superpowers are finding it difficult to compete with much hope of making political gains.

29 May 1987

Military Influence on the Wane in the Kremlin

Mikhail Gorbachev's willingness to contemplate radical cuts in the Soviet nuclear forces and the extended unilateral test ban which ended last month are both strong evidence that the influence of the Soviet military is on the wane in the Kremlin.

The new leadership sees its relationship with America and its allies in predominantly political terms. Despite the growth in US defence budgets under President Reagan, it regards the military parity it has achieved as solid. This basic confidence in the stability of the military balance between the superpowers underlies the more flexible Soviet approach to arms control over the past two years. Gorbachev shares the view of Georgi Arbatov, expressed in the mid seventies, that "military force has become all the more difficult to translate into political influence".

Today Gorbachev takes care to stress that high US defence budgets are an attempt to spend the USSR into bankruptcy or to sabotage economic reform. Last month he told the trade-union congress in Moscow that the Soviet Union would do enough to defend itself, "but we shall not take a single step over and above the demands and requirements of sensible sufficient defence."

Gorbachev's emphasis on the political rather than the military constituents of the balance of power with the USA has been accompanied by two other changes which have reduced the institutional clout of the Soviet military. Most important is the shift of control over foreign and security policy away from the military and towards the Communist Party secretariat. The appointment of Anatoly Dobrynin, for twenty-four years ambassador to Washington, to be Party Secretary in charge of foreign policy in 1986 means that the military has less say in determining the degree of threat the USSR faces from the US or anybody else.

Secondly, the election of Gorbachev as Communist Party General Secretary saw the passing of a generation of Soviet leaders who made their reputations in the Second World War and whose view of world politics was more militarised than that of their successors.

Gorbachev has also changed some of the older commanders—Naval Commander Admiral Sergei Gorshkov and General Aleei Yepishev, in effect the army's Chief Commissar. "Not all our commanders, political instructors and staff officers have fully realised the essence of reconstruction, defined their role and position in it, understood that it is necessary to begin with themselves," Marshal Sergei Sokolov, the Defence Minister and a non-voting member of the Politburo, said last month.

Certainly Marshal Sergei Akhromeyev, the Chief of Staff who succeeded Marshal Ogarkov, has publicly committed himself to all Gorbachev's disarmament initiatives. At the summit with President Reagan in Reykjavik he headed the working group which detailed the package of nuclear arms cuts, including the agreement on medium-range nuclear missiles now to be negotiated separately.

There is no sign, however, that the reduced political leverage of the armed forces has meant that they have a smaller share in the allocation of resources. US experts put Soviet military spending at between 13 and 15 per cent of gross national product, and there is no sign of a reduction.

An overall thaw in relations with the USA would ultimately allow the transfer of Soviet resources from the military to the civilian side, but in the short term a cut in medium-range or strategic nuclear weapons would have very little economic payoff for the Kremlin. Nuclear arsenals are cheap compared with high-technology conventional weapons. Gorbachev knows that a cutback on defence needs in this expensive area would significantly boost his plans for economic restructuring.

An assessment by the US Central Intelligence Agency and Defence Intelligence Agency last year concluded that as a result of investment in the defence industry, "almost all of the production capacity required to support Soviet force modernisation over the next six years or so is already in place."

No doubt the armed forces will fight hard to maintain their share of Soviet resources, but they have a vested interest in the success of Gorbachev's efforts to modernise economic management and raise the technical level of industry. It is this which ultimately determines the ability of the Soviet Union to maintain conventional military parity with the USA.

13 March 1987

Air Defence Flaws

The dismissal of Marshal Alexander Koldunov, chief of the Soviet Air Defence, by the ruling Politburo last Saturday for his failure to prevent a light aircraft flying across the Soviet Union from Finland and landing in Moscow's Red Square is only the latest embarrassing episode in the history of the organisation he headed. Marshal Koldunov was appointed nine years ago in circumstances similar to last week's fiasco. In April 1978 a Korean airliner, lost on a flight from Paris to Alaska, flew deep into Soviet airspace over key naval installations around Murmansk for a hour before it was forced down by fighters.

The incident was regarded as particularly humiliating because Soviet Air Defence (known by its Russian initials as PVO) deploys vast resources including 630,000 troops, 2,250 interceptor and reconnaissance aircraft, 9,000 anti-aircraft guns and 10,000 SAM missiles. Given that the cost of all this is 12 per cent of the Soviet defence budget, according to the CIA, it is not surprising that Gorbachev and the Politburo are so angry at the latest failure of Marshal Koldunov's men.

Irritation is all the greater since it was a PVO interceptor which shot down the Korean airliner KAL 007 after it had strayed off course into Soviet airspace on 1 September 1983. Soviet Air Defence had evidently mistaken the plane for a US reconnaissance aircraft. All 269 passengers on the aircraft died in the incident. The PVO may have been shielded from some of the blame for KAL 007 because Soviet military and political leaders were convinced that the aircraft's intrusion was deliberate.

Discounting the possibility of error by Soviet radar operators, Marshal Sergei Sokolov—who also retired last Saturday—and Marshal Koldunov remained convinced that they were victims of a US conspiracy.

There was no such excuse last week. The Hamburg Flying Club light aircraft piloted by nineteen-year-old Mathias Rust was seen by Soviet radar as it approached Soviet airspace and Soviet fighters flew around it twice, according to the angry Politburo communiqué. "At the same time, the political bureau pointed out that the aircraft defence forces command had shown intolerable unconcern and indecision about cutting short the flight of the violator plane without resorting to combat means," the statement says. It does not explain how this can be done without shooting the aircraft down.

In fact, the PVO has an impossible task. It is blamed for both failing and succeeding to intercept intruding aircraft. Established in 1948 as a separate branch of the armed forces, Soviet Air Defence was originally geared to stopping US bombers carrying nuclear weapons from reaching their targets. Its only real success, however, came in 1960 when it succeeded in shooting down an American U-2 spyplane piloted by Francis Gary Powers over Soviet territory.

Current Soviet military and political doctrine is to stress that defence is impossible against nuclear attack because of the destructive power of nuclear warheads and the diverse means of delivering them. The fact that the truth of this thesis was neatly, if humiliatingly, demonstrated by Rust's landing in Red Square has clearly not been appreciated by the Politburo.

The speed of the dismissal of Marshal Koldunov and the retirement of Marshal Sokolov is very much in keeping with the style of Gorbachev's leadership. Top officials are now held accountable for success or failure, in contrast to Brezhnev's years in power, when lower-ranking officials usually paid the penalty for fiascos such as last week's.

Overall, the input of the military into Soviet security policy has diminished since Gorbachev came to power. It is now very much in the hands of Gorbachev himself, Eduard Shevardnadze, and Anatoly Dobrynin. At the same time, Gorbachev has always said that his policy of offering concessions to the USA on nuclear weapons would never be pursued to the point where it compromised Soviet security.

By landing his aircraft in Red Square, Rust may well have handed ammunition to Soviet generals and party leaders who argue that the defence of Soviet territory has slackened. Given that ordinary Soviet citizens tend to be paranoid about any intrusion across the frontiers of the USSR, this could be used as a powerful argument against Gorbachev, particularly if his disarmament initiative fails. For the moment, however, he has demonstrated that he is very much in control.

1 June 1987

A Tactical Retreat

For a few days after Mathias Rust had landed his single-engined Cessna light aircraft in Red Square, Soviet officials were inclined to treat the affair as something of a joke. It was only after the Politburo retired Marshal Sergei Sokolov and sacked Marshal Alexander Koldunov did Soviet spokesmen begin to treat the affair as a grave threat to Soviet security.

The vigour of the Kremlin's response can be only partly explained by outrage at another failure by Soviet Air Defence. The real reason for taking Rust's escapade so seriously is that it provided an excuse to reorganise the Soviet High Command.

Marshal Sokolov, seventy-five and part of the military leadership in Moscow since 1965, was very much of the pattern of elderly senior officials inherited from the Brezhnev era, whom Gorbachev has been replacing wherever possible. Marshal Koldunov, the other casualty of the debacle, may already have had a mark against him as head of Soviet Air Defence in 1983, when one of its planes shot down the Korean airliner KAL 007.

To drive home the message that top officials, including members of the Politburo, are accountable for failure, Tass even reported approvingly an interview given by Zbigniew Brzezinski, former National Security Adviser to President Carter and long among the Kremlin's least favourite people. It quoted him as saying: "The Soviets have done what the American High Command and political leadership has not had the guts to do—namely, fire the top military men when there is a significant setback."

Nor was the departure of the two marshals the end of the affair. Recently, *Krasnaya Zvezda* said that the same deficiencies in organisation and competence exposed in air defence were also to be found in the fleet and ground forces. "We cannot take one step forward if we do not learn to work in a new way to overcome stagnation and conservatism in all their forms," the newspaper warned.

Exactly what perestroika means for the Soviet High Command and the 3.7 million servicemen is unclear, but it is evident that the position of the armed forces as an institution in Soviet politics and society has changed over the past two years. It now has less influence on Soviet security policy and foreign policy. It also looks less well placed to urge the claims of weapons procurement against investment in the civilian sector. Greater concentration of policy-making at the centre, in the Politburo and the party secretariat has been the trend in all branches of government under Gorbachev.

On coming to power in 1985, Gorbachev inherited policies in which the armed forces were playing a reduced role. The military intervention in Afghanistan in 1987, under the overall command of Marshal Sokolov, had become a running sore. The army could claim that the politicians had got them into the mess, but the failure of the 115,000-strong contingent to crush the anti-government guerrillas did not increase the military's prestige in its first prolonged conflict since 1945. In Afghanistan and other regional struggles Gorbachev's instinct has been to do enough militarily to hold the line, while looking for political success. Thus the government ceasefire in Afghanistan, inspired by Moscow, strengthens Kabul's political position, though it is doubtful whether it will do much to end the war.

It is also significant that the expansion of the Soviet warm-water navy has slowed. This does not mean that the USSR under Gorbachev is less interested in its influence in the Third World, but that its approach is more political.

This change is not confined to the top. The Soviet army plays a much larger role in the life of Soviet citizens than it does in the USA or Britain, primarily because all Soviets are liable to be conscripted into the armed forces for two years (three if it is the navy or border guards). However, dislike of the draft is increasing. At a discussion organised by *Literaturnaya Gazeta*, one scientist described it as "stupid and shortsighted" and other scholars asked: "Whom does our society need more—soldiers or young scientists?"

The question has become all the more relevant because students are no longer exempt from the draft. Before the 1980s, the majority automatically became non-commissioned lieutenants on graduation and never had to serve. But the fall in the birth rate—and accusations that the elite were dodging service in Afghanistan—put paid to this. A more traditional view of military service has been put by General M. Gareev, deputy chief of the armed forces' general headquarters. Writing in the same newspaper, he complains of certain scholars expressing "a negative attitude not only to conscription for students, but to service in the armed forces in general".

The armed forces are unhappy about some aspects of their position in Soviet society and about losing influence over policy formation, but this alone would not be enough to provoke a backlash against Gorbachev. For a start, the Soviet military, as a separate institution, has less leverage in the Kremlin than the Pentagon has in the White House. After 1917, the early Bolsheviks feared the rise of a Napoleon figure at the head of the army. The fact that the Communist Party is organised under military discipline ironically gives the military a less distinct identity. This does not mean that an armed forces revolt is not feasible, but that it would have real force only in support of a much bigger backlash, probably on economic issues, against Gorbachev by a majority of the Politburo and the Central Committee. There is no sign of this happening.

Nevertheless, there are rumblings in the party and military leadership that concessions on arms are interpreted in Washington as evidence of weakness, and that all Gorbachev's initiatives have yet to produce anything. None of this looks very serious because although there have been no great successes, there has been no great disaster. A successful summit in Washington later this year would be taken by the leadership in Moscow as proof of parity with the USA which they feel eluded them during the first period of détente between 1972 and 1977.

In the long term, an easing of the defence burden on the Soviet economy is essential if Gorbachev is to produce the desired surge in growth. Earlier this year, he said the Soviet Union would spend only enough to ensure "sensible sufficient defence". The dismissal of the two marshals for failure to stop Rust shows that the armed forces are expected to provide this defence—but through better organisation rather than a larger share of Soviet resources.

16 June 1987

Moscow and the Burden of the Arms Race

Is the Soviet economy in such bad shape that it can no longer afford the cost of competition with the US? Alternatively will the strain of high defence budgets force the US to play a diminished role in the world? Both arguments, advanced over the last year as motives for Moscow and Washington seeking renewed détente, miss the point that the capacity of either superpower to intervene in the world is going down, almost regardless of how much they spend on defence. The real change in international politics is that Third World nations are much stronger today than they were in the thirty years after 1945. States are no longer as vulnerable to outside interference as when newly established in the aftermath of the collapse of the European empires.

Up to the mid seventies, revolutions and coups provided numerous opportunities for superpower intervention. In 1969 alone, the Arab world saw coups which changed the governments of Iraq, Libya and Sudan. The fragility of newly emergent states created friction between Moscow and Washington as both sought to fill the temporary power vacuum left by the departing Europeans. This is no longer true. A characteristic of President Reagan's time in office is that the political reverberations of the collapse of the European empires are dying away. World politics have become much less fluid. US and Soviet leaders can now sit down and discuss regional conflicts in the Kremlin because new friction points are not developing as they used to do. Contrast this with the first period of détente under Nixon and Brezhnev, which took place against a background of hot wars between US and Soviet allies in the Middle East and South East Asia. Détente itself was in part undermined by the collapse in 1974 of the last European empire, that of Portugal, leading to a scramble for its former colonies of Angola and Mozambique.

By the 1980s states which emerged after the Second World War had developed powerful state machinery and armies. Outside intervention—be it of the Soviet army in Afghanistan or the US marines in Beirut—involves greater risks than it did before, and more expenditure on defence by either the US or the Soviet Union is not going to change this. Suppose, for instance, that the US had doubled the number of its warplanes, naval vessels and marines in and around Lebanon in 1982–84; or the Soviets had stationed twice as many troops as they did in Afghanistan—would there really have been any change in the outcome of either conflict? The real lesson of the last ten years is that in a less pliable world, increased military spending does not translate into greater political power in the way that it once did. This is an important conclusion because it makes largely irrelevant the current debates on whether the US and Soviet economies can any longer support their defence needs.

Given the smaller size of the Soviet economy, the arms race has always imposed more of a burden on Moscow than on Washington. Hence the argument that the US should now exploit its economic weakness to extract maximum concessions in foreign policy and other areas. The weakness of this approach is that it is doubtful if the Kremlin was getting its money's worth and Gorbachev's government knows this. The programme approved by the Communist Party's ruling Central Committee last month accuses the old leadership of allowing itself to be drawn into an arms race with the US which, once basic parity in intercontinental ballistic missiles was achieved, produced few political dividends. In other words, if the Soviet leadership believes that resources allocated to the military have produced a diminishing return in terms of security and political influence abroad, it has the additional option of unilaterally cutting its defence allocations during the next five-year plan.

A somewhat similar argument about the decreasing ability of the US economy to sustain its defence burden, recently popularised in *The Rise and Fall of Great Powers* by Professor Paul Kennedy, suffers from the same fallacy. By suggesting that the US may be unable to afford its military role in the world, it avoids the question of whether increased US defence budgets over the past decade brought any real increment in US security.

Intervention in almost any regional conflict by the superpowers today means they will face well-equipped armies capable of inflicting heavy casualties, and this puts up the domestic political costs of using or threatening to use force. As the world enters the 1990s the trend is not that defence is becoming too expensive but that it buys less and less political influence.

20 June 1988

PART VII

Afterword

Unusual Flowers

Soon after Mikhail Gorbachev came to power in 1983 a procession of editors and politicians began to arrive in Moscow to take the political pulse of the Soviet Union. Resident diplomats and journalists laboriously arranged for them to interview newly accessible Soviet officials, intellectuals and journalists about the prospects for reform. It was often a dispiriting experience. Few visitors knew enough about how the Soviet Union had worked of old under Brezhnev to distinguish what was new under Gorbachev. What makes the Soviet Union tick is obviously a complicated question and one not easily answered by a week of interviews conducted by visitors on edge because they fear some subtle entrapment by the KGB or, more simply, suspicious that they may be lured into premature celebration of change by plausible Soviets. The politicians, less knowledgeable about the Soviet Union than the professional pundits but by the same token less encumbered by the traditions of Kremlinology, were often the quickest to spot that something fundamental was changing in the way the Soviet Union ran its affairs. But, whatever their political instincts told them, they were nervous of giving too ringing an endorsement of Gorbachev which might make them vulnerable to charges of naïveté.

The result of such visits by senior journalists was usually a series of carefully hedged newspaper articles of the "continuity in the midst of change" type, in which the author backs all horses both ways. It also became evident during the four years I spent in Moscow that visitors were often influenced less by the interviews arranged with such trouble by the resident correspondent than by the state of the hotel in which they were staying and the restaurants where they ate. Residents of the comfortable National Hotel opposite Red Square tended to be noticeably more optimistic about Gorbachev's chances than people staying in the rather drab Intourist Hotel round the corner in Gorki Street; they, in turn, were that little bit more hopeful than visitors compelled to stay at the nearby Moskva Hotel built by Stalin in the 1930s. Lack of a bath plug, or a drunken waiter, makes more impact on the mind than complicated and contradictory interviews.

213

Study of visiting journalists, academics and politicians also showed that they were vulnerable to two other fallacies: an exaggerated belief that some small incident is indicative of the general state of the Soviet Union, and the conviction on the part of the visitor that he or she had just spotted some neat and comforting parallel with Western experience. A good example of the latter fallacy comes in an article written by Karen Elliott House, foreign editor of the *Wall Street Journal*, entitled "Moscow Innovations have Shallow Roots" and published in the *Journal* on 6 October 1988, in which she describes how "surveying a boisterous group of Russians and Americans downing vodka and debating a dozen different topics, one could easily mistake the scene for a New York arts and society gathering." This, mind you, is House's example of beneficial change under Gorbachev. It carries the implication that if a Russian journalist on a brief trip to the USA wanted to put his finger on the pulse of America, she would point him towards a New York arts and society gathering as the place to do it. Also commended are "small 'enterprise' restaurants where attentive service and broad menus make dining a pleasure", but the author adds warily that these are "unusual flowers" and may not survive outside the hothouse. The use of horticultural analogies, of which there are no fewer than seven (not counting the title) in House's piece, are a danger signal quickly recognised by students of the "continuity in the midst of change" style. They are favoured because they enable one to use terms such as "seeds of change" and "shallow roots", which sound concrete but commit the writer to nothing.

It is in—or, rather, just outside—a restaurant that a significant incident occurs illustrative of the tension between progress and reaction. House tells how Vitali Korotich, editor of the weekly magazine *Ogonyok* and the "very model of Mr Gorbachev's new free-thinking Soviet man, arrives to meet Westerners for lunch at the Riviera, a new French restaurant aboard a boat in the Moscow River." Korotich, "an urbane, outspoken disciple of glasnost and perestroika, is recently back from an overseas trip and is about to fly off to Brazil on another." He arrives at the boat early, five minutes before his foreign hosts, and this is the cause of the significant incident. Because the Riviera accepts payment only in hard currency, which Soviet citizens cannot legally possess, a militiaman orders him down the gangplank and off the boat. This, concludes House, shows that "the openness called glasnost, which blossoms in diplomatic circles and drawing rooms, hasn't put down the kind of roots that extend into Moscow's daily life", and possibly she is right. But hard currency restaurants are only a little bit more common in the Soviet Union than Buddhist monasteries in the USA, and it would be difficult to think of an example less typical of Moscow daily life than

Korotich's ejection from the Riviera, where a meal for two, including wine, costs about $120. (Ironically, there is a significant episode in the House article which the writer mentions without fully realising its importance. This is the tendency of Korotich and other perestroika supporters to spend time in Brazil and elsewhere on the international conference circuit, a habit which may ultimately create something of a reaction in Moscow as they themselves become as out of touch with daily life as their foreign visitors.)

The Karen Elliott House piece is useful because in the space of 1,500 words it contains so many of the misconceptions current in the mid 1980s about what was happening in the Soviet Union. Its conclusions are the polar opposite of those expressed in this book. House assumes that change is superficial and largely confined to the elite—implying that in the cities, towns and villages outside central Moscow, little has happened or will happen. The essays and articles I wrote between 1985 and 1989 assume, on the contrary, that within the Soviet state and society there was a confused but overwhelming propensity for change. This does not mean that Gorbachev was inevitable—any more than Stalin was half a century earlier—but that in the 1980s the Soviet Union was likely to become more free, just as in the 1920s the trend was in the opposite and more authoritarian direction. Both Stalin and Gorbachev represented the trend of the moment, but the extraordinary personalities of the two general secretaries ensured that each trend took a far more radical line than had been predicted even by those who forecast its general direction.

At the heart of Gorbachev's political strategy is a recognition that Soviet society is in a state of flux. The party can no longer act as a Praetorian Guard, and must try to channel and direct changes which it cannot hope to obstruct. To understand this puts a different political complexion on the principal crises of Gorbachev's years in power. At the time the nuclear disaster at Chernobyl in 1986 or the miners' strike in Siberia and the Ukraine in 1989 looked like serious crises or, at best, setbacks for perestroika. In fact Gorbachev was extraordinarily successful in seeing the creative potential in both conflicts. He used Chernobyl to discredit the secrecy which had previously prevented Soviet people from knowing about major disasters, and he used the miners' strike to speed up local elections and recognise unofficial strike committees. A recurrent pattern in Soviet politics after 1985 has been Gorbachev's tactical agility and daring in turning apparent setbacks to his own advantage.

This does not mean, of course, that the triumph of Gorbachev and perestroika is somehow preordained. Sectarian warfare and massacres in the Caucasus and Central Asia over the last two years show how difficult it is to ride the tiger. Conservatives in Moscow and in the local party hierarchy can convincingly argue that if Gorbachev had left well alone then none of this would have happened. By undermining local party and state authority he failed to increase the popularity of the government in Moscow and provoked an explosion of popular grievances. Gorbachev himself was clearly surprised at what was coming to the surface. After the killings in Armenia and Azerbaijan in the first half of 1988 he told the Supreme Soviet: "These are not just machine-gun bursts, but complete artillery salvoes from the past." Despite Gorbachev's tactical flair he has so far failed to resolve crises in two key areas: economic management and ethnic relations. Nor is there much time left. Alexander Yakovlev, Gorbachev's principal ally in the Politburo, said almost a year ago: "We probably have no more than two or three years to prove that socialism as formulated by Lenin can work." Otherwise he predicted the triumph of a vengeful conservative reaction.

The visit of Karen Elliott House in October 1988 was probably the last occasion that a foreign observer in Moscow could claim to see little moving in the petrified political landscape of the Soviet Union. On the contrary, the most striking feature of Soviet politics over the next twelve months was the pace of change. Gorbachev succeeded Andrei Gromyko as President at the end of 1988. The election of the Congress of People's Deputies on 26 April 1989 saw the defeat of members of the party apparatus and, above all, of the party leadership in Moscow and Leningrad, the two largest industrial regions in the country, and the heart of the Bolshevik revolution in 1917. Boris Yeltsin, sacked as head of the Moscow party in 1987, got 89 per cent of the vote in the capital. In Leningrad Yuri Solovev, long a senior member of the party apparatus in the city, failed to win enough votes to become a deputy. He had always been a famously remote figure with no known views on anything. At current affairs meetings in the city, officially organised but fairly free, it had become a standing joke to ask speakers about the attitude to recent events in the Soviet Union of somewhat obscure foreign leaders and of the Leningrad Party Secretary. Thus a member of the audience would ask: "What is the attitude to perestroika of the Prime Minister of Denmark, the President of Togo and the Communist Party Secretary for Leningrad?" A month after the elections Gorbachev persuaded 98 members and candidate members of the Central Committee, all of whom had lost the party and state posts which had originally earned them membership of the committee, to resign. This was an important victory for radicals in the party. Previously, men like Grigorii Romanov, former boss of Leningrad, who was dropped from the Politburo in 1985, had still retained their position on the committee, although their political careers had ended in all other respects. Now Gorbachev had a committee more to his liking and, by the summer of 1989, it was in any case becoming doubtful that a conservative majority against him on the Politburo and Central Committee could defeat him as he established another power base in the State Presidency and the newly elected Supreme Soviet.

The elections strengthened Gorbachev, but they also revealed something worrying for the party radicals. Were party conservatives defeated simply because they were in the party? Boris Kagarlitsky, an acute observer of the elections, said: "I don't see defeat for the conservatives as such—a lot of party functionaries were defeated, but they were not defeated because they are conservatives, but because they belong to the apparatus." As an example of this he cited the defeat of Bryachikhin, one of the most liberal of the Moscow party, who had allowed left-wing clubs to operate in his district. People were voting against almost any kind of official. Under Brezhnev the party had become an administrative apparatus: Gorbachev and Yakovlev want to transform this into a democratic party able to win votes in a free election. But this presupposes that the party has a base of popular support on which they can build. The April elections put this in doubt.

Gorbachev himself remains extremely popular. Moscow intellectuals often suggested that enthusiasm for perestroika was largely confined to themselves, but the success of Gorbachev's appeal to coalminers to end their 1989 strike showed his influence among the Russian working class. In the April election for the Congress intellectuals like Yuri Afanasyev the historian, who had sometimes doubted the depth of support for perestroika, were nevertheless elected for a working-class constituency. Gorbachev's personal popularity did not, however, seem to benefit the party, which was having enormous difficulty in shifting from being an instrument of coercion to one of persuasion. Is such a transformation in fact possible? In Poland, the victory of Solidarity in the elections on 4 June 1989 showed that the Polish Communist Party had almost no popular support. And what, in any case, would this new party, Gorbachevian rather than Leninist, look like? Lenin built the party as a disciplined body of cadres; professional revolutionaries organised along military lines. During the revolution it may have had mass support but it was never a mass movement. Authority flowed from the top. Khrushchev had shaken up the system by firing and reorganising officials and, in reaction, Brezhnev had instituted his policy of "kindness to cadres", whereby top officials in the bureaucracy were seldom moved. Now Gorbachev was asking the men who ran the party apparatus to acquire political skills which they had never previously had to exercise.

A politically animate party is also vital if Gorbachev is to succeed in containing the nationalist movements of 1988–89. In the Baltic states of Estonia, Latvia and Lithuania the fiftieth anniversary of the Hitler–Stalin pact was celebrated by demonstrations in favour of independence. "Stalinism and Hitlerism destroyed independent states by secret deals", a commission of the Lithuanian parliament announced in August 1989. "The independence of many of these states has been restored, but Lithuania, Latvia and Estonia still have not reacquired their independence." At the same time, in the Caucasian republic of Azerbaijan 80,000 protestors demonstrated in the central square of the capital Baku to demand greater autonomy, the recall of their deputies, considered unrepresentative, from the Soviet parliament and the settlement of the dispute with Armenia over the future of Nagorno-Karabakh in their favour. These demands were echoed in the other fourteen non-Russian republics, creating anxiety among the 50 million Soviets who live outside their home republic. In Estonia the large Russian minority went on strike to protest against an attempt by the local parliament to disenfranchise some immigrants by denying them the vote until they had been resident for two years.

The response in Moscow to demands for autonomy or even self-determination has been low key. Where the government has tried repression—as when soldiers killed some twenty people in Tblisi, the capital of Georgia, during a demonstration on 8 April 1989—the results have been disastrous. Obviously the balance of power between the nationalities is shifting. The republics and autonomous republics will get greater financial and economic independence. Promotion within the republics will increasingly require a knowledge of the local language (making bilingualism in Russian and the local language obligatory for all jobs is probably not feasible). Above all, Gorbachev needs to give the local elite access to power in Moscow. Under Brezhnev, powerful local party leaders like Dinmukhamed Kunaev of Kazakhstan, Sharif Rashidov of Uzbekistan and Vladimir Shcherbitsky of the Ukraine were long-time members or candidate members of the Politburo. Accused of corruption and other crimes, few of these regional party barons, with the exception of Shcherbitsky, survived long under Gorbachev—with the result that local party and state leaders can only exercise influence within the confines of their own republic. Gorbachev therefore needs not only to devolve authority downwards to the republics, autonomous republics and districts but to give the non-Russian nationalities greater access to power in Moscow.

Do the nationalist movements in the Baltic, Caucasus and elsewhere threaten the break-up of the Soviet Union? Could they provoke a conservative backlash in Moscow which would tip the Central Committee and the revivified Soviet parliament towards repression? Moscow is clearly worried. A statement from the Central Committee read on the news of 26 August 1989 warned people in the Baltic states not to over-step the mark in pressing nationalist demands. It warned of "the real threat in some places of a true civil conflict, with mass clashes in the streets". Nor were the Baltic, Caucasus and Central Asia the only areas to see an upsurge in nationalism. As the Central Committee was issuing its warning 300,000 people in Moldavia demonstrated in the capital Kishinev in favour of making Moldavian the republic's official language. Ethnic Russians, who make up 35 per cent of Moldavia's population were already on a one-week strike against any such law. Gorbachev seems to be prepared to grant any degree of autonomy short of self-determination. If this becomes the demand of Estonia, Latvia and Lithuania, Moscow may respond with repression, which it is well able to do in the smaller republics. The balance of power remains very much in favour of the centre so long as demands for independence do not spread to the Slav heartlands of Russia, the Ukraine and Byelorussia where some 70 per cent of the Soviet population lives. In recognition of this, the authorities are noticeably more repressive towards nationalists in the Ukraine, with a population of 50 million, than in Estonia with a popu-lation of only 1.5 million, 40 per cent of whom are not Estonians.

These changes in Soviet ethnic politics are more likely to produce conflict because they take place against a background of deteriorating economic performance. In Moscow and other cities, queues outside the shops lengthen as food supplies diminish. Economic reforms, the broad outlines of which were drawn up in 1987, have stalled ever since. Gor-bachev needs to have sufficient political strength to carry out a radical price reform. This has been the key test of the political acceptability of Communist governments in Eastern Europe. So far, the degree of change brought about in the management of the economy by Gorbachev has, if anything, made the situation worse. In Moscow a more demo-cratic parliament means greater pressure for increased spending, despite the budget deficit. In the provinces, plant and enterprise managers have used their greater authority to raise wages. Since the price of goods has not gone up and the same quantity is being produced, the result is that inflation has been expressed by worse shortages, with more people standing in queues.

In the face of growing disorder in the non-Russian republics and deterioration in the economy, Gorbachev has argued that the least risky course for the party is to pursue a radical policy now. The party can only survive if it transforms itself from an administrative to a truly political organisation. Once this is accomplished, once the party can command a measure of consent, then the present economic and ethnic problems, which look so intractable today, become more soluble. The process has clearly proved much slower than Gorbachev originally hoped, and by giving priority to political change—in contrast to China—he has in practice postponed economic reforms for a dangerously long time. Strikes and demonstrations have become commonplace. The very pace of change seems in danger of overwhelming Gorbachev and the reformers. But they retain certain crucial advantages. Opponents within the party have never produced an alternative programme to Gorbachev's. The defeat of the party apparatus in the April 1989 elections to the Congress of People's Deputies makes it very unlikely they could do so now. A second centre of power has developed. And even the upsurge in nationalist feeling, dangerous though it looks from Moscow, represents a series of crises rather than a single united movement. Yet, amid these extraordinary events, there were observers as late the end of 1988 who saw little of consequence happening in the Soviet Union, only "unusual flowers".

August 1989

Index

Abalkin, Leonid 38, 174, 175, 178, 179
Abuladze, Tenghiz 41
  Repentance 11
Admiral Nakhimov, sinking of 19, 56, 111, 112
Afanasyev, Yuri 217
Afghanistan 26, 30, 45, 46, 47, 48, 72, 88, 89, 93, 114, 196, 201, 207, 208, 209
Agenbegyan, Abel 38, 41, 73, 163, 187, 188
agriculture 46, 52, 84–6, 88, 89, 90, 91, 93, 95, 117, 118, 158–62, 175, 176, 181, 189
Akhromeyev, Sergei 56, 200, 204
Akoyev, Vladimir 172
alcoholism, clampdown on 33, 90, 103, 125–7, 133, 134
Aleyev, Geidar 73, 112
Alma-Ata, unrest in 67, 71, 72, 86, 91, 92, 94, 95
Altai region (Siberia) 184
Andreyeva, Nina, letter purportedly from 33, 36
Andropov, Yuri 3, 4, 29, 35, 52, 90, 103
Angola 48, 196, 209
Arbatov, Georgi 17, 138, 194, 203
armed forces 41, 45, 66, 71, 76, 100, 101, 193, 194, 204, 207
Armenia 27, 43, 49, 65, 66, 69, 72, 73, 75, 76, 77, 90, 100–101, 216, 218
Armenian ethnic group 7, 27, 33, 43, 65, 66
arms race 46, 52, 54, 56, 196, 198, 199, 204, 209–10

atheism 88
autonomy
  financial, of businesses 83, 183, 185
  nationalist demands for 27, 43, 44, 65, 74, 218, 219
Azerbaijan 27, 43, 65, 66, 72, 73, 75, 90, 100, 101, 216, 218

Baikal, Lake 32, 79, 81
Balduyev, V. 79
Baltic Republics 27, 33, 43–4, 49, 65, 66, 70, 74, 75, 76, 90, 145, 167, 175, 218, 219
  see also under specific republics
Baltimore Sun 6
Barayev, A. 85
Baruzhdin, Sergei 121
Beirut 3, 4, 8, 202, 209
Belfast 8
Berlin, status of 48
bilingualism 220
black market 13, 110, 128–9, 132, 167, 169, 173
Bogomyakov, G. 156
Bolsheviks 13, 36, 53, 67, 117, 208
Bonner, Yelena 113
Bovin, Alexander 17, 48, 194
Brezhnev, Leonid 45, 52, 53, 107, 114, 153
  agricultural policy of 86, 158
  death of 3, 25, 34, 36, 50, 68, 90, 94
  and the economy 37, 83, 173, 175, 177
  energy policy of 38, 80, 81, 154, 157
  era of 5, 10, 12, 17, 28, 33, 42,

46, 49, 58, 59, 66, 103, 105,
  113, 128, 213, 216
legacy of 16, 29, 30, 33
military policy of 47, 109, 191,
  195, 209
and nationalities question 70, 71,
  221
old guard appointed by 4, 32, 51,
  73, 91, 92, 106, 115, 206, 217
religious worship permitted by 72
Brodsky, J. 122
Bryukanov, V. 149
Brzezinski, Zbigniew 206–7
Budapest 20
Bulgaria 159
Bukharin, Nikolai 117
bureaucracy 32, 35, 60, 164, 217
Burlatsky, Fyodor 17
Byelorussia 144, 145, 219

Cambodia 196, 201
Canada 17, 82
capitalism 166, 179, 186, 187
car
  industry 129, 170–72, 180
  ownership 90, 99, 163, 167–9
Carter, Jimmy 196, 202, 206
Catholic Church 74
Caucasus 65–9 *passim*, 73, 75, 215,
  219
  see also under specific republics
censorship, relaxing of 16, 32, 70,
  105, 114, 116, 117
Central Asian Republics 68, 69, 71,
  72, 76, 86, 88, 92, 93, 94, 95,
  118, 147, 175, 215, 219
  see also under specific republics
Central Committee 141
  and the arms race 195, 197, 198,
    210
  and demands for change 29, 34,
    57, 58, 59, 106, 153–4
  economic agenda set by 27, 38,
    179, 182–3, 187, 188
  Gorbachev's position in 21, 26,
    28, 30, 31, 41, 53, 55, 185–6,
    208, 216
  and nationalist unrest 219
Central Dentistry Research Institute
  106
Central Intelligence Agency (CIA)
  36, 195, 204, 205

Chebrikov, Konstantin 29, 33, 34
Chechen-Ingush ethnic group 66
Chekhov, Anton, *Uncle Vanya* 122
Chernenko, Konstantin 3, 4, 10, 21,
  29, 35, 40, 47, 50–51, 52, 153
Chernobyl, nuclear disaster at
  14–16, 19, 26, 28, 56, 101, 103,
  107, 108–9, 110, 111, 137–9,
  140, 142, 143–50, 215
China 31, 46, 47, 48, 49, 167, 176,
  181, 196, 201, 202, 220
Churbanov, Yu. 71
CIA *see* Central Intelligence Agency
class struggle 30, 33
Club for Social Initiative 119, 120
clubs, political and social 18, 118–20
Cockburn, C. 9–10
Cold War 11, 22, 47, 48, 191
collectivisation 42, 159–60, 178
Comecon 157
Congress (US) 195, 198, 200
Congress of People's Deputies 198,
  200
Conrad, Joseph, *Under Western
  Eyes* 17
conservatism
  of Central Committee 57, 58, 187
  in cultural unions 117
  in Party 66, 76, 177, 182, 183,
    215
  in Politburo 4, 25, 28–9, 30, 31,
    35, 41, 60, 162, 165, 166
  of Soviet system 21, 33, 36, 42,
    48
consumer demand
  for goods 37, 159, 163, 164, 169,
    174, 175, 179
  for services 166, 167
consumption 46, 53, 106, 156, 157
co-operatives 176–9, 183
corruption 90, 92, 93, 95, 105, 106,
  115, 118, 127–33, 134–6, 182,
  218
Council of Ministers 141
Crimean Tatars 65
Cuba 78
Czechoslovakia 98

Daily Telegraph 9
Daily Worker 9
Daniloff, Nick 13, 19, 55, 56, 108
defence

industry 8, 46, 175
    spending 153, 175, 194, 195,
        196, 197, 203
    see also arms race; détente
Demichev, P. 107
democratic centralism 36, 77, 186
Department for Struggle Against
    Embezzlement of Socialist
    Property and Speculation
    (OBKHSS) 129
détente 14, 25, 46–8, 56, 109, 146,
    194–204, 208, 209
dissident movement 10–11, 32
Dobrynin, Anatoly 38, 56, 197, 203,
    206

East Germany 153, 175, 176
Eastern Europe 26, 27, 165, 185,
    219
economy, Soviet
    and arms race 46, 56, 195, 206,
        210
    command 37, 38
    problems of 26, 27, 28, 35, 37,
        83, 108, 141, 147, 209, 219
    reform of 39, 41, 49, 50–51, 52,
        53, 54, 56. 57, 58, 60, 69,
        151, 153–89, 219
Ecopolis Club 119
Ekonomicheskaya Gazeta 13–14
education 40, 172
    spread of higher 26, 121, 122
environmental concerns 32, 119
Estonia 27, 33, 43–4, 65, 68, 69, 70,
    73, 74, 76, 77, 98, 110, 179, 184,
    218, 219
Ethiopia 196

Federation of Socialist Clubs 120
Financial Times 6, 8, 15
Finland 14, 15, 96, 204
five-year plan 37, 38, 46, 53, 162,
    186, 198
Fomin, N. 149
Foreign Ministry 5, 8, 13, 14, 15, 16,
    19, 20, 33, 56, 110, 139, 144
Foreign Office (British) 13
foreign policy 30, 32, 33, 38, 45–8,
    56, 57, 58, 109, 146, 194–210
Foreign Trade Bank (FTB) 181
Foreign Trade Ministry 134, 135,
    136, 165, 171, 175, 180, 181, 182

France 164
Frolov, Ivan 16
fur trade 96
Fyodorov, Andrei 176
Fyodorov, Pyotr 78

Gapurov, M. 89
Gareev, General M. 208
Gastronom Number One 128, 130,
    131, 132
Gedye, Robin 8–9
Gefter, Mikhail 11–12, 121
Gemayel, Bashir 4, 5
Geneva Summit 51, 53, 194, 195,
    197, 198
Georgia 69, 89–91, 97, 98, 218
Georgian ethnic group 7, 76, 90
German ethnic group 87
Gladky, Ivan 166, 167
glasnost 11, 14, 15, 18, 20, 29, 32,
    44, 45, 59, 69, 70, 73, 76, 77,
    103, 105–11, 114, 118, 120–21,
    136, 214
Glavtorg 131
Glushkov, N. 162, 164, 165, 170,
    187, 188
Gorbachev, Mikhail 5, 13, 16, 17,
    19, 20, 25, 42, 49, 50, 51, 52,
    213, 215
    and agriculture 158–62
    and conservatives 4, 21, 26, 29,
        30, 33, 34, 35, 58
    economic reforms of 27–8, 37–9,
        53, 54, 55, 80, 81, 82, 83, 87,
        91, 98, 99, 140, 141, 147,
        151, 153, 154, 155, 157, 171,
        172, 174, 175, 177, 182–9
    foreign policy of 45, 46, 47, 48,
        54, 56, 57, 142, 191, 194,
        195, 197–201, 203, 207, 208
    and glasnost 11, 14, 18, 59,
        105–9, 111, 114, 115, 117,
        118, 137, 146
    reform of party by 31, 36, 40,
        60–61, 90
    use of media by 41, 121, 122
Gorbachev, Raisa 16, 160
Gorshkov, Sergei 203
Gosagroprom (State Agro-Industrial
    Committee) 161
Gosnab (State Supply Committee)
    38, 163, 178, 182, 184, 186, 188

Gosplan (State Planning
  Organisation) 38, 106, 182, 184,
  185, 187, 188
Graham, Katharine 20
Great Britain 6, 18, 127, 164, 207
Grishin, Viktor 29–30, 31, 51, 71,
  115
Gromyko, Andrei 21, 29, 33, 34,
  38, 51, 53, 109, 216
Grossman, Vasily, *Life and Fate*
  116, 117
Grossu, S. 118

hard currency earnings 37, 47, 158,
  181, 214
health 133–4
  sector salaries 172
Herzen, Alexander 127
Hitler, Adolf 218
House, Karen Elliott 214, 215, 216
Hungary 20, 37, 176, 185

industrialisation 40, 42, 53, 80, 87,
  164, 165
Institute of Economics 38, 174, 178
Institute of State and Law 183
Institute of World Economy and
  International Relations 46
intelligentsia 105, 107, 116, 117,
  119, 120–23
International Atomic Energy Agency
  145
International Herald Tribune 10
Iran 72, 87, 88, 89, 93, 94, 196, 202
Irangate 202
Iraq 182, 202, 209
Islam 67, 72, 75, 88, 89, 92, 94
Israel 201
Italy 135
Ivanov, Vilen 122
Izvestia 41, 84, 106, 112, 115, 122,
  132, 133, 155, 171

Japan 46, 79, 81, 87, 182
journalism
  foreign 3–4, 5, 6, 8, 9, 12, 18–19,
    109, 110, 176, 213–16
  Soviet *see* press, Soviet

Kagarlitsky, Boris 117, 217
Kalashnikov, V.I. 98, 99
Kazakh ethnic group 7, 68, 69, 72,

  87, 91, 92, 93, 94
Kazakhstan 8, 30, 65, 67, 68, 70, 71,
  72, 75, 76, 84–6, 86–7, 91–5,
  143, 218
Kennan Institute for Russian Studies
  (Washington) 25
Kennedy, Paul, *The Rise and Fall of
  Great Powers* 210
Kerblay, B., *Modern Soviet Society*
  163
KGB 4, 5, 6, 18, 29, 34, 41, 108,
  131–2, 213
Khomeini, Ayatollah 72, 88, 179
Khrushchev, Nikita 12, 13, 17, 25,
  26, 28, 40, 41, 48, 50, 85, 86, 92,
  93, 98, 114, 115, 116, 121, 122,
  160, 170, 217
Khudaiberdyev, N. 95
Kirghizia 68, 94, 108
Kissinger, Henry 109
Klimov, Yefim 41
Kolbin, Gennadi 70, 71, 72, 91, 94
Koldunov, Marshal 204, 205, 206
Koltsov, Mikhail 9–10, 16
Kommunist 16, 32, 173, 184
Komsomol 120, 140
Komsomolskaya Pravda 115, 193
Koralenko, Alexander 149
Korean airliner incident 204–6
Korean ethnic group 87
Korotich, Vitali 16, 17–18, 41, 114,
  115, 116, 214–15
Kosygin, Alexei 28, 32
Krasnaya Zvezda (Red Star) 116,
  196, 207
Kremlin 50
  balance of power in 41, 203, 208
  economic policies of 27, 54, 80,
    82, 127, 134, 140, 141, 157,
    158, 159, 160, 170, 179, 183,
    188, 195, 204
  foreign policy of 45, 52, 57, 146,
    196, 197, 202, 209, 210
  leadership of 28, 103, 106–7, 194
  and national question 65, 66, 67,
    75, 76, 87
  and openness 14, 15, 35, 109,
    142, 198
  popular view of 10, 12, 46
Krupyenkov, B. 171
Kunaev, Dinmukhamed 30, 31, 71,
  72, 86, 91, 92, 94, 95, 218

Kurashvili, B. 183, 185
Kuzminykh, Yevgeny 135
Kuznetsk coalfields 82

Latsis, O. 184
Latvia 27, 33, 43, 65, 68, 70, 73, 77,
    167, 218, 219
Lebanon 3, 20, 48, 101, 196, 209
Lenin, Vladimir 3, 4, 12, 13, 21, 40,
    50, 98, 103, 105, 106, 153, 179,
    186, 193, 216, 217
Lenin Prize for Literature 107
Leningrad 7, 18, 31, 96–7, 120, 129,
    153, 156, 164, 216
Leninism 30, 217
Levikov, A. 183–4, 185
Lewin, Moshe 42
Libya 182, 209
Ligachev, Yegor 26, 27, 29, 30, 31,
    33, 34, 35, 36, 55, 58, 67, 70, 71,
    103, 107, 145, 158
Literaturnaya Gazeta 95, 184, 207
Lithuania 27, 33, 43, 65, 66, 68, 70,
    73, 74, 75, 77, 177, 218, 219
Lukonin, N. 147
Lyubimov, Yu. 107

Malaya Zemlya 45
Maltsev, Nikolai 156
Marchenko, Anatoly 113
Markov, Georgi 16, 107
Mayorets, A. 147
media, mass 41
    foreign 108, 138, 139, 142
    Soviet 59, 115, 121, 122, 135
    ses also press, Soviet; journalism,
        foreign
Medvedev, Roy 11, 33, 109,
    112–13, 114
Medvedev, Vadim 31, 34
Mexico 198
mining industry 78–9, 217
Ministry of Automobile Manufacture
    171
Ministry of Chemical and Petroleum
    Machinery 155
Ministry of Construction for Oil and
    Gas Enterprises 140
Ministry of Culture 11, 12
Ministry of Health 106
Ministry of Heavy Machine Building
    55

Moldavia 118, 179, 219
Moldavian ethnic group 68
mortality rates 118, 133–4
Moskovskaya Pravda 130
Moskovsky Komsomolets 110
Moscow 7, 9, 10, 18, 59, 68, 119,
    156, 164, 176, 215
Moscow News 16, 32, 41
Mozambique 48, 209
Murakhovsky, Vsevolod 161

Nagorno-Karabakh 27, 33, 43, 65,
    69, 70, 73, 75, 100, 218
Napoleon Bonaparte 111
national minorities, question of 26,
    27, 42–4, 48, 49, 65–77, 89–90,
    94–5, 100–101, 217–220
National Security Agency (USA) 25
Nazi-Soviet non-aggression pact 74,
    220
Nedyak, L. 111, 112
New Economic Policy 179
New Left (West European) 120
New York Times 6
New Zealand 112
newspapers *see* press, Soviet
Newsweek 20
Nicaragua 196
Nikiforov, L. 178
Nikolaev, A. 171
Nikonov, V. 35
Nixon, Richard 47, 109, 201, 209
Nobel Prize for Literature 122
North Korea 79
North Wales 15
Northcliffe, Lord 5
Northern Ireland 21, 101
Novy Mir 41, 161

Odom, William 25, 26
Ogarkov, Nikolai 56, 196, 204
Ogonyok (Little Light) 9, 16, 17–18,
    32, 41, 114, 115, 116, 122, 215
oil industry 38–9, 47, 80–83, 91, 93,
    106, 140, 141, 147–8, 154–7
Oktyabr 116
Orthodox Church 8, 73

Pakistan 45
Paleo-Siberian ethnic group 66
Pamyat (Memory) 71, 120
part-time employment 166, 167

the Party 151, 177, 186, 215–16
  conservatism in 31–2, 33–4, 35,
    36, 76, 216
  as instrument of reform 31, 215
  and Popular Fronts 44, 74
  reduced role of 123, 176
  reform of 51, 54, 55, 57, 73, 92,
    153, 216–17
Pasternak, Boris 69
Patiashvili, Dzhumber 90
Pavlov, Valentin 163
Pavlovsky, Gleb 119, 120
Pelman, Grigory 120, 122–3
Pentagon 208
perestroika 18, 20, 26, 27, 29, 30,
    34, 36, 37, 39, 42, 43, 44, 49, 58,
    60, 61, 66, 69, 70, 74, 77, 19,
    120, 121, 122, 123, 151,
    207, 214, 215, 216, 217
Petestroika Club 119
Peter the Great 25, 42, 48, 97
Petrikov, A. 130, 131
Petroleum Industry Research
  Institute 155
The Pickwick Papers (Dickens)
    118–19
Pietela, A. 6
Poland 39, 42, 47, 52, 181, 185,
    201, 217
Politburo 4, 12, 19, 45, 59, 145, 193
  conservatism of 26, 29, 30, 31,
    33, 34, 41, 162, 165–6, 183,
    185, 216
  and defence 204, 205, 206, 207
  Gorbachev's position in 21, 27,
    28, 35, 38, 48, 51, 53, 55,
    186, 208, 216
  members of 3, 20, 66, 70, 71, 73,
    91, 95, 103, 117, 144, 156,
    203, 218
  and nationality question 72, 76
  and openness 14, 109, 115, 142
  policy decisions of 81, 82, 111,
    155, 172
Popovic, Miroslav 6
Popular Front, Estonian 43, 74
populism, of Gorbachev 36, 53
Portugal 48, 209
Powers, Francis Gary 205
Pravda 9, 16, 33, 41, 42, 50, 55, 59,
    82, 89, 95, 107, 110, 115,
    122, 143, 144, 158, 162, 194, 196

press, Soviet 41, 53, 55, 106, 107,
    109, 110, 111, 114, 115, 116,
    117, 137
  see also media, mass, Soviet
prices
  food 7, 132, 159, 161, 166
  system of 39, 99, 162–5, 182–3,
    185, 187, 188, 219
Primyakov, Yevgeny 17, 46
prisoners, political 45, 113
Prohibition (USA) 127
Protapopov, Professor 59
Pushkin, Alexander 97
PVO see Soviet Air Defence

Rashidof, Sharif 70, 92, 94, 95, 218
Reagan, Ronald 40, 47, 48, 51, 52,
    53, 56, 57, 68, 113, 146,
    194–204 passim, 209
Red Star see Krasnaya Zvezda
Reddaway, P. 25, 26, 27
refuseniks 10
Rekunkov, A. 129
Reuters 15
Revolution, October 13, 22, 36, 40,
    42, 50, 53, 67, 87, 153, 158, 159,
    163, 193, 216
Reykjavik Summit 54, 56–7,
    199–201, 204
Romanov, G. 31, 53, 216
Roosevelt, Franklin 25, 187
Russians, as ethnic group 67, 68, 69,
    70, 71, 74, 75, 76, 86–7, 89–94
    passim, 218, 219
Rust, Mathias 101, 191, 205, 206,
    208
Ryabkov, Mikhail 129
Rybakov, Anatoly, Children of the
    Arbat 116
Rybakov, A.I. 106
Ryzhkov, Nikolai 54, 71, 145, 185

Sakhalin Island 81, 87
Sakharov, Andrei 16, 112–14
SDI see Strategic Defence Initiative
Second World War 45, 52, 65, 76,
    87, 90, 98, 111, 154, 193, 203,
    209
Shah of Iran, overthrow of 88
Shatrov, M. 114–15
Shcherbina, Boris 81, 139–41, 143,
    144

Shcherbitsky, Vladimir 66, 71, 218
Shevardnadze, Eduard 30, 31, 33,
    38, 47, 56, 68–9, 90, 91, 108,
    185, 191, 197, 206
Shmelev, N. 184
Shultz, George 47, 108, 194, 197,
    200
Shushkov, V. 134–6
Siberia
    Eastern 78–9, 81
    Western 38, 80, 81, 82, 83, 84,
        93, 106, 140, 141, 147, 153,
        154–7, 215
Slav ethnic group 69, 72, 76, 94
Slyunkov, N. 188
Smolny Institute 53, 153
socialism, Soviet 25, 32, 138, 184,
    187
Socialist Industry 184
Sociological Research Institute 122,
    177
Sokolov, S. 203, 205, 206, 207
Sokolov, Yu. 130–32
Soleiman, M. 84
Solidarity union, in Poland 47, 217
Solomentsev, M. 34
Solovev, Yu. 216
Solzhenitsyn, Alexander 41, 107,
    116
South Wales 87
Soviet Air Defence (PVO) 204, 205,
    206
Soviet Embassy (Washington) 19
Sovietskaya Rossiya 33, 156
Spanish Civil War 9, 10
Stalin, Josef 4, 7, 13, 36, 42, 44, 52,
    70, 70, 98, 121, 215
    and collectivisation 159–60
    era of 11, 12, 17, 21, 122
    and industry 93
    and nationality question 87,
        217–8
    purges ordered by 9, 116, 117,
        119
    show trials of 58
    state machine of 40, 48, 186
Stalingrad *see* Volgograd
Stalinism 11, 113, 218
Star Wars *see* Strategic Defence
    Initiative
state, Soviet 12, 13, 35, 36, 40, 48,
    51, 111

State Committee for Statistics 37
State Committee for Labour and
    Social Issues 166
State Committee for Prices 162, 163,
    164, 187
State Construction Committee 59
State Enterprise Law 38, 185, 188
State Foreign Economic Commission
    of the Council of Ministers
    (SFECCM) 180
State Planning Organisation *see*
    Gosplan
State Supplies Committee *see*
    Gosnab
Strategic Defence Initiative (SDI)
    194, 196, 197, 198, 199, 200
strikes 39, 215, 217, 219, 220
Sudan 209
Supreme Soviet on Nationalities 66
Sweden 14, 137, 144

Tajikistan 68, 70, 72, 94, 97
Talyzin, Nikolai 54, 185, 187
Tass 72, 91, 92, 133, 206
Trotsky, Leon 13
television 15–16, 27, 33, 40, 41,
    121, 122, 146, 200
Temperance Movement (British)
    127
Third World 48, 191, 196, 197, 198,
    201, 202, 209
Tikhonov, N. 51
Transport Ministry 177, 179
Tregubov, N. 130
Trud 115, 134, 135
Trushin, V. 127
Turkey 72
Turkic languages 72, 94
Turkmenistan 68, 69, 87, 88, 89
Twentieth Century and Peace 18

Ukraine 14, 44, 71, 75, 76, 85, 91,
    112, 115, 137, 138, 139, 140,
    142, 144, 145, 146, 149, 156,
    183, 215, 218, 219
Ulyanov, M. 32
United Nations (UN) 46, 100, 108,
    194, 200
United Press International (UPI) 15
United States 6, 18, 19, 44, 46, 47,
    48, 54, 56, 57, 120, 127, 128,
    130, 134, 158, 164, 172, 187,

191, 194–201 *passim*, 204, 206, 207, 208
Unitedc States Department of Agriculture 84, 117
USA and Canada Institute 17, 138, 194
US News and World Report 13, 108
Usmanov, V. 93
Ustinov, D. 3
Uzbekistan 68, 69, 70, 71, 92, 93, 94, 95, 118, 132, 149, 218
Uzbek ethnic group 7, 69, 93, 94

Vaino, Karl 74
Valyas, Vaino 43, 74
Vietnam 47, 196, 201, 202
Vladivostok accords (1974) 195
Volga provinces 85, 87
Volgograd 98–9
Von Paulus, Field Marshal 98
Vorotnikov, V. 156
Voznesyensky, Andrei 17, 105, 111
Vremya (television news) 41

wages 78, 172–4, 177, 219
Wall Street Journal 214
Washington Post 20
Washington Summit 56, 57, 61, 208

Watergate 19
Weinberger, Caspar 142, 195
West Germany 6, 46, 164, 201
Western Europe 82, 196, 201
Wilson, Harold 21, 52
World Economy Institute 17
World Service (BBC) 15
Writers' Union 16, 32, 105, 107

Yakovlev, Alexander 16, 17, 28, 31, 33, 38, 117, 185, 186, 116, 217
Yakovlev, Yegor 16, 41
Yakutia 78–9
Yaroslavtsev, Gennady 149
Yeltsin, Boris 30–31, 33, 45, 57–61, 144, 186, 216
Yepishev, A. 203
Yevtushenko, Yevgeny 17, 41, 107, 108
Yugoslavia 39

Zaikov, L. 60
Zakharov, G. 108
Zamyatin, Leonid 198
Zaslavskaya, Tatyana 119, 173, 174
Zhivotachenko, V. 198
Zorin, Valentin 138